THE FACES OF VIOLENCE

Publication Number 1089
AMERICAN SERIES
IN
BEHAVIORAL SCIENCE AND LAW

Edited by
RALPH SLOVENKO, B.E., LL.B., M.A., Ph.D.
Professor of Law and Psychiatry
Wayne State University
Law School
Detroit, Michigan

THE FACES OF VIOLENCE

By

GEORGE B. PALERMO, M.D.

Clinical Professor Psychiatry and Neurology
Director of Criminological Psychiatry
Medical College of Wisconsin

Adjunct Professor of Criminology and Law Studies
Department of Cultural and Social Sciences
Marquette University

Lecturer, Department of Psychiatry and Bioethics
Loyola University, Stritch School of Medicine

CHARLES C THOMAS • PUBLISHER
Springfield • Illinois • U.S.A.

Published and Distributed Throughout the World by

CHARLES C THOMAS • PUBLISHER
2600 South First Street
Springfield, Illinois 62794-9265

© *1994 by* CHARLES C THOMAS • PUBLISHER

ISBN 0-398-05934-9

Library of Congress Catalog Card Number: 94-31664

Printed in the United States of America
SC-R-3

Library of Congress Cataloging-in-Publication Data

Palermo, George B.
    The faces of violence / by George B. Palermo.
       p.   cm. —(American series in behavioral science and law)
    "Publication number 1089"—Ser. t.p.
    Includes bibliographical references and index.
    ISBN 0-398-05934-9
    1. Violence—United States. 2. Violence—United States—
Psychological aspects. 3. Crime—United States—Psychological
aspects. I. Title. II. Series.
HN90.V5P33   1994
303.6—dc20   94-31664
                                      CIP

Dedication

To the memory of my parents
To the presence of my wife and children
To the future of my grandchildren

FOREWORD

Dr. George B. Palermo has observed criminal violence for over twenty-five years and he is concerned about the absence in the United States of a coherent culture, its material obsession, the destructiveness of welfare, and the disintegration of the family. In this book on violence, Dr. Palermo expresses those concerns.

Dr. Palermo offers a lifetime of experience and observation about human nature that includes thirty-five years in psychiatry and twenty-five years observing criminal behavior as a psychiatrist. He examines criminal cases as a forensic psychiatrist for Milwaukee County. He is well known for his plainspoken, unpretentious testimony in the trial of serial killer Jeffrey Dahmer.

Dr. Palermo argues that the upsurge of violence in our society is basically due to the lack of the formative influence of the family unit on its members, especially children and adolescents. He considers the family as the primary social agency. Poverty, drugs, access to guns, joblessness, poor education and inadequate housing are what he considers tangential issues.

Most of the people whom Dr. Palermo sees accused of crimes do not know their fathers. They lack the stability that comes from an integrated family. The family not found at home is found in a gang.

The welfare culture, he says, is a disincentive for families to unite as a single economic unit—as a unit of emotional support. With welfare, a mother and father are not encouraged to team up for the support of their children. At the same time, he points out, there is a culture of desire that makes people feel incomplete if they do not have all that the society offers materially. That encourages violence, as illustrated by the killing of children by children for a pair of sneakers or a jacket.

Dr. Palermo was born in Italy, the third of ten children. His passion has been to observe America and to write and share his point of view, especially, of late, on violence. The *Milwaukee Journal* has described him as "a sort of an Italian Alexis de Tocqueville, the 19th century French historian famous for his analysis of American democracy."

With a medical degree from the University of Bologna, he undertook a medical internship at St. Michael Hospital in Milwaukee in 1952. During his first years in the United States, he was poor and he learned English—an immigrant's story. He completed residencies in psychiatry, and then went into the private practice of psychotherapy in Milwaukee from 1960 to 1969. At the same time he took forensic cases in Milwaukee County. In 1969, he returned to Italy for a prolonged stay; then, in 1988, he came back to America.

In 1955, he married Adriana, a nurse, and they had five children, three girls and two boys, between 1956 and 1964. Three of them followed their parents into health care. Their oldest daughter is a pediatrician in Rome; their older son is studying acupuncture in Denver; their younger son is a specialist in neurology who is currently following in his father's footsteps by taking a specialization in psychiatry at Johns Hopkins University; their second daughter is an artist and illustrator of children's books in Milan; and their youngest daughter is a professor of foreign language and literature in Rome, where she works for the Food and Agricultural Organization of the United Nations.

Dr. Palermo is renowned as the poet-philosopher of Milwaukee psychiatry, a man of charm, good humor, and likability. He is enterprising, engaging, ebullient. He has written and lectured widely. He is an associate editor of *The International Journal of Offender Therapy and Comparative Criminology.*

This book is a work that will stand the test of time. It is marked by honesty of thought and moral nobility.

Ralph Slovenko
Editor
American Series in Behavioral Science and Law

INTRODUCTORY NOTE

The topic of this book, violence, is not a figment of the imagination. In the United States, and in many other nations, violence stands there, upright, similar to Mt. Everest, daring to be scaled and conquered. Unlike Mt. Everest, however, crime and violence are growing larger, both in the United States and in other countries. In most opinion polls in the United States, they are often the number one concern.

Depending on one's angle or scaling efforts, specific problems are encountered and become canonized as *the avenue* to take. Around this opinion, which at times becomes a "faith document," cluster like-minded, and well-intended people. If they are powerful enough, laws are enforced to lessen violence. There is currently no vaccination that eliminates, or will eliminate, violence.

To even attempt to grasp violence, human nature needs to be known. It is the twin peak, higher and more devious than Mt. Everest. Mt. Everest is there. Where, or what, is human nature? Does human nature exist?

Given such a formidable task as the above, only a veteran need apply. One has: Dr. George Palermo. Dr. Palermo has not scaled the Mt. Everest of violence, but he has scaled lesser mountains; the reader of this book will rather quickly observe this phenomenon. What mountains has he scaled? Dr. Palermo has not resorted to a comfortable office, dancing at a safe distance from the major issues of violence. His chapter on Jeffrey Dahmer clearly establishes his rite of passage on the difficult and at times baffling topic: the serial murderer. In this chapter, Dr. Palermo portrays the instincts of a bloodhound.

When the need arises, for example in his chapter on "The Biology of Violence," he is at home in a variety of laboratories—the intricacies of neurology, genetics, and psychopharmacology.

In truth it can be said, Dr. Palermo is a climber for all seasons and on all sides of the Mt. of Violence. Readers will learn this for themselves as

ix

they travel through the pages of this informative, provocative and scholarly book.

Edward M. Scott, Ph.D.
Professor Emeritus of Psychiatry
Editor, *International Journal of Offender Therapy and Comparative Criminology.*

PREFACE

Before accepting the invitation to write this book on violence, I wondered whether it would be redundant to further investigate a topic that has been the focus of so much writing during the past twenty years. However, my hesitation was overcome, first, by my personal interest in the subject, and second, by the realization that there is a lack of a global assessment of this issue in most of the very interesting papers and books that have been written about violence. Most of what I read, while certainly enlightening, appeared to me to be one-sided and dispersive. In addition, I thought that this would give me the opportunity to raise some questions, and to introduce to others some insight derived from my professional experience and personal reflection.

During the course of my professional life, I have been intrigued by the possible reasons behind human acts of violence against other humans, either as an impulsive raptus or as the result of elaborate programming, and which reach, at times, destructive proportions. I have often wondered about the motivations of those people who break social taboos and direct their instinctive destructive aggression towards other persons, both nown and unknown to them. I have reflected on the different perceptions of violence that people have, and on the distinctions that are made between crimes of violence that are committed during wartime—in wars both declared and undeclared—and the present day non-collective violence, highly disregardful of human life, and to which we have become all too frequently involuntary witnesses, and to which we have also become gradually desensitized. I have been puzzled by the acceptance of these killings of masses of people for just or unjust social reasons, and the obvious non-acceptance of the killing of peaceful citizens by their unexpected murderers in their homes and on the city streets. Faced with the devastating effects of social and interpersonal violence, I ask myself, as we all must do, as individuals and part of the collectivity, why does such destructive violence exist? Is this human nature? What can be done about it?

The appreciation of human behavior—normal, abnormal or deviant—calls for an analysis that should take into consideration the social context. The suddenness, unpredictability and randomness of street violence, which is becoming ever more prevalent, is not only highly frightening, but disruptive of our daily lives, even more so than the frequent occurrence of domestic violence; it is the unexpectedness of street crime that makes it so frightening. These crimes against persons generally have dire consequences, physical or psychological, on both the individual and on the immediate family. Those of us who have had direct professional contacts with these unfortunate people are well aware of this, and it is certainly not difficult even for the reader who has not had this professional experience to appreciate the shattering effects of aggravated assault, rape, and murder. There is no doubt that the upsurge of the phenomenon of aggression in our society calls for a relentless search for a comprehensive understanding of its causes and, obviously, an attempt to find a remedy for them, or, better yet, a means for their eradication at the origins.

My intention in writing about violent behavior is not only to reassess the variables commonly accepted to be at its basis, but primarily to search for, and reflect on, whether there is a single, most important factor—a common denominator—at the origin of that violence against the person that is flooding our homes, our cities and our country. A great number of scholars and writers have stressed, at different times and from various perspectives, the multiple factors at the basis of violence and crime in society at large and in American society in particular. However, it is my impression that this topic should be assessed from the point of view that considers the individual as an actor and as a reactor to various internal, external and environmental stimuli, a member of a social community that holds certain mores and values—mores and ethical values that determine the social conduct of each one of us when interacting with one another. Some of these values seem to have been with us from time immemorial; others, instead, seem to have a more fluctuating course, depending on the particular social or historical period. In order to better understand my approach, I would like to suggest that the reader visualize the individual at the center of concentric circles: the first is that of the family with its constellation of members; the second, that of the community; the third is that of society and its culture; and the fourth, that of the world at large—the cosmos, with or without the presence of an omnipresent cosmic power or a superior entity that many believers call

God, and with whom many individuals have a silent spiritual relationship. This approach will, I believe, give us a better dynamic view of the violent person.

I will limit my discussion principally to the problem of individual violence, bearing in mind that the variables so far addressed by many scholars, even though important in themselves are, in my estimation, co-factors, or, as I prefer to call them, facilitators. Addressing these variables alone as the cause of violent crime has not, thus far, produced any great changes in the frequency of crime in our society. The rate of crime has soared while these investigations have mushroomed throughout the recent years. Modern man, as well stated by Zillmann, "in furthering his self interest has shown little reluctance to inflict pain, injury, mutilation and death upon his fellow man."[1] p.1 It seems reasonable, therefore, that a further inquiry and a global assessment of the behavior of the violent individual in his or her own social habitat, as a psycho-bio-socio-ethical self in a continuously changing society, within or without a family structure, will bear better fruit in clarifying the factors and co-factors at the basis of violence and in a search for means to combat its manifestations in the attempt, ultimately, to make our daily lives safer.

I have divided the book into two main sections. The first section includes four chapters, each of which examines violence from a different perspective, i.e., historical, sociological, psychological, etho-biological, and statistical, even though statistics are necessarily reported throughout the book. Various theories regarding each argument are reviewed and critically appraised.

The second section of the book deals with the major manifestations of crime against the person in our society. I have dedicated a great deal of attention to these chapters because of my active involvement in community forensics and criminological psychiatry. I have included chapters on rape and domestic violence, both very timely subjects. I also discuss at length the antisocial personality disorder, and finally, in a chapter on serial killers I offer a brief historical analysis of this type of violent behavior. In particular, I describe the serial killer Jeffrey Dahmer, whom I examined for many hours as a court-appointed psychiatric expert, and about whom I testified for many hours in Milwaukee Circuit Court.

My basic thesis, which runs throughout the book, is that the many variables so far amply studied, and unfortunately often poorly addressed by our society, are not the primary cause of violent behavior. Nonetheless,

I have also written two chapters, one on illicit drug and alcohol abuse, and one on guns and other variables, or facilitators, as I prefer to call them, and their importance as co-factors in the genesis of crime.

Before concluding, I have attempted to reinforce my thesis by focusing my attention on the importance of the family in the formation of a person's good character as the only real prevention of crime and violence. I hope that this chapter, "At the Roots of Violence," will enlighten the reader about the ever present importance of the family as a source of physical and moral support, a means by which values are passed on and virtues are acquired.

In concluding, I propose that the upsurge of violence in our society is not due primarily to the facilitators/variables which should continue to be addressed, especially the cancerous spread of illicit drug and alcohol use and abuse and the easy availability of guns, but is basically due to the lack of the formative influence of the family unit on its members, especially children and adolescents. Violence in our homes and streets is at a high never before encountered, families are slowly disintegrating, people feel lost. Alexis de Tocqueville would be surprised to see present-day America.

I do not offer any specific cure for this state of affairs because it is not within the scope of this book and would certainly involve another Herculean work. I can only say that my professional work and my experience tell me that if the social cell goes awry, the fabric of society tends to decay. Under such circumstances, violence, the outcome of many frustrations and dysfunctions, and a manifestation of almost genocidal proportions, ensues. That is what we are witnessing and this is what we must do: reintegrate the family at its best and help it to once again assume its role as the foundation for the good character of our citizens.

As a final note, I would like to alert the reader to my frequent use of a semantic approach to commonly used words. I feel that the etymological roots of words frequently give insight not only into their historical origins but also into their present day meaning.

NOTE

1. Zillmann, D.: *Hostility and Aggression.* Hillsdale, NJ, Lawrence Erlbaum Associates, 1979.

ACKNOWLEDGEMENTS

I n writing this book I was overwhelmed by the plethora of publications on violence. A great deal of my effort was spent in selecting literature pertinent to my topic of interest. In this process, I came across many interesting scientific articles and books which enlightened me about issues pertinent to my topic and some that were somewhat peripheral to it, and which, because of space limitations, I could not include. In addition, I have tried to avoid repetition in reporting studies concerning violent behavior. Therefore, I wish to apologize to the many scientific investigators whom I have not mentioned for not doing justice to their scholarly works. However, I wish to thank the many authors from whom I drew information. They have given me not only data but inspiration.

I wish to thank the editor of *Dynamic Psychiatry* for permission to reprint the historical background of cocaine, previously published in the journal in 1990, in my article, "Cocaine Paranoia or Paranoid Schizophrenia—A Diagnostic Dilemma."

In collecting the data for this book, I was helped tremendously by Anna Green, the dynamic librarian of the Milwaukee County Mental Health Complex. She was prompt and efficient in complying with my requests for material, and with her kindness she made my work more enjoyable.

Professor Ralph Slovenko, Professor of Law and Psychiatry, Wayne State University, had enough esteem for me to suggest that I write a book on the topic of violence. He was basically thinking of the serial killer Dahmer, but because of my interest in violence I decided to enlarge the topic, also in order to avoid giving too much attention to the destructive deeds of one person. I wish to thank Prof. Slovenko for his critique and suggestions, and primarily for his kind introduction to the book. Sociology is the cradle of criminology, and as a psychiatrist one should view the human being in his or her totality. Thus, his mention of me as the Milwaukee Tocqueville, even though incorrect as far as fame is concerned, is certainly correct for my interest in American society.

There are also several other people whom I wish to thank for their support of my efforts and for reading and commenting on some of the chapters in the manuscript. I owe special thanks for the Introductory Note of Edward Scott, Ph.D., Professor Emeritus of Psychiatry at the Oregon Health Sciences University. We have been closely associated professionally for the past several years. He is an individual full of human empathy, greatly concerned with large social issues and a man of vast knowledge who, at the same time, has that humility that makes people special. I thank him for reading many of the chapters and for his comments and suggestions.

I also wish to thank Harry Prosen, M.D., Professor and Chairman of the Department of Psychiatry, Medical College of Wisconsin, for reading and commenting on the chapter, The Psychology of Violence. His confidence in me has been a source of strength.

A friend for many years, Edward J. Gumz, Ph.D., Associate Professor of Social Work and Chair Undergraduate Social Work Program, School of Social Work, Loyola University, Chicago, was kind enough to read the chapters, The Sociology of Violence and The Roots of Violence. His perceptive and at times challenging criticism has been of great help.

I wish to thank my collaborator on several articles, the statistical wizard, Maurice Smith, Ph.D., Research Associate, Comprehensive Assessment and Treatment Outcome Research, in Minneapolis. His obsessive trends helped keep my work on stable ground.

Special thanks are due to Barbara Liccione, M.A., Executive Director of the Task Force on Battered Women and Children; and to the National Coalition Against Domestic Violence for their help in obtaining statistics on domestic violence and rape; and to Thomas Christopher, B.S., Detective Lieutenant, City of Milwaukee Police Department, and to the Federal Bureau of Investigation for their assistance in obtaining recent statistics regarding violence in Milwaukee and in the United States.

But above all, I wish to thank my wife, Adriana, who has been close to me during the entire period of my work, with her loving presence, her stimulating and challenging thoughts, her continuous constructive criticism, her untiring use of the word-processor, and her pre-editorial survey of the entire book. I am grateful to her and I consider her contribution to have been the greatest of all. I wished to dedicate this book to her; then, in discussing it with her, we came to the conclusion that, in tune with my thesis which pervades the book, the dedication should embrace a longitudinal span of my life: parents, wife and children.

Lastly, a grateful thought goes to the hundreds of violent persons whom I have had the opportunity to encounter in my professional life as an expert forensic psychiatrist, because they are basically the ones who taught me what I have attempted to divulge to others in this book. I hope that during my encounters with them my words were a source of reflection and a stimulus to change their behavior.

CONTENTS

THE FACES OF VIOLENCE

Chapter One

AN HISTORICAL PERSPECTIVE OF VIOLENCE

Violence has a history that begins with humankind, and humans, throughout their historical course, have been both prey and predator, suffered hatred and aggression, enjoyed feelings of love and tenderness, been energized by courage and petrified by fear. In order to better understand the problem of human hostility and violence, therefore, one should look at humankind's historical evolution. It is safe to assume that humans, viewed from an anthropological perspective, evolved as biological units, who, in contact with their surroundings, reacted to the many sensorial stimuli present. For the sake of discussion, one can assume that these primitive beings were more spontaneous in their relationships and simplistic and realistic in their appreciation of the world around them and in their contacts with one another.

One can argue that at that stage of evolution the social necessity of repression or suppression of emotions and feelings was not felt as it later came to be. They were close to nature and unsophisticated natural reactors, obviously still more impulsive and less defensive in a Freudian sense. Since emotion and feelings do not develop in a vacuum, it can be safely accepted that they became a part of the human psychological self as a responsive reaction to their contacts with nature and their fellow humans.

Human beings progressively developed their potential mental capacities, and slowly passed from a rudimentary psychic life to the complex selves that we know today. Attraction, fear, love, and hate must have become, of consequence, the natural emotional feelings in this Eraclitian dynamism in the life of these primitive people and the feelings that they experienced as genuine tended, with the passage of time, to camouflage themselves, either consciously or unconsciously.

It is one of the tenets of psychoanalysis to remove the repressed from the unconscious, i.e., to make the unconscious conscious, and in so doing to make the individual aware of the repressed emotions that are, at times, not only strictly personal but also atavistic in character. Thus, one can assume that primitive humans were more impulsive reactors and more readily showed not only their positive emotions but also their negative ones. Modern humans, instead, have tried to suppress or repress many of these feelings and emotions—and they are often quite successful in doing so—in order to live in a society that continues to evolve in its civility. Occasionally, however, these repressed or suppressed emotions, such as anger, or feelings such as hostility, come to the fore, disrupting the life of the individual and of those around him or her.

Violence and victimization have been part of collective life and daily relationships from time immemorial and the use of crude force instead of good reasoning is a long-standing habit of humankind. The current spiral of violent behavior in our communities is, unfortunately, a cyclical return of the past. Testimony to that comes to us from the Old and New Testaments, the Homeric writings of the Iliad and the Odyssey, the fables of Aesop and Phaedrus, and the long tradition of mythology and fairy tales. Narration and legends have passed from generation to generation, through word of mouth, papyri, tables, and later through scripta, and in a conscious or subconscious way, the awareness that human beings, in addition to their positive drives and high ideals, have their own frailties, their own vices, their own shortcomings, their own aggressiveness and their own violent tendencies.

Studies of violence indicate that its presence reached high peaks at different historical periods, and it is common knowledge that at any given period violence has been felt by society and those people who live it to be the worst possible kind. Thus, since it is relevant to the socio-historical period under consideration, it is unfair to say that present day violence is greater than that which was experienced by people in previous societies. Indeed, if present day humans had a better knowledge of the history of violence through the past millennia, they would have, I believe, a more objective appreciation of present day violence. This does not mean that today's violence is not frightening or highly disruptive socially, or that it does not cause a great deal of pain and suffering for many of us. It means that when viewed in an evolutionary perspective it may, without losing those qualities that we think specific to it, share basic commonalities with violence throughout the centuries.

In the Old Testament, the prophets emphasized man's propensity to corruption and violent behavior. In Psalm 14:2–3, one can read the following: "The Lord looks down from heaven upon the children of man to see if there are any that act wisely, that seek after God. They have all gone astray. They are all alike corrupt. There is none that does good, no, not one." Further, in Psalm 55:9, one can read about the deceit and violence of man as described by the psalmist: "Destroy, Oh Lord and divide their tongues; for I have seen violence and strife in the city;" and in Psalm 55:23, "Bloody deceitful men shall not live out half their days. . . . " In reading Genesis, one comes to realize that the narrator of that particular period was quite aware of man's violent instincts, so much so that he reported the voice of God lashing out at humankind because it was corrupt, wicked and violent: "And God said unto Noah, the end of all flesh is come before Me, for the earth is filled with violence through them; and behold, I will destroy them with the earth."[2] Violence is, indeed, a central theme of the Old Testament. Scholars such as Horsley, Schwager, and Williams, who delved into the study of the Old Testament, came to separate but similar conclusions as those of the narrators of the biblical stories: that men and women, since the beginnings of humankind, have been creatures of passion, who easily become enraged and angered, and that violent anger is so powerful that often reason and good will can barely resist it; and that at times violence may not only be expressed against a given individual, the intended target of their hostility, but also against unrelated persons or innocent bystanders.

It seems that what was passed on to us from previous generations, especially the early civilizations, was the anecdotal report of good or bad deeds about which the narrators themselves attached a value judgement. Early mythologic stories and folktales were simple, almost concrete, but were highly illustrative, and conveyed either condemnation or exultatory statements regarding human behavior. They were easily understandable by the majority of people and usually hit home with the striking familiarity of their reportage. Whether their concreteness was the expression of an evolving mind, or was due to the incapacity to conceptualize and abstract is hard to say. In his description of various myths, G.S. Kirk[3] tells us that Isiod, in his *Theogony,* describes the first act of violence, even though not occurring among mortals but among the so-called gods of that period: Kronos, son of Uranus and Gaia—Mother Earth—castrated his own father at the instigation of his mother: "And with his right hand he grasped the monstrous sickle, long and jagged toothed, and swiftly ripped off the genitals of his dear father, and flung them behind him to be carried away."[p.114] This mixture of eviration and castration certainly has the flavor of what would today be called sexual sadism, even though Uranus was being punished for unidentified shameful deeds. Isiod, the ancient source for tales, confronts us with another act of violence by a god against his own father, of Zeus against Kronos. Zeus subdued his father Kronos, who had himself castrated his father Uranus, and drove him from his honored position because his father apparently had swallowed each of his newly born children of Rhea, the mother of Zeus; Zeus, himself, was the only survivor of this programmed infanticide.

These early mythological tales well portray the degree and quality of human aggression against one another. They are, indeed, the recounting of the hostility, anger, vengeance, and aggression perpetrated by human-created anthropomorphic gods, expression of humankind's emotions. They are the forerunners, and they epitomize the ubiquitousness, of much domestic violence, that violence that has been clearly illustrated throughout the allegorical periods of mankind's history.

Another act of biblical violence was the murder of Abel by his brother Cain. Cain killed him because he believed that he, Abel, was the pre-ferred one of the Lord. In Genesis, 4:46–50, is written, "And the Lord had regard for Abel and his offering but for Cain and his offering He had no regard." Again in Genesis 4:9, when the Lord says to Cain, "Where is Abel your brother?" and Cain answers, "I do not know, am I my brother's keeper?" one can appreciate the intuitiveness of the early narrator of what we understand as human negative emotion: hostility, prevarication and defiance. In a simple way, almost in a story telling fashion, we are forced to recognize that the bad instincts of humankind, such as the disobedience to parental authority, rivalry with one another—even with one's own sibling, at times exasperated to the point of murder, was already within the sphere of awareness of early man. We can certainly agree that "there is no new thing under the sun,"[4] even after seven thousand years.

In reading the biblical studies of Williams,[5] and Schwager[6] I was struck by what they call mimetic violence, violence between twins, and curious about its possible meaning in the minds of the narrators in the Old Testament. There is a profusion of violence between brothers in the Bible: Cain and Abel; Jacob and Esau; Isaac and Ishmael; Paris and Xirah; Ephraim and Manasseh; Moses and Aaron. I believe that the reference to this violence among brothers in the Bible is an obvious indication of the human tendency for possible conflictual relationships, often destructive in character, and which the narrators felt justified in emphatically reporting, even among blood relations, and even between twin brothers. Could the purpose of the narrator have been to show that hostility and destructive violence is so ingrained in the human race that it actually needs this type of dramatization: brother killing brother? Could it be that man should not trust even his own self? the twin being a reflection of that self? "Let everyone be aware of his brother and put no trust in any brother for every brother is a supplanter. . . . ."[7]

The stories of Uranus and Kronos, of Kronos and Zeus, of Cain and Abel, may indicate the beginning of a human and humane awakening. The narration of God's recognition of Cain as the murderer of his brother may have served as not only the condemnation of Abel's murder, but also as the prohibition of murder itself. God's commandment forbade the murder of Cain, and the story of Cain and Abel became the foundation of one of the most important commandments: "Thou shalt not kill." The possibility that the story of Cain and Abel is a condemnation of murder is also reflected in the passage regarding the prohibition of any vengeance towards Cain: " . . . so that no one that came upon him would kill him."[8]

The Bible describes the struggle of humankind in confronting its own basic nature, its puzzlement about its own existence, its difficulty in relating to others and to God, and the negative emotions of hostility, anger and destructiveness to which humans may become easy prey. At the same time, it lays the foundation for ethical standards that after millennia are still considered valid. Retribution for the offender in order to rectify his sinful actions was demanded by God, through his prophets, as reported in the Bible. Millennia later, like an echo from Genesis, the resounding voice of a young lady was heard in one of our courtrooms when, utterly distraught, she called out against the killer of her brother, "I hate you. I hate you. May you never find peace, even after death!" That condemning statement in the midst of a deep silence seemed to come from above while it actually came from the sadness of a human soul, stricken by the violent murder of her beloved brother by a serial killer. She demanded that same retribution from the offender in order to rectify his sinful actions that had, centuries before, been demanded by the biblical God.

Retribution is also asked for by the Islamic religion and violence always called for immediate punishment. Indeed, in the Holy Koran is stated: "The punishment of those who wage war against God and his apostles and strive with might and main for mischief through the land is execution or crucifixion or cutting off of the hands and the feet on opposite sides or exile from the land."[9]

The Ten Commandments, centuries old, epitomize humankind's desire to put a hold on human violent behavior, to give people a social order—even though often the outcome of compromise—a sense of connection, and ethical rules to live by. One could say that, even though previous civilizations held similar codes of moral human conduct, the Ten Words of the Jewish tradition have been used to lay the foundations of the beginning of modern Western society, the respect for authority and for one's fellow human, and for the dignity of all. That humankind was aware of its own negative destructive emotions even prior to the existence of the kingdom of Israel can be inferred by codes of law compiled by civilizations just prior to and around that same period, certainly written in order to curb the unsanctioned behavior of their people and keep in check their violent instincts against one another. The Mesopotamian, the Syrian, and the Hammurabi Codes, the Assyrian and Hittite Codes, and the Mosaic Laws, the Greek Draconian Code, later the Twelve Roman Tables, the German Salic Law, the Napoleonic Code and present day legal codes are all confirmation of the continuous awareness of people at different times in history of the ubiquitousness of violence and crime; violence that required preventive codification or exemplary punishment.

Aggressive violence is reported throughout the major Homeric works, the Odyssey and the Iliad, both dating back to the eighth century B.C. These two epic poems describe a world in chaos, where war and violence appeared ubiquitous, and where angry and violent gods, possibly the expression of humankind's search to understand itself and a reflection of human emotions, often quarreled with one another and with mortals as well. Odysseus's killing of his loyal wife's suitors, even though justified, still assumes the semblance of a slaughter. In The Iliad, Cassandra, during the siege of Troy, sought refuge in the Temple of Athena, and there, at the foot of the statue of Minerva, she was battered and raped by Ajax. Is there any difference between the rape of Cassandra and the rape of many women in our society while walking the streets or even in their own homes?

Another mythological example of destructive violence is that of the killing of Agamemnon, King of Mycenae, slaughtered by his wife and her lover: "And now she comes with the double ax, raises it up . . . and the head is almost off but hangs by a precarious thread of skin. And now he comes again, and hacks at the corpse."[10] And what can be said about the disfigurement of Hector's cadaver after he fell under the blows of

Achille's sword in the Iliad?[11] "... and you [Hector] the dogs and birds will mall you, shame your corpse . . . " said Achilles to Hector. To which Hector answered, "I beg you, beg you by your life, your parents, don't let the dogs devour me . . . so Trojan men and Trojan women can do me honor . . . ", and not a man came forward who did not stab his body.pp.352–353

Throughout history, as we proceed from Greek to Roman legendary epic, the expression of human hostility with its accompanying violence frequently appears as a reminder that it is halted neither by friendship nor kinship, as when Romulus killed his brother Remus. As previously mentioned, the killing of one's brother, especially a twin, is quite a recurrent episode, obviously highly symbolic, throughout historical and legendary literature. Recently, I had the opportunity to examine two pairs of identical male twins. Both of them had come to the attention of a psychiatrist and were eventually hospitalized in a psychiatric unit because of depression. Contrary to what has been the common assumption that twins usually have good feelings about one another, these twins easily verbalized their hostility towards the other twin together with their non-appreciation of the other's behavior, described by them as destructive and antisocial in character. This, strangely enough, was a reflection of those characteristics for which they, themselves, had entered the hospital. Could this support the idea that mimetic violence as reported in mythological legends is nothing else than the expression of man's awareness of his own shortcomings, of his antisociality, of his own hostility and aggression, and that the narrators of the mimetic legends had been attempting to advise us not to trust even our own selves because of our propensity to act out in a hostile, destructive way against our own blood, our people, ourselves?

In the history of later Rome, the figure of Nero (Nero Claudius Caesar Drusus Germanicus) stands out as one of the most destructive. He killed his step-brother Britannicus, his mother Agrippina, his first wife Ottavia, his teacher Seneca, and eventually he himself asked one of his freedmen to kill him. The murder of Julius Caesar by his adopted son Brutus is also tragic, and Caesar's reported exclamation, "Et tu, Brute?" seems to resound as the recurrent echo of parricide throughout the centuries, and is in some way similar to the treason of Judas Iscariot leading to the death of Jesus Christ.

All civilizations have grappled with the problem of crime and violence. We are told, for example, that in ancient Greece, Plato, around 400 BC, aware of the social problem of violent behavior, described homicide as voluntary, involuntary, or homicide in anger, and suggested a new model of penology to be instituted in the utopian city that he called Magnesia, where the reformation of the offender's character would take place.[12] Later, as humankind's knowledge about its propensity for violent behavior grew through the centuries, codes of law against crime and violence were written and varied with the historical period: from simple, reactive or almost talionic laws, to the later codes of Justinian, Napoleon, and to those found in English law. Crime and violent behavior slowly came to be appreciated not primarily as the idiosyncratic acts of violence of an individual against a fellow human, as had been accepted for centuries, but as the product of an individual's antisocial conduct, an individual viewed principally as a reactor to ecological and environmental stimuli. The above has especially been true in the last decades with the advent of phenomenological theories which have primarily upheld social factors as criminogenic, shifting the attention from the individual to society. With this approach, a socio-pathogenic view of human violent behavior slowly began to undermine personal responsibility, and the historical religious control of human behavior clashed with the doctrine of individualism and the new radical social theories. Personal responsibility, that has always been an integral part of the history of our American society, has been substituted by social responsibility.

Much has been said recently about the amount of gratuitous violence in the various media, but violent events seem always to have had a certain attraction for people in the arts, and dramas and tragedies are a frequent part of artistic productions; many writers and poets have immortalized this violent behavior, the most well known, perhaps, being Shakespeare. There are numerous examples of violence in his works: The Rape of Lucrece, the many tragedies—Macbeth, Hamlet, Othello, and others. The chain of murderous actions that take place throughout them vividly portrays human jealousy, greed, and the quest for power, and the obsession with killing is vividly portrayed. In Macbeth, for example:

"Is this a dagger which I see before me,
The handle towards my hand? Come, let me clutch thee.
. . . art thou a dagger of the mind, a false creation
Proceeding from the heat-oppressed brain?
I see thee yet, in form as palpable
As this which now I draw.
. . . I see thee still;

And on thy blade and dudgeon gouts of blood, . . . "[13] In Hamlet the theme of violence is again presented. Claudius, the usurper King of Denmark, kills his own brother, but will eventually be killed by Prince Hamlet just before his own death by the poisoned sword of Laertes.[13] Many personages of these Shakespearean tragedies are doomed to death and the author painstakingly depicts chaotic intrigues and the evil of human destructive instincts.

Prior to Shakespeare, Dante, the thirteenth century Italian poet and wandering persecuted Florentine, could not resist placing the violent sinner in his Divine Comedy. The perpetrators of violence are located in the Inferno and they are portrayed as still actively violent and angry, even after death. He wrote: "And I, who was intent on watching it, could make out muddied people in that slime, all naked and their faces furious. These struck each other not with hands alone, but with their heads and chests and with their feet, and tore each other piecemeal with their teeth."[14] He so despised violent persons that he continued by saying that those souls, "whom anger has defeated," and who were suffering infernal pains while underneath the water that was bubbling because of their size, were bitter swallowers of slime. Did Dante's profound understanding of human nature lead him to believe that violence is so ingrained that it does not leave the violent person even after death?

Together with the theatre, many operatic productions have indulged in themes of violence: Verdi, with Othello, and Leoncavallo, with I Pagliacci, another human tragedy, to name only two. Paintings such as the Rape of the Sabines, by Jacques Louis David, Clarissa, the novel by Samuel Richardson, and films such as Anatomy of a Murder and Roshomon, as well as Psycho and The Silence of the Lambs, are also representative of artistic and literary representations of violence.

About a century before the Shakespearean tragedies that portrayed the violence of man against man, on the Italian peninsula, Cesare Borgia, a violent and dissolute individual who had his own brother assassinated, achieved legendary status for the horror of his many murders. Around that same period, in Russia, Ivan IV Vassileyvich, called the Terrible, imprisoned and tortured his son and apparently inflicted on him the coup de grace which truncated his son's life. Individuals have also been tortured by fascist and nazi and communist secret police throughout periods of dictatorship. But violence is not always as obvious as when it is overtly directed against individuals and may be a part of unjust laws aimed at populations at large. Even though there have been innumerable acts of individual violence against persons reported by historians, violence has also assumed collective characteristics, from the devastation of invaded territories by the victorious Roman armies to the barbaric invasions of Europe, the destruction of human lives during the Napoleonic campaigns, the genocide perpetrated by dictators like Stalin and Hitler, or the killing of thousands by liberators who felt forced to use atomic bombs in order to put a halt to a wave of destructive war that could have continued interminably.

Unquestionably, recorded history deals with facts and teaches us the vicissitudes and struggles of the ever evolving human race, but unless their motivation is explored it remains an interesting learning of successive human events. Necessarily, this investigative psychology of history is relegated to a select group of scholars and not to the masses, and while mythology, religious texts, art and history may have been good teachers for the illustration of human violence to the educated and observant person, the so-called common people had other ways of learning about their negative emotions of hostility, anger and violence.

The fables of Aesop and Phaedrus and the centuries old use of fairy tales still present in our society are good examples of the above. Indeed, through oral tradition and since the time of earliest recorded history, stories of violence have been passed down from one generation to another. They were a means of entertainment, but also a means of teaching moral values. Even in the most violent fairy tale there is a lesson to be learned, as opposed to the gratuitous violence seen in many films and television programs today. The story of Little Red Riding Hood, who is eaten by the wolf, is certainly one of the most violent of these tales. But Little Red Riding Hood escapes and returns home, having learned the importance of obeying her mother and realizing that violence may be just around the corner. And there are few children who have grown up without hearing the tale of Hansel and Gretel and their cruel step-mother, and the witch who wanted to eat them. And yet, the two children are able, with their own resourcefulness, to trick the witch and destroy her, and return home to their loving father. This can be seen as the mastering of evil through the use of ingenious thinking acquired in the process of coping with adversity.

While there are also fairy tales which tell of the positive side of humankind, the above mentioned ones, as well as many others, attempt to convey to children the message of the human tendency to violence, almost a gentle preparation or introduction to the concept of *homo homini lupus.* They have been and still are a popular means of conveying a message about the nature and life of man: they teach about positive and negative emotions of the gods, semi-gods and the common man. They use allegorical descriptions in order to explain the anger of humankind, its love, aggressivity, violence, selfishness or altruism. They also serve the useful purpose of alerting children to the existence of violence and of its unpredictability, and they may help them to be more objective in their assessment of human conduct, both their own and that of others.

Fairy tales and mythology seem to have a similar aim even though at different levels of human ontology. Fairy tales are less elaborate than myths and, even though probably born out of a desire to entertain children and open new vistas beyond that which is usually restricted to their often protective family environment, these stories employ a teaching procedure that, usually unknowingly, has made the best of the Piagetian and Kohlbergian developmental maturational stages. Through them the child is helped to learn methods of dealing with anger, hostility and violence, part of his human nature and part of his future. The child's interest is stimulated by stories which involve human conduct, often camouflaged as animal behavior, and through them and their interaction with their family and their world, they are helped to crystalize their own model of moral conduct. Child psychologist Bruno Bettleheim[15] believed fairy tales to be important in the life of the developing child. Indeed, he wrote, "Fairy tales . . . confront the child with the basic human predicament [life and death]" and for the growing child "the conviction that crime does not pay is a much more effective deterrent [than punishment or fear of it] and that is why in fairy tales the bad person always loses out."[p.8-9] Similar to Bettleheim's ideas regarding fairy tales is Kluckhohn's belief that one of the functions of myth is to achieve a "sublimation of antisocial tendencies."[3 p.76] And as Kirk wrote, "myths about murder or incest . . . purge us of an unhealthy preoccupation with these things, whereas ritual bloodshed directs our sadistic desires into a socially acceptable, even useful, form."[3 p.76]

Since the advent of television, fairy tales are most probably not as important a channel of communication between parents and children as they were in the past. Children are often placed in front of the television set and exposed to unrealistic, violent cartoons without the counseling presence of their parents. One may even wonder whether the diminishing of story telling that has accompanied the appearance of television has produced youngsters unprepared for an interactional life which demands problem solving almost on a continuous basis and occasional moral decisions. Could the above be counted as another cofactor in the genesis of adolescent violence in our society? While that is probably an exaggeration, I do believe that an intra-familial type of educational approach regarding acceptable behavior is essential for the development of good non-violent adolescent, and even adult, behavior.

Obviously, this short chapter can only touch upon the history of violence, but with this very brief review I have attempted to point out that it has always been present in society, particularly violence against the person. Since the beginning of time, humankind, aware of harboring violent instincts, has tried to contain them with sublimating approaches through the employment of religious teachings, myths and fairy tales that vary according to the period of ontological-moral development, or to control them with the adoption of commandments, codes, rules, and teachings that have developed over the centuries. But violence, in spite of all the well meaning approaches to it, continues to exist. This seems to testify to the fact that it is an integral part of humankind.

Chapter Two

THE BIOLOGY OF VIOLENCE

In an attempt to explain why people often seem to opt for a violent solution to problems encountered in their interpersonal relationships, numerous ethologists have attempted to establish a theory of aggression on the basis of animal studies. However well done and interesting these experiments may be, one should not forget that it may be unwise to relate or adapt the results of ethological studies to human behavior. Human behavior is much more complex than animal behavior. The human neocortex is extremely developed and differentiated and humans have developed feelings and emotions, a quid that clearly distinguishes them from an instinct driven animal. Humans are able to think, reflect and express their thoughts. Their behavior is object related or person related. They imagine, they create, and they destroy their creations, and through the plasticity of their neocortex have devised myriad ways to make their lives better — and at times worse. The plasticity of the brain is typical of humans. They are led not only by knowledge but also by acquired social-ethical norms which they use — or do not use — during the course of their lives, for both good and bad purposes.

Humans certainly are only minimally comparable to animals in their behavior. Therefore, a word of caution should be pronounced regarding the investigative operationalization of aggression in humans and its reproduction in laboratory studies with animals. Laboratory experimental studies of human aggression, even when performed with voluntary humans, can not recreate a natural setting with the spontaneity and impulsivity that is present in almost any type of violent behavior.

Lorenz,[16] with his hydraulic energy model, attempted to explain that hostility is in continuous flux, and tends to accumulate, like the flow and accumulation of liquid in a container. In his container, when the liquid reached a certain pressure threshold, it would open a valved spout and a sudden flow of accumulated liquid would escape. Lorenz equated basic instinctive actions with various gradients of pressure of the liquid in his hydraulic model. He then proposed, on the basis of this experiment, that

15

the force behind any instinctive behavior, a force that energizes aggressive behavior, has cumulative effects, and, if not regularly discharged, accumulates and eventually finds a target on which to release itself. He further theorized that when a specific target is not available the aggressive behavior may be triggered without an external stimulus. His experiment is quite intriguing because it could explain how hostility builds up in people, often to the point of explosive acting out, and that could possibly be the reason for the random violence that we witness so much today. Lorenz also supported the thesis that aggressive behavior may be philogenetically determined, and that ontogenesis itself only accounts for possible minor behavioral modification.

This equation between the accumulated liquid in a container that under high threshold pressure escapes and the energy that is usually present in humans, while interesting, appears, however, rather simplistic. Indeed, it does not explain the dynamics of the human emotion of hostility, of aggressiveness and violence, or the quality of feelings that generate them. It does, however, tell us that emotions or feelings may increase, charged by an energy that we could call *elan vital* and which fluctuates like a musical crescendo and diminuendo as a psychobiological force. Is this energy produced by feelings, or are the feelings produced by the energy? Are thoughts and feelings themselves energy? Possibly, in the future, molecular biology will be able to answer this puzzling question.

Lorenz viewed man as inheriting drives, among which that of aggression. In assuming that ontogenesis could involve only minor modifications of innate aggressive behavior, he explained that some philogenetically determined aggression remains in a state of latency, but may, at times, manifest itself under the pressure of environmental factors. He believed that humans have a propensity within themselves to react to stimuli that elicit fighting. He talked of releases of aggression and counter-releases, and also of modifiable aggression through learning.

Kuo[17] investigated the adaptability of animals to different forms of behavior when in different environments. Even though asserting that a flexible adaptation at the ontogenetic level is philogenetically determined and part of a reservoir of behavior potential which strengthens it throughout life, he was inclined to think that it would be safe to infer even stronger ontogenetic dominance in the developmental behavior of both primates and humans, giving more determining power to the self in its developmental choices.

In support of Lorenz's idea of an inborn aggressive drive in animals and possibly in man, the studies by Kruijt[1] of fighting cocks found that when in isolation the cocks manifested an instinctive aggressive behavior pattern. Can one suppose that when humans are isolated or marginalized in society they build up a similar tendency to strike out? The violent behavior that is present among some disadvantaged marginalized persons in our areas at a high risk for violence may find its explanation in Kruijt's studies. These studies have also been supported by Rasa's studies on chichlet fish which apparently demonstrated the most direct evidence so far of the spontaneity of aggression.[1]

Craig,[18] contrary to the inborn theory of aggression in animals, denied any biological urge for conspecific fighting and declared that such fighting in animals is motivated by fundamental needs and is often unavoidable, but is engaged in for the procurement of food, territory, the securing of reproductive mates, status among the group, and for control, adding that if these needs were satisfied without a conflict of interest with other animals, no fighting would ensue. Therefore, aggression in animals may serve the function of purposeful adaptation to the ecological surroundings. It is quite possible, however, that the animal, responding to stimuli from its immediate environment that at times convey a message of attack, counterattacks in self-defense, using behavioral patterns that may be either innate or learned.

Zillmann[1] proposed the theory that competitive activities may lead to violence and stated that aggression should be viewed as the force behind the preservation of the self and the species. However, he claimed that Lorenz's assertion that all species, including man, "are equipped with instinctive aggressive forces that when not discharged by appropriate external stimuli will result in a discharge towards potentially inappropriate targets or in a vacua . . ."[p.56] was unfounded and unwarranted. Zillmann[1] reports that Bigelow supported the theory of instincts and to some extent reminded us of the three brain theory of philogenetic evolution, when he stated that our animal responses have not evolved because we have evolved from lower animals.

Smith[19] gives an excellent basic explanation of the theory of the triune brain which has received wide publicity. He describes it as a belief that the vertebrate brain has evolved through three stages (protoreptilian, palaeomammalian and neomammalian) and these three complexes persist in primates as a highly integrated system, as stressed by MacLean's term triune. In the human, the protoreptilian layer is represented by the basal nuclei. The limbic system corresponds to the palaeomammalian layer which is involved in such behavior patterns in mammals as nursing and maternal care. The neocortex and thalamic structures, instead, correspond to the neomammalian layer and are concerned with "finely tuned sensory analysis and motor coordination, with memory association, and, in *Homo sapiens* with linguistic communication."[p.151]

That there may be a natural predisposition to aggression was the contention of Berkowitz,[20] in 1958, when he proposed that frustration, in itself, represents a threat. Later, while trying to establish which cues may stimulate an aggressive reaction in a stimulus response model, he put forward the proposal that the easy availability of guns in zones at risk may function as a stimulus for aggression because not only do they permit violence but they can also stimulate it. "The finger pulls the trigger, but the trigger may also be pulling the finger," he wrote.[21][p.2] He further wrote that a state of frustration may stimulate an individual's aggressive drive, placing him in a state of readiness for aggression as usually occurs in other animal species.[22]

In reviewing the possible similarities between human aggression and animal aggression, one should be reminded that the higher the organism the more flexible its adaptability. In humans, the adaptability should be viewed as being at a maximum compared to that of animals. The effect of knowledge, education, and moral values acquired through ontogenesis certainly have modifying power over those tendencies to aggressivity that have been acquired philogentically. One wonders whether it is wise and sound to make aggression an inevitable expression of the human condition.

Bandura[23] proposed that aggression, even though inborn as an aggressive instinct, may stimulate people who witness aggression being either rewarded or not punished to behave in a similar way. This could certainly reinforce the necessity for the exposure of children to a good role model in the family.

The reaction of American psychologists interested in animal behavior to the work of Lorenz and other European ethologists was at first somewhat skeptical. This seemed to be somewhat incongruous if one considers that Darwinism pervaded much of American culture at that time. However, Zillmann reports that as early as 1950 Beach partially accepted Lorenz's ideas and proposed that animal behavior was not simply a matter of heredity or environment, but a combination of both, with a predominance of the factor heredity. The ideas of Lorenz and their implications for human behavior also found some partial acceptance in the field of sociology. His work, even though not upheld by the general scientific community in the sixties and seventies, became a source of interest for social scientists investigating the genesis of human aggression. The world of science began to look at human behavior not only as the result of environmental, cultural, social and political factors on a *tabula rasa*, but also as due to predisposing biological and genetic factors. Johnson[24] reminds us that Ginsburg and Allee stated that the selective mating of animal species in order to obtain aggressive animals has been a rather successful common practice for many years. One can assume that an interplay of genetic inheritance in humans could also produce a predisposition to aggression and violence or that a similar effect may be the consequence of a chance mutation.

Is it possible that people may have a constitutional predisposition to aggressive behavior upon which socio-economic variables may act? And in what would that constitutional predisposition consist? Genetics may hold the answer in so far as the genome is present within an individual's particular constitution, with its biological information in a well defined set of genes. A phenotype subsequently manifests itself as the product of an interaction between the genotype and the environment. This is facilitated by cellular enzymatic processes which also lead to the myelinization of the brain structures, to the development of the neuro-endocrine system and to the action of growth hormones on the organism as a whole. It is a very complex play of DNA and RNA and nucleic and nucleinic acids that seems to be at the basis of our biologic selves.

In the seventies, American anthropologists, in their investigation of the origin and evolution of humankind, adopted a broader approach which included genetics, biology, ecology, medicine, and psychology, and ventured the idea that neurology would be the possible future link between biology and cultural anthropology.

There is no doubt that animal studies on aggression and their correlation to human behavior have stimulated the curiosity of social scientists and promoted biological and genetic contributions towards the understanding of human violent behavior. Through the years, the dichotomy of environment or genetic-biological factors as the basis of violent human behavior has been of paramount interest in scientific research.

As a young doctor in psychiatric training I spent several months of my educational period in the electroencephalographic department of Dr. Frederick Gibbs at the University of Illinois in Chicago. While becoming acquainted with the brain waves inscribed on what seemed to be interminable strips of paper, I often wondered about the possible relationship of those spikes not only to epileptic manifestations but to fluctuations in mood and behavior, and I envisioned the possibility that the tracings might one day reveal the abnormality of human thinking and of human behavior in general and specifically that of schizophrenics, manic depressives, or of the criminal and criminally aggressive and destructive people.

That was in 1957, and we were at the beginning of what I call the third psychiatric revolution—the advent of psychopharmacology. It was interesting—actually fascinating—to observe, during that historical period of psychiatry, those patients who had been mute, catatonic, detached, with loosely organized cognitive faculties or prey to disturbed affective behavior and delusions and hallucinations return to reality, reacquire a calm, relation oriented behavior and be freed from psychosis because of those newly discovered medicaments. I also wondered whether any of those brain cells influenced by those medications might be the site of biochemical activity, a biochemical activity that produces some kind of energy which might be that *quid* that enables us to think, behave and relate to others.

Degler[25] reports that Carmichael[26] and Hirsch[27] rejected the idea that it is only the environment that is determinant of human behavior and stated that "both behaviorists and vitalists overlooked the inherited determinants of behavior."[p.232] In fact, during the past two decades there has been a partial rejection of the theory that complex human behavior is due primarily to environmental conditioning, and scientific interest in the search for possible biological factors became stronger. Social scientists, such as Mazur and Robertson,[28] and Barkow,[29] have, indeed, questioned the stress that has been placed on the environment, almost to the exclusion of the biological approach, in trying to understand human conduct.

Indeed, it may be wiser to look at people as functional psychobiological units, with feelings generated by interpersonal encounters, idiosyncratic in their reactions. People should not be considered as cybernetic machines, but as a composite of an exquisite inherited substance influenced by an interplay of genetics, biology and environment.

At times we are confronted with criminal behavior or violent actions perpetrated by people who have been the recipient of good demographic variables. That should indicate, indeed, that personal, biological, genetic components, and not only socio-environmental demography, are also determinant of conduct. I have personally encountered in my professional life many young people who, regardless of race and social status, exhibited violent behavior and who, prior to their violent explosions, lived in well-functioning families, surrounded by devoted parents, participant of no more than the average financial ups and downs, and exposed to the best education within the limits of their family possibilities. They also claimed a good relationship with their significant others but, nevertheless, exhibited explosive, destructive behavior even against them.

In many of these cases it would be hard to believe that their behavior was due to the type of environment they were raised in. And, if not the environment, what can account for their destructive behavior if not their biological selves? In the words of Willhoite,[30] "We are genetically programmed to learn and persist in certain kinds of behavior much more readily than is the case with other possible behavior.... this does not necessarily mean that a particular behavior is inheritable, rather than that heredity significantly affects the probability of its development."

As Bergson[25] aptly stated, "We are fond of saying that society exists and that hence it inevitably exerts a constraint on its members.... but in the first place, for society to exist at all the individual must bring with it a whole group of inborn tendencies; society, therefore, is not self explanatory so we must search below the social accretion."p.270 Below that social accretion there are people with their individuality who defy any stratification or robotization, and who still remain an unknown in their totality because of the complexity of their nature.

That is why ethological studies of animal aggression can serve us only as a working hypothesis. They cannot serve as a specific interpretation for human behavior and aggression. One should not forget that the human brain/mind is so extremely developed in its functioning that it defies any generalizations of behavior. Generalizations, even in human studies should be limited to working hypotheses.

It is established, then, that any scientific study of human violence should address the subject being investigated—the violent person—as a bio-psychological functional unit reacting to a specific ecological milieu. This approach recognizes the unique, idiosyncratic reaction to stressful stimuli that is proper to all humans. This is a personal predisposition, which, even though distinguishing one person from another, rises above any racial issues, and limits itself to the interaction between a genetic, biological, inheritable self with social-environmental factors. Only if the scientific study adheres to the above can it retain its objectivity and usefulness.

Statistical analyses are conducted on groups of people, usually with similar characteristics, and even though allowing for the drawing of conclusions on a larger scale, they should also take into consideration the individual components of that group. Any studies involving groups should always be taken with a grain of salt, however I do not agree with Murdock, the Yale anthropologist, who, according to Degler,[25] already in 1972, repudiated the conviction that had been held until then that studies of social aggregates are preferable to individual studies. He proposed that social scientists center their research on the individual as is commonly done in biological research.

However, in reviewing the literature on violence from a biological point of view, I see that most of the research continues to take into consideration not individuals, but groups of people with similar behavior. This method of analytical study has become widespread in scientific circles, and is thought to be more objective than the investigation of one or two people which is then projected to a larger population group, with questionable generalizations.

The biological assessment of violent people is as important as the socio-demographic one. It is, indeed, the human brain at the basis of behavior that moves people towards one another, either with friendly or with hostile, destructive thoughts. It is reasonable, then, to ask what takes place within our brains: are there biochemical reactions during periods of affection or of hatred, at the moment of making love or of killing?

The possibility that biological factors affecting an individual's body, and especially the brain, may be at the basis of violent behavior has long attracted the interest and scientific attention of clinicians and researchers. Cesare Lombroso,[31,32] who lived more than a century ago, and whom many regard as the father of the criminal anthropological school, in opposition to the then dominant school of thought which upheld free will as the determining factor in crime, originated the theory of the "born criminal," based on a biological and moral degeneracy.[32] This born criminal, according to Lombroso, was driven to his antisocial act by a particular atavistic inheritable makeup, which he believed was akin to a rather primitive evolutionary stage of the human race. The born criminal was averse to socialization and not amenable to adaptation.

This Lombrosian idea of degeneracy brought about the belief that the born criminal was some kind of sub-human creature who had a natural drive for crime. One could argue that his ideas were influenced by the theories of Darwin, or even by some botanical theories of the time which regarded the groups of plants recently discovered to be carnivorous because they have a tendency to capture insects and use them as nourishment. This may have influenced Lombroso's theoretical hypothesis that destructive aggression in the human species is also inborn, as in carnivorous plants. These botanical theories were later refuted by H. Wagner in Die Fleischfressenden Pflanzen,[33] when he stated that carnivorous plants are such due to a process of adaptation to a ground lacking in nitrogen substances. Could this process of adaptation explain much of our present day violence in the poor, disadvantaged areas of our cities, where many inhabitants destroy one another?

The Lombrosian school also attempted to compare animal aggressive behavior to human aggressive behavior. It equated homicide by necessity (self-defense) to the animal killing another animal in order to procure food; homicide in defense of personal dignity was likened to the attempts by the animal to maintain a dominant role within the group; and homicide due to jealousy to animal aggression toward other male members of the herd in order to keep possession of the female.[34] In addition to the above, similarities between humans and animals were seen in the killing for self preservation or as a defense of one's territoriality.

Around that same period, Adolf Lenz,[34] an Austrian jurist, proposed a broader view of criminal biology. He included in his view of the criminal not only somatic inherited or acquired characteristics, but also the criminal's psychological self, product of life experiences, which he termed *Erlebnis* (life experience). This is one of the earliest mentions that the characteristic psychological attitudes of the criminals may be involved in their criminal actions. In so doing, Lenz emphasized the totality of the personality in action of the offender.

Kretschmer,[35] in his Korper Bau und Character, attempted to assess criminals on the basis of their physical habitus dividing them into four distinct types: the pyknic, the asthenic, the athletic, and the dysplastic. He believed that a particular type of criminal behavior corresponded to each of them: the pyknic, he said, was prone to crimes of passion, anger states, and suicide; the asthenic type tended towards misdemeanors and would be frequently recidivist; the athletic type, instead, frequently was associated with brutal criminal actions, violent murders, armed robberies, and was impulsive in his emotional expressions. How remindful this particular athletic habitus is of many violent offenders I meet in visiting the jails and prisons!

Kretschmar described the dysplastic type as hypogonadic, deficient in his sexual characteristics, intellectually and morally inadequate, and prone to mental diseases such as schizophrenia. This latter type would probably form, today, the cohort of sexual paraphiliacs as defined in DSM–IV. Kretschmar believed that criminals manifest their antisocial tendencies primarily between the ages of eighteen and twenty-four. He also thought that they would be frequent recidivists. Penrose criticized the theories of Kretschmar as well as that proposed by Sheldon which classified humans into endomorphic, mesomorphic and ectomorphic types, believing that typology has only marginal importance in the determinism of crime.[34]

At the beginning of the nineteenth century, writing around the same time as Kretschmar, Gall,[32,36] a Viennese physician interested in neuro-anatomy, theorized that the protruberances of the human skull correspond to the various cerebral lobes lying underneath the bony structure. He formulated the idea that the size and shape of those cranial protuberances reflect the individual's mental ability/capacity and predispositions to a given conduct. In so doing, he gave birth to what was called craniology, a forerunner of phrenology. Dr. Gall believed that he could detect in his jailed prisoners, through the study of their skulls, their tendency to fight, to lie or to steal.

In the United States, physicians and alienists, such as Cardwell at the Transylvania University in Kentucky, and Dr. Amariah Brigham at the New York State Lunatic Asylum, also firmly believed that faculties of the mind were reflected in the shape of the skull.[32]

Following Lombroso's theory of degeneracy and his born criminal, a wave of scientific and social interest was created. The Lombrosian trend to see the criminal or the mentally deranged person as socially diverse also opened the door to a great deal of socio-political prejudice. In 1857, Augustine Benois,[32] a French physician, had pointed out innumerable varieties of physical degeneration in people, which he thought matched their moral depravity, their socially abusive and offensive behavior, and their mental deficiencies. Bromberg[32] stated, regarding the last half of the nineteenth century, "Degeneracy of the mind and the moral sense was accepted as the cause of crime," and added that Lydston had put forward his view that criminality is determined by neurological forms of inherited degeneration when he wrote, "The closer we get to the marrow of criminality . . . the more closely it approximates pathology."p.56

The above obviously calls for reflection and interpretation. Beliefs that physical attributes, an inharmonious development, unattractive features, or at times actual ugliness, have been held since time immemorial as an expression of inner attributes of evilness of mind, enviousness, and hostile thoughts. These are popularly held convictions and superstitions which have clung tenaciously in different cultures. They probably derive from the associations made by primitive people of bad with ugly and good with beautiful. In reporting the ugliness of the deformed Thersites, Homer described him as a man with "harsh or scanty hair, and like a pot that had collapsed to a peak in the baking," and he associated his physical features with the possible behavior of a criminal mind. This early thinking of ugly—bad and beautiful—good, also has some Platonism in it.

One cannot always dismiss popular beliefs *tout court,* however. The ancient Romans believed that *vox populi vox dei,* and current popular belief is that "where there is smoke there is fire." Should we disregard the observations and beliefs of many observers of human nature and scholars in their own disciplines, or, rather, should we attempt to see if there is an actual basis for their beliefs, in this case the relationship between personal attributes and antisocial behavior? Could it be that these observers were principally concerned with the external appearances or behavioral manifestations of criminals while we, instead are more interested in how the human mind thinks, feels and acts? Can the two observations and interests, theirs and ours, be reconciled? Can they become complementary instead of being regarded as antagonistic and exclusive?

There is no doubt that the physical characteristics of present day offenders with antisocial personalities are not at all remindful of the well known description of the Lombrosian born criminal with long ears, broad cheekbones, scanty beard, strongly developed canines, thin lips, frequent nystagmus and contractions of the sides of their faces, and with the span of their arms often exceeding their height. Indeed, many of them are healthy, well-developed and good looking persons. Nevertheless, I would like to propose that at times some individuals, born with some physical or constitutional defects, may develop feelings of inadequacy, feelings of resentment and hostility toward family and society, for having received a "bad deal," in their life. Because of these feelings, could they, at times, be prone to express more hostile and destructive behavior than the average individual towards those people whom they feel are critical of them, are rejecting them or whom they feel are "better" than they are? That type of feeling, in my experience, even though not necessarily acted upon, is frequently expressed by neurotics who are unable to accept their physical self. Many criminals belong to the large category of neurotics and psychodynamically many of them have hostile feelings of resentment which often stem from this non-acceptance of the self. This may contribute to the dynamics of their misconduct.

One can certainly theorize that the above interpretation could bridge the gap between the external, physical objective facts emphasized by the Lombrosian theory and the modern psychodynamic interpretation of criminal behavior. It is undeniable that we all experience the effect of our looks on our psychological self. If one accepts that poor socioeconomic factors may be at the basis of crime, why should poor physical attributes not be taken into consideration as a possible cause of angry, hostile behavior? Demographic variables and personal attributes may be a source not only of pleasure and positive attitudes, but also of anger and resentment.

The theory of degeneracy continued to be accepted as a basic predisposing cause of criminal behavior, and dominated the scientific and cultural scene for a long period, both in the United States and abroad. It was not until the time of Charles Goring's longitudinal study of more than 3,000 English criminals that the theory of degeneracy was refuted. In his report, he clearly stated that there was no correlation between physical degeneracy and criminal conduct.[32] However, even though the Lombrosian theory was disproved and came to be rejected, the feeling remained among clinicians that moral characteristics were the expression of a psychic morbidity or psychic degeneracy. This belief continued up to the time of Esquirol and Pinel, and was later substituted by the term "constitutional psychopathic inferiority" proposed by Adolf Meyer.[32] This new terminology reflected the importance that scholars were then giving to interpersonal relationships.

After this short historical excursus into some of the most important biological theories of the phenomenon of violence, it seems appropriate to discuss some of the physiological dysfunctions and disease entities of which aggressive behavior is a clinical manifestation. The investigative study of selected clinical entities which have as a manifestation disordered, often violent, behavior can help grasp the possible organic factors in violence. Although there is a wealth of reports on the presence of biological noxae in aggressive and violent individuals, it is still premature to determine whether they are causative factors or just unrelated findings.

I would like to take into consideration the episodic dyscontrol syndrome, the syndrome of temporal lobe dysfunction, the attention deficit disorder or minimal brain disorder. I will attempt to show that at the basis of each of them there are, at times, neurological disturbances, occasionally quite serious. Indeed, when confronted with what is called motiveless, aggressive, destructive behavior, it is natural to think that such explosive conduct may have an organic cause at its basis, most likely involving a neurophysiological short circuit. I will also briefly discuss the importance of twin studies and chromosomal abnormality studies in the genesis of aggression.

Smith[19] writes that molecular biology has made spectacular progress in recent years, not least in the analysis of the central nervous system, and there is no doubt that new understandings of neural functioning will follow. The syndromes of sudden explosive behavior, minimal brain disorder, temporal lobe epilepsy, and partial complex seizures should be viewed as descriptive terms behind which there is functional or anatomic pathology of specific brain structures. Fenwick,[37] stated that automatism, sane or insane in type, representing a split-second disruption of consciousness, may explain impulsive aggressive behavior in previously law abiding citizens.

Papez's[38] discovery of the limbic lobe as a substrate of emotion in 1837 opened a new vista for the interpretation of aggressive behavior, and not just for the common emotions of love, affection and hate. The possibility that the structures of the limbic lobe may be affected by traumatic brain pathology, small tumors or encephalitis, must be taken into consideration when investigating aggressive behavior. At times, aggressive behavior may result from the dysfunctional interplay of brain structures like the antero-lateral hypothalamus and the posterior thalamus, the preoptical nuclei, the antero-median part of the amygdala, and the more superficial structures such as the frontal or pre-frontal cortex. This interplay is well evidenced when there is the presence of lesions of the orbital frontal regions, as pointed out by Luria[39] in 1969, when, because of the decreased inhibitory effect of this part of the brain over the deeper structures, the individual becomes impulsive, aggressive, prone to rage and predatory aggression, and at times exhibits a psychopathic type of behavior.

A study by Jarvie[40] showed that frontal lobe lesions may act as a disinhibitor of social control and this was also corroborated by a study by Blumer and Benson.[41] Grafman and collaborators[42] put great emphasis on their observation that personality changes, often to the point of psychiatric symptomatology, are also common after frontal lobe damage. A pseudo-psychopathic personality characterized by a lack of impulse control, irritability, anger, and hostility usually ensues following injury of the orbital frontal regions. Results of the above studies suggest that chronic recidivistic violent behavior, even though a minimal part of the larger bulk of criminal offenses, may be due to a biological or neuro-physiological predisposition.

Miller[43] suggests that "impairment of language related skills and regulative functions controlled by the frontal lobes have been found with some consistency in antisocial populations. He regards this as indicative of developmental failure rather than neurological damage, and proposes that delinquents, more particularly those identified as violent and impulsive, may have a relative inability to use inner speech to modulate attention, affect, thought, and behavior under conditions of stress."

The earliest studies of EEG abnormalities of violent people by Hill and Waterson[44] in 1942, and Silverman[45] in 1944, reported various non-specific abnormalities in the electroencephalogram of the criminals they tested. However, in 1947, Gibbs, Bagchi, and Bloomberg,[46] in a study of 452 prisoners and 1,432 non-prisoner controls, found no significant differences in the EEG tracings of the two groups, concluding that "subclinical forms of [epilepsy and organic brain disease] are not contributing factors in a significant faction of the 'sane' criminal population."[p.297] Mednick and Volavka,[47] believing that Gibb's results were due to the misinterpretation of data, reanalyzed them and found a higher number of abnormalities among the tracings of the offenders. Buikhuisen,[48] states that the reanalysis by Mednick and Volavka of the above mentioned study was of great importance because people, influenced by the results of Gibbs and collaborators, had accepted their conclusions that the EEGs of criminals are not abnormal. He wrote, "Most of the studies carried out agree that the proportion of abnormal EEGs is higher among criminals than among controls,"[p.209] and he added that this is especially true of studies regarding violent offenders, citing Williams,[49] Monroe,[50] and Bach-y-Rita[51] in cases concerning episodic dyscontrol. Buikhuisen seems to support the opinion of Yeudall[52] and of Mednick and Volavka[47] that there is ample evidence to support the "hypotheses of brain dysfunction in aggressive patients. . . . and the weight of research finding strongly supports a conclusion that criminal EEGs are more frequently classified as abnormal than those of non-criminal control subjects."p.209

Zilboorg[53] reports that already at the time of Kraeplin, the epileptic's mood was described as ranging from good natured to angry, coupled with occasional explosive behavior, at times to the point of threatening physical violence. Unfortunately, because of their rapid mood swings, people suffering from temporal lobe epilepsy often alienate themselves from friends and relatives. During the course of my professional experience, I have frequently encountered persons suffering from epilepsy who exhibited, in addition to an aggressive disposition, a highly emotional state and frequent attacks of anger mixed with paranoid ideation, and also noted, at times, viscosity of speech.

Delgado-Escueta and collaborators[54] pointed out that as a rule a complex partial seizure, CPS, shows behavior that is short and self limited, fumbling and purposeless, and with only occasional minimal aggressive behavior during seizures. Today's clinical investigation has shifted from the ictal seizure to the interictal seizure discharge. Interictal explosive behavior and irritability are common occurrences in seizure patients with temporal lobe involvement, and this behavior is thought to be due to excessive neural activity and often associated with a confusing variety of mental and behavior features.[54] At times, such patients show moodiness and explosiveness in the form of intensive verbalized anger and threatened physical violence or suicide and paranoid ideation, and because of this may cause many problems within a family.[41]

The literature on hostile attacks or violent manifestations in epileptics is controversial. Epileptic violence has been thought by some to be a reaction to the restraining attempt on the part of onlookers who are trying to help the epileptic during a seizure, especially the partial complex type. However, that should refer, if at all, to the ictal period of the seizure. Fayette and collaborators, Witkin and collaborators, and Williams have reported the presence of concomitant abnormal electroencephalographic findings in individuals classified as amotivated murderers or psychotic murderers and who exhibited recurrent violent behavior.[55]

At times, in patients who are suffering from clinical psychomotor seizures or limbic ictus, but who have a normal surface electroencephalogram, epileptogenic foci may be detected only with depth electrodes. Stone[56] believes that people suffering from limbic epilepsy, alias interictal dyscontrol explosive syndrome, are persons adapting to a bewildering type of disorder, and suggests that the organic factors in this type of behavioral manifestation should be sought out very diligently and thoroughly. The episodic dyscontrol syndrome usually occurs during the interictal period. At that time, the individual shows rage attacks against people or things, often of a very violent nature. It is common knowledge that a positive electroencephalogram finding is infrequent in persons suffering from epilepsy; therefore, as a criterium ex adiuvantibus, violent people who are suspected of suffering from temporal lobe epilepsy or a partial complex seizure, or whose violence is diagnosed as explosive, may benefit from antiepileptic medication, especially Tegretol.

Rickler[57] reports that Bach-y-Rita[51] and collaborators found electroencephalographic abnormalities in fifty percent of their violent patients, mostly consisting of spiking in the temporal region; thirteen of one hundred twenty-three patients had undiagnosed temporal lobe epilepsy. Elliot[58] noted significant EEG abnormalities in more than sixty percent of his cases; and Monroe[59] reported abnormalities, both focal and generalized in fifty-eight percent of ninety-three aggressive criminals with two EEG tracings.

Bear[60] stated the following: "We and others have observed aggressive behavior in many patients with temporal lobe epilepsy," adding that it is obvious that this is not the only important cause of aggression. "In selected cases neurosurgical intervention has been shown to be effective in reducing aggression, . . . The severity of any interictal behavior changes, including aggressiveness, appear to be independent of or even inversely correlated to seizures frequency."

In addition to recent research on the limbic lobe, the amygdala, and the mesio-temporal lobe, researchers have investigated what have been considered innocent electroencephalographic spikes. Some have reported that the presence of spikes may affect cognition, even though briefly and, at times, recurrently.[61,62]

Recent studies with new brain imaging techniques, such as Positron Emission Tomography studies (PET), Single Photon Emission Computed Tomography (SPECT) and Magnetoencephalography, reveal that specific dysfunctions visualized by these techniques correlate with behavioral manifestations, as, for example, in the dyscontrol syndrome. Fenwick[37] postulates that the advent of magnetoencephalography, the measurement of magnetic brain activity, contrary to the electroencephalographic tracing, may enable us to detect and monitor those deep areas of the brain where spikes usually arise before spreading to the cortex, giving us the tracings of the firing activity of deep-line nigro-hippocampal structures.

Scandinavian studies show that children who exhibit epileptic spikes without suffering from tonic-clonic convulsive seizures or fits of any other type exhibit cognitive dysfunction and difficulties in learning.[61] This is due to frequent *lapsus mentis* while the firing activity is present. However, it has been shown that single spikes are also seen in hyperkinetic children with or without brain damage, and in people suffering from schizophrenia or depression during the acute remission of their illnesses.[63] One can question whether isolated spikes in the electroencephalogram have the same meaning as the ST changes that are observed on a normal electrocardiogram, or if they are really the expression of brain dysrythmia which may be accompanied by fleeting and recurrent impairment of cognition. This could be quite useful in properly diagnosing those children who appear to be rather distractable or restless and who are usually diagnosed as suffering from conduct disorder or hyperactive behavior.

Karl Menninger[64] attempted to explain human aggression with his theory of dysfunction/dyscontrol. He claimed that an explosive destructive act, or a series of acts, is the outcome of internal disorganization and the individual's incapacity to control basic, dangerous impulses and he thought that this could explain chronic, repetitive, aggressive behavior, or episodic impulsive violence such as homicidal assaultiveness.

A recent study states the following, "A decompensating patient with poor impulse control may be at risk for violence in the community regardless of the diagnosis."[65] p.731 In the study, the diagnosis of both schizophrenia and mania were associated with dangerous behavior. Many patients were more unpredictable and emotionally explosive during the first period of their hospitalization. The attack is often sudden and preceded by a very short period of dysphoric mood. The behavior is usually incongruous with the individual's usual behavior, and is described as a sudden change of the personality.[66] The individual so affected usually seems to have a pleasant personality between episodes of violence. This episodic dyscontrol syndrome is often the cause of wife beating and child abuse, aggressiveness, suicide, motiveless homicide. In fact, Ervin and Mark,[67] describing the episodic dyscontrol syndrome and its four characteristic symptoms, give the first as being a tendency to physical assault, especially of the wife and children. Monroe[50] characterized the dyscontrol syndrome as a highly impulsive and unreflective act, sudden and paroxysmal. In addition, it is often associated with developmental or acquired biological defects, often involving the medio-temporal lobes of the brain.

Among the developmental disorders, there is a disruptive type of behavior called attention-deficit hyperactive disorder which is classified in the DSM–IV[68] as a disturbance of at least six months duration, during which at least six of the following symptoms of inattention or of hyperactivity-impulsivity have been present to a degree that is maladaptive and inconsistent with the individual's developmental level. Symptoms of inattention are: (1) often fails to give close attention to details or makes careless mistakes in schoolwork, work, or other activities; (2) often has difficulty in sustaining attention in tasks or play activities; (3) often does not appear to listen when directly spoken to; (4) often does not follow through on instructions and fails to finish schoolwork, chores, or duties in the workplace; (5) often has difficulty organizing tasks and activities; (6) often avoids, dislikes, or is reluctant to engage in tasks that require sustained mental effort; (7) often loses things necessary for tasks or activities; (8) is often easily distracted by extraneous stimuli; (9) is often forgetful in daily activities.

Symptoms of hyperactivity are given as: (1) often fidgets with hands or feet or squirms in seat; (2) often leaves seat in classroom or other places where remaining seated is expected; (3) often runs about or climbs excessively in inappropriate situations (this may be limited to subjective feelings of restlessness in adolescents or adults); (4) often has difficulty in playing or engaging in leisure activities quietly; (5) often "on the go" or acts as if "driven by a motor"; (6) often talks excessively. Symptoms of impulsivity are given as: (1) often blurts out answers before questions have been completed; (2) often has difficulty awaiting turn; and (3) often interrupts or intrudes on others.

In order to apply this diagnostic labeling, the onset of some of the symptoms should have been present before the age of seven; there is some impairment due to the symptoms in two or more settings; there is clear evidence of clinically significant impairment in functioning socially, academically or in the occupational setting. Finally, the symptoms do not occur "exclusively during the course of a Pervasive Developmental Disorder, Schizophrenia, or other Psychotic disorder and are not better accounted for by another mental disorder . . . "[p.65]

The severity of this attention deficit hyperactivity disorder goes from mild to severe, involving the cognitive or behavioral sphere, and may manifest itself, as above stated, in the home, at school or in social functions. In my experience this disorder is more common in boys than in girls and one of the most common manifestations of the condition in these children or early adolescents is that they have a short attention span, they appear to be rather impulsive, hyperactive, hypertalkative, and often endowed with average or superior intelligence. Indeed, their inattentive behavior at school may often be due to the fact that the school does not challenge their intellectual capabilities. The attention deficit disorder may accompany various other syndromes such as the borderline syndrome, the episodic dyscontrol syndrome, delinquent behavior in the young, and antisocial behavior in the adolescent and adult. Children suffering from the syndrome may become antisocial and involved in disruptive behavior. Occasionally these youngsters benefit from methylphenidate in appropriate dosages.

The syndrome of minimal brain dysfunction or hyperactive brain syndrome is at times observable in adults who, even though possessing average or above average intelligence, are not functioning at their best. Their behavior fluctuates from apathy to restlessness. They often change employment, and may be unable to pursue goal directed endeavors to completion. They usually end up being jobless, using drugs, and often go on welfare. At times one can notice in these persons soft neurological signs as well as various handicaps that have been with them for a lifetime and to which they have become so accustomed that they no longer think of them as abnormalities.

Elliott[66] reports that these individuals may, at times, be unable to knot a tie or to catch a ball, or to read with a certain easiness. They may be unable to distinguish the right hand from the left or follow a map. They also have more specific cognitive problems such as learning deficits; they may be dyslexic, have difficulty in spelling or in doing simple arithmetical problems. An underlying organic disorder should be sought. The pathological syndromes which at times lead to aggressive behavior such as the episodic dyscontrol, the hyperactive minimal brain syndrome, and the antisocial personality may be influenced by genetic factors. Even though the majority of people think that this type of behavior is just a reaction to environmental influences and a sign of character disturbance, there seems to be a good possibility that they are based on genetic or organic inherited factors.

In his review of the literature on violence and biological factors connected with it, Elliott[66] differentiates various types of aggression. For example, he reports that aggressive rage, with restless unprovoked violent behavior, is probably due to the lack of the inhibitor effect of the prefrontal cortex on lower lying, midline cerebral structures. Predatory aggression is thought to be due, in all probability, to the stimulation of antero and lateral hypothalamic structures, the preoptical nuclei of the thalamus, and, at times, the amygdala in its antero-median side. Lastly, Elliott reports a syndrome of compulsive aggression in which he includes temporal epilepsy, tumors of the temporal lobes, minimal brain syndrome, encephalitic sequelae or encephalopathic states. This compulsive aggression may be subsequent to hippocampal, cerebellar and pontine lesions. It is also found in subarachnoid hemorrhages, multiple sclerosis, tumors, hemorrhages, pressure hydrocephalus, cerebral malaria, hypoglycemia, Cushing's disease, phencyclidine, alcohol, benzodiazepine release effects, and, Alzheimer's disease.

It is a common observation that boys are more aggressive than girls. Even though, to most of us, this is obviously a natural biological condition, attempts have been made to attribute the behavior to social, cultural, and familial influences. Suggestions have been also made that in order to influence boys' natural tendency to aggression they should be exposed more to the educational teachings and values to which girls are generally exposed.[69] This seems to reflect the present day culture of equalization of the sexes at all costs and needs no further comment.

In supporting a developmental neuro-organic theory of human aggression, one should take into consideration the effect of testosterone on the brain. Androgens, and especially testosterone, exercise their influence on the development of the brain and, in particular, of the preoptic hypothalamic nucleus, already during the prenatal period. The hormone testosterone is also responsible for maintaining a normal level of aggressivity in both men and women, who, when under the effect of higher doses of this hormone become more aggressive in their behavior. In fact, while impotence in men may be a cause of physical, and at times attempted sexual violence against women, hypersexuality due to hormonal influences may also be at the basis of assault and rape. The counterpart of the high testosterone level leading to aggressive tendencies in men is the premenstrual syndrome in women. It is a well known fact, indeed, that during the premenstrual period many women become tense, irritable, aggressive, and more easily lose their self control. This seems to be due to lowered levels of progesterone and higher levels of prolactin.[70]

A very interesting metabolic dysfunction that may cause violence, either verbal or physical, is hypoglycemia, which may be due to pancreatic insulinoma, hyperinsulinism, diabetes, or pre-diabetic states. In hypoglycemic violence there is usually a state of confusion prior to and during the period of aggressivity or anger attacks. At times, there have been concomitant electroencephalographic abnormalities. Wilder[71] believed that hypoglycemic states, even below 40 milligrams/hundred, may lead to serious violent crime. A study done at the Karolinska Institute in Sweden was also related to hypoglycemic states.[72] Forty-three impulsive and fifteen non-impulsive alcoholic offenders and twenty-one healthy volunteers, all inpatients of a forensic psychiatric department, "underwent lumbar puncture and oral and aspartame challenges and their diurnal activity rhythm was measured with physical activity monitors."[p.20] The authors found that Finnish alcoholic impulsive offenders and fire setters had a relatively low cerebral spinal fluid 5-hydroxy indolacetic acid (5-HIAA) and their response to oral blood glucose tolerance tests showed a low blood glucose nadir. The purpose of the study was to relate the association of unprovoked interpersonal violence with a low concentration of 5-HIAA in cerebral spinal fluid. The authors theorized that the low serotonin level in their subjects was a part of a defective central serotonin turnover which would affect the supra chiasmatic nuclei whose function is believed to be the regulation of the metabolism of glucose, as well as being an endogenous circadian pacemaker. The subjects of the study also exhibited irregularity of sleep. Whether their unprovoked interpersonal violence and their irregularity of sleep was due to a low serotonin level or to a low blood sugar, which also may precipitate interpersonal violence, is still unclear.

In a further study assessing the personality profile and the state of aggressiveness of a similar type of subject, the same authors concluded that alcoholic violent offenders with low cerebral spinal fluid of 5-HIAA concentrations have high irritability, impulsivity and anxiety ratings in the KSP (Karolinska Scale of Personality). A subgroup of antisocial personality disorders which exhibited high free testosterone and low corticotropic concentration demonstrated a low socialization and high monotony avoidance in sensation seeking rates on the same Karolinska Scale of Personality test.

The relationship between age and aggression may also be the expression of a biological parameter. Aggression is most frequent between the ages of sixteen and thirty-four. It is thought that this may be due to high levels of testosterone in men and even in women. However, Kaes,[73] already in 1907, and much later Yakovlev and Lecours,[74] proposed that the above could be due to an impaired process of the myelinization which is necessary for the development of mental discriminatory capacities, good judgement, self control, and the development of a social conscience. These mental functions are thought to be localized in the frontal and temporal lobes. Corresponding to the recognized period of highest aggression in humans, poor or delayed myelinization is frequent in the age bracket of sixteen to thirty-four. Myelinization of these important parts of the brain is reported to be sometimes delayed up to the third or fourth decade of life, while a process of synaptic connections and dendrite sprouting continues until late in life. This would support the possibility that physiological immaturity is at the basis of violence among young people, and is an important factor to be considered in any rehabilitation program. Could the late completion of brain myelinization and continuous dendritic sprouting be correlated to the diminishing violent behavior during middle life in previously violent young adolescents and young adults? The above appears to indicate that there is a good possibility that this is true.

Searching for other manifestations of organic deficits at the basis of violence, we should also consider the intelligence level of the offender. Based on my clinical interviews and psychometric testing, I have found that a large number of inmates have a low-normal Intelligence Quotient. The contention that IQ scores are strongly related to crime is supported by Hirschi and Hindelang,[75] who concluded that the weight of evidence is that IQ is more important than race and social class for predicting criminal behavior. The above statement is also supported by more recent research by Moffitt, Gabrielli, Mednick, and Shulsinger.[76] In their Danish studies they concluded that children with low IQs may be more prone to engage in delinquent behavior. Those children also failed in school because of their poor verbal ability. They stated that these early experiences may contribute to later delinquency by creating in the children a negative attitude towards authority, or by encouraging them to seek acceptance in a less socially desirable setting, and by being more sensitive to delinquent peer pressure. A study in 1977 by Kirkegaard, Sorenson, and Mednick,[77] concluded that those juveniles who later committed criminal acts were shown to have a lower tested intelligence than their more law abiding peers.

The study by Jacobs and colleagues[78] brought to the attention of the scientific world the possibility of chromosomal aberration as the basis of disturbed, at times violent, behavior. Nevertheless, since this first paper, as often happens, contrasting views regarding the connection between chromosomal variations and possible violence/criminality have been reported. The results of the Copenhagen study of Witkin and collaborators,[79] perhaps the most well-known, do not support a direct link between XYY and XXY populations and criminality or violence. However, in evaluating their review of the aggression hypothesis, Witkin stated that according to this view an extra Y chromosome increases aggressive tendencies and may lead to increased criminal behavior. Their interesting and well documented study did reveal that the frequency with which XYY (five of twelve, or 41.75%) and XXY (three of sixteen or 18%) were involved in criminal behavior was higher than the XY controls (9.3%), a statistically significant result. They also found that most of the offenses were against property and only one of the XYY individuals committed an act of aggression against people and only one of the XXY individuals "assaulted his wife in an extremely brutal way . . ."[p.551] Witkin concluded by stating that "the data from the documentary records we have examined speak of society's legitimate concern about aggression among XYY and XXY men. . . . [even though] no evidence has been found that men with either of those sex chromosome complements are especially aggressive."[p.555] Craft stated that just as with other immature offenders the XYY, XXY, and XXX offenders need the safety, time, and education necessary to achieve maturity.[80] "I am aware of the controversial nature of the subject and I am also cognizant of not holding the final answer, but I feel that regardless of statistical studies, pros and cons, and until that answer is found, the screening of XXY and XYY chromosomes in violent individuals should be done in order to be more thorough and objective. That is essentially what is suggested here. Obviously, I do not consider all those persons carrying the XYY and XXY chromosomes to be violent/dangerous individuals. Violent crime is due to a combination of variables and a personal predisposition."

Persons with XXY chromosomes have been described as being individuals who may be highly irresponsible and immature and whose misconduct causes concern at a very early age. The family background does not appear to be responsible for their behavior. They come into early conflict with the law, and while their criminal activity is primarily aimed at property, if antagonized their violence may also be directed against persons.[79]

As a curiosity, a recent report from Nijmegen, The Netherlands,[81] concerning a rather large family, shed some light on the possible link between an excessive amount of neurotransmitters in the brain and violence. A pattern of aggressive behavior was noted in eight males in this family who demonstrated ups and downs of aggressive behavior over time. It was found that the eight subjects shared "a syndrome of border-line mental retardation and a tendency towards bouts of impulsive aggression, often in response to stress," and "a genetic defect in the eighth exxon of the MAO–A structural gene on the X chromosome" was present. Could a deficiency in the enzymatic MAO–A activity in metabo-lizing neurotransmitters such as dopamine, serotonin, and noradrenaline in the anatomic structures of the limbic system and amygdala— sites for emotions and aggression—possibly be at the basis of violence? While this is an interesting hypothesis, I fully agree with the researcher that "it is oversimplistic to attribute aggressive outbursts in these patients to a genetic defect alone," and that other variables must be taken into consid-eration when evaluating violent persons.

Twins and adoption studies have been used to prove the relationship between inherited biological characteristics and violent behavior. In perusing studies of Mednick and Finello[82] regarding psychopathy and criminality in monozygotic and dizygotic twins, including that done by Lange in Bavaria in 1929, that of Yoshimasu, in Japan, in 1961, and others from Holland, the United States, Germany, Finland and England, I found that there is enough evidence to state that hereditary factors are important determinant variables in the genesis of crime and violent behavior. The concordance for monozygotic twins was sixty-seven per-cent while that for dizygotic twins was almost thirty percent. A larger twin study by Christiansen,[83] in 1977, of 3,586 pairs of male twins from a well defined region of Denmark, suggests that identical twins inherit biological characteristics that predispose them to a risk for future crimi-nal behavior. He found a thirty-five percent concordance for identical twins and twelve percent concordance for fraternal twins.

Mednick and Finello[82] researched 14,427 adoptions in Denmark, registering the court convictions for the adoptees, their biological par-ents and their adoptive parents. Their results pointed out that the conviction rates of both the male adoptees and their biological fathers were considerably higher than those of the adoptive fathers. The adop-tive fathers' rate, in fact, "is just about the average rate for men of his age group in this time period—minus eight percent."[p.5] They also found that recidivism was rather frequent among both the male adoptees and their biological fathers. They found that adoptive parent criminality is not associated with a significant increment in the son's criminality; instead, the effect of the biological parent's criminality was marked. They stated that "long linear analysis reveal that the relationship is highly significant for property crimes and not significantly significant for violent crimes."[p.6] This result, unless due to a low level of violent crimes in Denmark, may cast doubts on the theory of genetic transmission of a predisposition to violence.

Coid, Lewis, and Reveley[84] examined a sample of psychotic probands over a period of four decades and found more psychotic patients with a criminal history in the later decades than earlier. After an interesting analysis of the data they conclude that their study "lends weight to the theory that criminal convictions are increasing among the psychotic population, particularly schizophrenic men. . . . [but] appears more of an outcome of psychiatric illness in this population than of genetic factors."[p.91]

The above genetic and the biological studies have not shown indisputable correlations supporting the relationship between organic factors and violence. Nonetheless, they have stimulated, and continue to stimulate, a search into the anatomical, biochemical and physiological bases of human behavior, both in health and in illness. The discovery of the limbic system and its circuits has shed some light on the understanding of human emotions and aggressive hostility. A vast amount of knowledge has been accumulated during the past decades regarding the functional importance of some anatomical structures in the human brain, and of the interplay of its numerous neurotransmitters and modulators. It is to be hoped that aforementioned new brain imaging techniques will aid in reassessing the mind-brain interaction and that more rapid tests of brain perfusion, and the special EEG techniques of sphenoidal and foramen ovale type, will, together with a thorough knowledge of neurotransmitters and their combined functioning, enlighten us about the factors involved in impulsive aggressive behavior. Hopefully, we will one day find a logical trait d'union between what occurs in the brain and what is manifested in the behavior of aggressive people.

However, some skepticism is warranted, since throughout the years there has been a fluctuating interest on the part of the scientific community in support of either the biological or the socio-environmental factors in the genesis of violence. This dichotomy was present already among early philosophers and still vexes modern scientists. Human behavior is, indeed, multifactorially determined. While it is my personal belief that organic factors are as important as the psychological and environmental ones in the genesis of aggressive and violent behavior, I can certainly understand the stance of environmentalists and psychologically oriented researchers to the possible biological determinism of human conduct. However, this controversy between organic and psychological factors at the basis of aggressive and violent behavior will perhaps, in the future, be overcome by the recent recognition that brain tissue growth may be influenced by environmental stimuli. Experience will change behavior via biological mechanisms.[85] This will not undermine those feelings that humans cherish: that they are not merely the clay that will acquire predetermined and unmodifiable behavior, but the sculptor who molds the clay, the sole masters of their destiny.

Chapter Three

THE PSYCHOLOGY OF VIOLENCE

Until 1965, the rate of destructive violence remained within certain "acceptable" limits in our society. Since then, it has continuously increased reaching new peaks annually. Even now, in 1994, although the rate of all violent crimes has statistically declined since 1993, the murder rate has continued its escalation. The forerunners of the increasingly unbridled and antisocial, or for that matter anti-anything attitudes, at the basis of this escalation originated in the post-war culture of the sixties with the anti-authority and anti-establishment protests. That unrest was fueled by the then new philosophical egalitarian, neo-libertarian theories. A social, cultural and ethical dysfunction slowly but progressively established itself and was present at all levels of interpersonal relationships. People, since then, are not only more open towards one another but easily express even their hostile feelings, at times without exercising any form of control. This social phenomenon, possibly part of an existential confusion, and disruptive of the stable social mores that had been present for many years, has increased almost to the point of absurdity, creating a horrible panoramic view of our society. Children kill children, children kill parents, parents kill children, men abuse women and children, both psychologically and physically, rape is rampant, people assault and brutally murder one another at random. Confronted with this discomforting scenario of violence in our communities, it is natural to ask oneself why such behavior has almost become routine in some people's lives.

Human behavior, from personal to collective, has undergone a great deal of scrutiny during the past thirty years in an attempt to search for the psychological drives, motives or dysfunctions that may be causative of man's violence against his own kind. Already more than a century ago, William James[86] wrote that human behavior could be explained by understanding humankind's instinctive tendencies. Later theories, such as those of McDougall,[87] also supported the possibility that behavior patterns are instinctual in nature and that aggression is the end result of

41

an outburst of instinctual force. In 1927, Adler,[88] also stressing the instinctual force at the basis of all human behavior through which people could overcome their environment, gave to this force, for which Bergson had coined the term *elan vital,* the name "will to power." Ardrey[89] also thought that human conduct is driven and motivated by instincts. Thus, the Adlerian view of people as humans striving for superiority, and the Ardrian view of them as principally interested in something they could call their own, be it space, property, or territory, combined with the biological theory of the sexual instinct and formed a triad of instinctual drives. Sex, power and possessions became the most important driving forces of human conduct.

An understanding of the instinctual theories of Freud[90,91] and others, and of the role that emotions and feelings play in the genesis of hostility and aggression calls for a clarification of what we mean when we speak of instinct. In animal life, instinct is equated with that internal *quid* which promotes actions useful to the life of the animal itself, for example, the survival instinct. In humans, it signifies the natural propensity of the individual to perform acts or behave in ways that usually are specific in themselves in order to achieve anticipated aims. In psychology, the characteristics of what we call instincts are that they are inborn, unchangeable and hereditary. Thus, we have the survival, the maternal and the sexual instincts. Basically, they are, by their own definition, independent from intelligence, even though a certain degree of memory is essential for their expression. In human behavior, instincts are less determinant of behavior than in animals, because neo-cortical humans use their various intellectual capacities to inhibit or modify their instinctive reactions. Indeed, in the process of emotional growth, they also develop notions and emotions that aid in controlling their basic instinctual tendencies.

Freudian psychoanalysis accepts the presence in all humans of a libidinal force which, when properly directed, helps the individual to achieve cherished goals. Freud viewed aggression as being only a reaction to frustration, consequent to the thwarting of the successful pursuit of libidinal inclination. This is somewhat remindful of the ethological frustration theory which is discussed elsewhere in this book.

Freud further theorized that any person, during his or her lifetime, is under the dominance of two major drives: *eros* and *thanatos,* the Greek names for life/love and death. This apparently manicheistic approach of Freud, exemplified by these two oppositional forces of life and death, has a certain similarity to the anabolic and catabolic phases of human metabolism. It may be interpreted in a general sense as a form of polarization used in the past to define human existence—the alpha and omega of the ancient Greeks. This interplay between the forces of life and those of death—eros and thanatos instincts—seems to be central to our lives.

In his later writings, Freud, possibly more involved with his theories of the various defense mechanisms, began to view human aggression towards others as a displacement of the primary aggression against the self. Freud theorized that primary aggression against the self—the death instinct—if turned away from the self would become an aggressive, destructive force against others. In fact, he believed that humans cannot escape their violent nature and that if interpersonal aggression were curbed the unchecked self destructive impulses would cause people's self annihilation. Freud probably did not trust the will power of humans or believed that their epicritical faculties could not control their emotions. For him, aggression, unless sublimated, was either inwardly or outwardly directed. Freud's view of man's violent nature as a natural drive may find support in his life experiences during the Nazi invasion of Austria—his own country—and in the European genocide and the destruction of the Second World War.

If drives are important in determining violent behavior, or any type of behavior, so are emotions. What we call emotions, so important in the genesis of human conduct, normal or pathological, are difficult to define. We can say that an emotion is a feeling state, a feeling tone, present in an individual at a certain time. Some people define emotion as an augmentation beyond a certain level of a feeling that may be of joy, sadness, anger, fear, anguish, surprise, shame, disappointment, and which is the outcome of an external stimulation perceived by the individual or an imagination internal to the individual himself. Are the psychic and physical manifestations of emotions dressed-up drives? Are they the expression of philogenetic drives, vested with ontogenetically derived feelings?

Emotions are recognized as the *primum movens* of any human interaction. In an imaginative comparison, one could equate an emotion with the engine of a car that, even though having a beautiful chassis, has no usefulness unless given power by its engine. It is especially through the power of the emotions that facial mimicry and body attitudes portray love or hostility, fear or aggression. An emotional life when balanced in its oppositional antinomic feelings becomes homeostatic and allows an individual to develop in accordance with the moral dictates of the society in which he or she lives.

In analyzing aggression and violence, I have realized that the individual's instincts usually come under the control of emotions and the power of human rationality. Emotions are frequently described, whatever their quality, as shallow, superficial, even, appropriate, congruous or incongruous with the thought content, intense and uncontrollable. They are strictly connected with affect and mood and together form that dynamic force that motivates behavior and that we call affectivity. At times we are confronted with people who show irrational, or more often, arational emotions.

At the time of Plato, the soul was considered to be the seat of emotions. In his book, *The Rationality of Emotion,* de Sousa[92] reminds us that Plato, in assessing the soul, used a model which included not only emotions, but also reason and desire. Aristotle, instead, viewed the soul of a person—the psychic part of a human—in a functionalistic way, assuming that the soul's faculties were "layered series of increasingly complex capacities, where the higher presupposed the lower: nutrition and growth, sensation, movement, desire, emotion, reason."[p.21] Sousa writes that Descartes, in explaining behavior, combined both the Platonic and Aristotelian views with their componential and functional aspects, viewing man as the dynamic expression of the interplay of different faculties.

William James[93], in 1884, suggested the so-called periphery theory of emotion which explained emotions as a confused perception of some physiological dysfunction of the human body. Sante de Sanctis,[34] instead, in 1926, in attempting to explain the origin of emotions, proposed the so-called circular theory which stressed that for an emotion to be felt, people had to first become aware of and recognize a particular affective value in perceptions. This would be followed by physiological changes that would, in turn, bring about, he said, a complete emotional state.

The most common emotion behind any violent criminal act is hostility which usually leads to aggression when the combination of hostile thoughts and feelings is acted upon. With this shift, previous attitudinal thinking is changed to motor or action oriented behavior. The aggressive act consists in the process of approaching another person with the intent of doing harm; the quality and the intensity of the aggressive act, however, is referred to as violence. Psychologically, at the basis of hostility/aggressivity one may find feelings of dependency, passivity, helplessness, a need to be loved frustrated in childhood, or even a wish to control or dominate, the last usually a reaction formation against tendencies to dependency and passivity. At other times, fearing abandonment, an individual who has avoided any close relationship, often feeling lonely and resentful, may exhibit explosive, inexplicable behavior towards those against whom he harbors ambivalent feelings or even against persons who are unknown to him.

Often, the upsurge of feelings of frustration precedes destructive acting out. These feelings of frustration, of fear, or of ambivalence are usually of long standing, and deeply buried within the unconscious or the subconscious of the individual who acts them out. Often, neurotic, repetitive negative behavior is the facade of more deeply based hostile and aggressive thoughts, a compromise that some people make during their lifetime in order to avoid realistic or fantasized narcissistic injuries. At times, feelings, usually negative in character, are ego dystonic and are perceived by the individual as dangerous to the psychological homeostasis of the self. Aggression may be the outcome of overwhelming feelings of boredom and monotony in a lonely life. The sudden break may signify a call for attention, acknowledgement, or for love. Fromm-Reichmann[94] believed that while humans usually repress their basic hostility, this repression is often unsuccessful and may manifest itself not only in physical illness, which is the most common, but also in disruptive conduct.

A distinction should be made between the so-called biologically inherited aggressiveness which is obviously instinctual and the hostile type of aggressiveness which usually has an interpersonal origin and arises during the course of early life, when the infant incorporates the mother's attitudes, including her hostility. This will be discussed later in this chapter.

Impulsivity is frequently connected with aggressivity, especially in the most explosive destructive acts. During a rage reaction, people unable to contain their feelings behave in a socially unacceptable way, careless of those boundaries of good interpersonal civilized conduct. They usually do not reflect on their thoughts or their feelings, but suddenly lash out in antisocial behavior. This is often observed in the psychopath/antisocial personality and is remindful of children who are unable to exercise their reflective capacity to the maximum of their potential because they are still immature.

A forty-four year old, white, married male, chronic alcoholic, but sober
for the past six months, had recently moved to a new home. He shared a
circular driveway with his neighbor. He became increasingly suspicious
of his neighbor's actions and felt that he was making disparaging remarks
about him, and because of that he became restless. He usually mis-
interpreted innocuous statements as having a double meaning. He became
intolerant of both the neighbor and his family and, at times, when
encountering him found a way to disagree with him and made veiled
threatening remarks. One day, he decided that he was becoming too
anxious, because he felt that his neighbor was looking down on him. He
took his car, went to the nearby liquor store, bought himself a case of beer
and several bottles of whiskey. He sat in his backyard and while checking
every move and listening to every word of his neighbor, trying to see or
hear what he did not like. All of a sudden, again misinterpreting some
remark that he overheard as being denigratory of him, he became furious.
He went to the second floor of his house, loaded his shotgun, came down,
and facing his surprised neighbor who questioned his intentions, fired his
gun and killed him. He then returned to his house, reloaded the gun, and
from his window he began to fire at a shadow in the front door of the
neighbor's house, believing it to be his neighbor, badly wounding the
neighbor's wife. He then jumped into his truck, and sped away, with the
police, called to the scene, in pursuit. At one point, he stopped the truck
and began firing at the police. He was later apprehended. When I examined him several days later he was obviously sober and in touch with
reality. However, he still believed that his neighbor had had it in for him,
even though he was remorseful for what he had done and obviously
depressed about it. The diagnosis rendered was paranoid personality
disorder with acute alcohol intoxication. He is serving a twenty-year
sentence in prison.

Anger, hostility, aggression and violence should be viewed as progressive manifestations, in a stepwise fashion, of the displeasure felt about his
or her life by the violent person who already has a shaky emotional
equilibrium. Emotional aggressive states are, at times, similar to the
so-called anger attacks described by Fava and Rosenbaum,[95] and are also
a frequent part of a depressive reaction. Depressed individuals may also
be agitated and irritable and show psychomotor retardation. When treated
with antidepressants, they may act upon themselves and commit suicide
or behave in a violent way against others. This reaction seems to support
the assumption that hostility and aggressivity are often repressed and
that depression is the only possible compromise that some people can
make in dealing with that type of feelings. Anger attacks, preceded by
irritability, are also part of the dyscontrol syndrome described years ago

by Menninger,[64] and the limbic syndrome more recently described by Monroe.[59] This may occur when, for fear of losing a love object or a cherished relationship, the violent person turns his or her aggression against the self.

As previously stated, Freud recognized a strong propensity toward aggressivity in humans. Indeed, in his book, *Civilization and Its Discontents*, he wrote that "men are not gentle creatures who want to be loved, and who at the most can defend themselves if they are attacked; they are, on the contrary, creatures among whose instinctual endowment is to be reckoned a powerful share of aggressiveness."[96] p.68 In further analyzing violent behavior on the basis of his theories, he hypothesized that behind a criminal action there may be a conflict at the level of the Oedipal relationship for which the crime itself could be the means to call upon oneself punishment for the Oedipic guilt.

Since it is never a good idea to generalize, projecting this Freudian interpretation to the large group of violent offenders that we see in our society is a bit hazardous. Nonetheless, reflecting on the above Freudian hypothesis, and being quite aware of the fleeting presence of the father in the early lives of a large number of present day offenders, one must ask whether present day children who exhibit violent behavior and who seem to relate in their early years mostly to their mother or mother substitute, established, *a fortiori*, a strong relationship with her which can still be of an Oedipal type, even though the presence in the house of a father/father substitute may be completely lacking. This could create guilt, fear of reprisal, rebellion against authority, and sexual confusion. The above state of emotions may generate violence in these children and create a craving for what they feel, at an unconscious level, to be deserved punishment.

Several theories on the psychological development of the infant may shed light on understanding aggressive behavior. Kohut,[97] in 1971, theorized that a child achieves individuation and self-esteem when he is able to tame the archaic, grandiose and exhibitionistic self. He believed, indeed, that this is a necessary process for an ego-syntonic purposeful adult personality development. However, he also thought that occasionally, due to a narcissistic trauma in early infancy, the child may not progress towards maturation and may still retain within himself the presence of a parental imago disappointing to him. At the core of his psychological self, even during his adult life, there would be the presence of what he calls an "archaic transitional self object that is usually required for the maintenance of a narcissistic homeostasis."

Mahler,[98] in 1972, proposed that the child, through a process of individuation, achieves intrapsychic autonomy, and with the separation from its mother obtains "differentiation, distancing, boundary structuring and disengagement...."[p.407] She also stressed the importance of the necessity for the optimal emotional availability of the mother in a mother-child relationship, believing it to be essential for a wholesome resolution of a prior symbiotic relation and for the achievement of the child's autonomy and self-concept. She felt that an infantile neurosis may ensue when the child becomes frustrated in his effort to force the mother to be an extension of his omnipotent self. During this period, according to her hypothesis, the child also fears being reincorporated by the mother and thus unable to separate himself from her.

Mahler's ideas are pertinent to the problem of aggression because she believes that the foundations for aggression are laid down in a child's psyche during the period of early infancy. At that time, delusions of omnipotence, feelings of dependency, and also self denigratory tendencies, are part of the budding psyche of the child. It is during this period that the child may also become aware of his rage and hatred towards a castrating mother towards whom he is highly ambivalent. Mahler's thoughts may be an explanation for aggression in our present society, and particularly pertinent to rape. The past history of many offenders often reveals ambivalent feelings about their mother, who, by force of circumstances, has assumed both paternal and maternal roles during the child's upbringing, and in so doing increased their ambivalent attachment to her. Emotional separation from her, then, often becomes difficult, provoking feelings of hostility, frustrated dependency and rage. At times these feelings may be at the basis of their violent behavior towards people in general and females in particular, and of suicide attempts.

A twenty-year old white male, a polydrug abuser since age twelve, has had serious interpersonal problems, especially with his parents. He is a shy young man who has difficulty in relating to people and who appears detached and amotivated. This young man harbors ambivalent feelings towards the female figure, possibly due to his early disturbed relationship with his mother. He has a history of explosive physical abuse against his girlfriends. One night, after leaving a tavern with his girlfriend, the mother of his child, and while at home, obviously drunk, he quarreled with her, grabbed a kitchen knife, and stabbed her four times before cutting both his wrists and stabbing himself in the abdomen. Bleeding heavily, he was taken to a local hospital where he was in critical condition from exsanguination. When he regained consciousness the following day, he was unaware of what had happened and shocked to learn about it from a television news program. He had complete amnesia for the event. A SPECT examination revealed zones of hypoperfusion in the left temporal and frontal areas. The defendant pled guilty and was sentenced to prison.

Kline[99] believed that the child necessitates a good relationship with its mother, and that the first few years of life are very important for resolving the early paranoid anxiety generated by the introjection and projection of those good and bad "imagos . . . fantastically distorted pictures of the real objects . . . in the outside world . . . [and] also within the ego."p.145 It has been proposed that during this early period of life the child perceives the mother's breast both as a source of nourishment and as a frustrating object and that this may lead to later tendencies towards depressive states and to paranoid fears.

Dollard and collaborators[100] thought that since frustration brings annoyance, a continuous reinforcement of the frustrating situation will promote feelings of hostility and eventually an aggressive response. The response, however, can be modulated in its expression by inhibitory forces when the individual realizes the possibility of ensuing punishment. Gratification versus punishment is, indeed, a dilemma that the individual has to face in determining the degree of aggression that he will express.

In his explanation of violent behavior, Fenichel[101] subscribed to the theory that views frustration as a prerequisite of aggression. In fact, many of the violent offenders I have examined reported having encountered a great deal of abuse and frustration throughout their childhood and adolescence.

A twenty-two year old shy but pleasant white male attempted to physically attack his older employer while at work during a heated argument over a pay-raise. The young man was considered to be a good worker but it had been frequently noted that he was prone to mood swings and had a tendency to be uncommunicative. His past history revealed that he had grown up in a dysfunctional family. His father was a chronic alcoholic, a poor provider, and had an unpredictable type of behavior. The offender often felt frustrated in his emotional and physical needs. He developed feelings of hostility for his father and was greatly ambivalent about him. His mother was described as a duty-bound person. The young man recognized that his explosive behavior towards his employer was uncalled for and was the expression of his repressed hostility towards his father. He classified for a diagnosis of passive-aggressive personality with explosive outbursts. He was referred to a counselor for psychotherapy.

It must be recognized that only a small percentage of people encountering those same frustrations shows aggressive behavior in dealing with others. It may be that aggressive reactions are due to factors idiosyncratic to each person, or that some people are aided in containing their aggressivity by the restraining effect of moral values to which they were exposed within their family. It is only at a later point in their life that further frustrations may unleash their removed hostility. It is doubtful, however, whether the frustration-aggression theory, even though interesting, can totally explain people's violent behavior.

There is no doubt that an early good relationship between the child and its mother, and the child and its environment, is essential for the healthy emotional development of the child, and one can safely assume that the lack of development of feelings of trust, security and love in the child may be fertile ground for a propensity to hostile, aggressive, or destructive behavior not only in childhood and adolescence, but in adult life as well. Bowlby[102] advanced the thesis that good parenting enables the child not only to develop normally and to become emotionally balanced, but also to develop the capacity for a certain degree of resiliency, that will enable it to withstand frustrating and unpleasant events that are often encountered in life. When, during its developing years, a child does not have the possibility of internalizing parental dictates because there are no parents present, or because, as in the case where there is only one parent who is usually overwhelmed by myriad stresses, the child becomes easy prey to the many frustrations and negative emotions that may lead to aggressive behavior.

Many other scholars have also attempted to explain the origin of aggressive violent behavior. Ammon[34] p.77 also described aggression as being the result of a primary disturbance in the very early mother-child relationship. Hartmann thought that aggression is a reaction to feelings of dependency.[103] Carl Menninger, as stated previously, described aggressive behavior as a progressive "dyscontrol" type of reaction while Jung thought it was the expression of an unconscious drive. Massermann,[104] in 1961, stated that aggressive behavior is an attempt to eliminate any obstacle found on the way to self-interest and pleasure. In fact, at times the interplay between loss of self-esteem and conflictual narcissistic aspirations may result in explosive dyscontrolled behavior.

Deviant identification, as Blackburn[105] suggested, could be another way of acquisition of delinquent behavior. It implies that the delinquent behavior in a son is the reflection of normal identification with a criminal father, the son having introjected his father's attributes.

A middle-aged white male and his nineteen year old son attempted to rob a bank. They were heavily armed but were unsuccessful in their criminal offense because of the rapid intervention of the local police. However, after breaking into a nearby home, taking a young woman hostage and stealing her van, and attempting to escape, they killed a police officer and then engaged in a fierce exchange of gunfire with the police at a roadblock. The two offenders were using a submachine gun. They eventually hit a tree with the van and were captured by the police, both of them seriously wounded in the crash. The young hostage managed to escape. The father had a previous criminal record and a love for firearms. His son, reputed by school authorities to be a good, well behaved student, was completely mesmerized by his father's aggressive personality to the point that he not only went along with him as he perpetrated his offense but apparently criticized his father's poor performance during the offense.

In cases of this type it is possible that "the child's delinquent behavior reflects an absence of guilt, but not abnormality of psychic structures."[105] p.115

Blackburn[105] stated, "Busch et al. (1990) found that 58% of 71 adolescents who had killed had a criminally violent family member compared with 20% of demographically matched non violent delinquents," adding that the above is "consistent with the social learning view that the family provides a learning environment where violent behaviours are modelled, rehearsed, and reinforced."p.234

Aggression can be distinguished as primary aggression and reactive aggression. Primary aggression is a goal directed self-assertion of a hostile nature and destructive in character. The reactive type of aggression, instead, is usually concomitant to, and part of, an emotional reaction brought about by frustrating life experiences. Violence in our society is representative of these two types of aggression: the programmed, organized criminal and the impulsive criminal.

Horney[106] felt that hostility and the urge to kill or injure someone, were often the result of feelings of humiliation or abuse suffered by the individual during earlier periods of his life. Schilder[107] proposed that as the child grows in the definition of its body image, he becomes more active and tries to master the world around itself. That entails a certain amount of aggressivity which at times is mixed with sexuality. Eventually, however, he is usually able to master his aggressivity, helped by the controlling influence of the family and social mores.

Homosexuality and paranoia may be an unconscious defense against feelings of aggression. Indeed, there is a possibility that passivity and aggressivity are defenses for each other at different times, and that the passive-aggressive type of personality could be an expression of this. Persons who commit murder or other assaultive crimes at times manifest an unconscious passivity behind an excessive show of masculinity. The possibility that explosive antisocial behavior may be due to a "surcharge of aggressive energy or an unstable ego defense system that periodically allowed the naked and archaic expression of such energy" was postulated by Satten, Menninger and others after studying a group of murderers who were not psychotic.[108 p.48]

There is no doubt that since the psychological self is in continuous dynamic flux, each time that strong emotions are felt by the ego there is a temporary dysfunction or a slightly impaired organization of the self. The term "dyscontrol reaction," in fact, was coined by Menninger to describe a series of events during which the ego or the self are overwhelmed by strong impulses that lead to aggression and violence. This was described by him as his third order of dyscontrol reaction to describe a third stage of regression, disorganization or disequilibrium, or dyscontrol character-ized by the escape of the dangerous, destructive impulses which the ego had difficulty in controlling. He considered these to be the outbursts, the attacks, the assaults, and the social offenses resulting from a considerable degree of ego failure.[64] This is distinguished from a further ego failure usually exemplified by psychotic behavior, and a complete ego failure leading to suicide. The effect of alcohol, especially on an individual with a weak and unstable ego may be disastrous.

A twenty-six year old white male with a history of hyperactivity as a child and a diagnosis of Tourette's Disorder had made a marginal adjustment to his school and social life during adolescence. He frequently resorted to drinking alcohol in excessive amounts to medicate his borderline person-ality, prone to depressive reactions, schizophrenic confusion or hyperac-tive behavior. He was of above average intelligence but extremely tense, timid, and self-conscious. On three different occasions he was reprimanded by his school principal for improper behavior in school and towards female teachers, in particular. On one occasion the police were called by the vice-principal because the student was roaming around the school even though he had already graduated. The young man's drinking increased through the years and he began to think that it was important to vindicate his dignity. One day, armed with a handgun, he went to the school, met the vice-principal, who again reprimanded him for being on the school grounds, and shot him to death. The offense was premeditated, and even though classifiable as a borderline personality the offender was aware of his actions at the time of the offense. He was found legally sane and guilty of the crime.

It is my belief that aggressive violent behavior against persons is to be understood as ego failure. Indeed, the failure implies that the ego has lost its capacity to divert or neutralize destructive impulses during a disorganization-reorganization process when confronted by stressors. This state of dyscontrol is often repetitive or irrational and the violent persons are oblivious of the consequences of their actions and of the disapproval of society.[64]

Already at the turn of the century, Ramon-y-Cajal[109] had proposed the possibility that mental activity stimulates dendritic growth and improves memory and behavior. At the World Congress of Psychology held in Moscow in 1966, Krech, Rosenzweig, and Nitikenko[34] presented an interesting scientific communication reporting that psychological factors influence the growth of dendritic ramifications in the cerebral cortex with functional changes in the brain associative areas.

The mind-body dichotomy has been a fluctuating presence throughout history in the attempt to explain human behavior, and the so-called psychosomatic approach has tried to overcome this unrealistic schism. Psychological and biological factors tend to integrate one another during the course of a lifetime. It is assumed that with the biological process of maturation of the self there will be a corresponding psychological and emotional development that we call maturity, which allows the individual to meet life's events with a reasonable degree of objectivity and decisional capacity. The character of any individual is shaped by his or her experiences in life, especially when confronted by adversities while moving towards the maturation of the self. During the process of maturation, a person's emotional attitudes are of the uppermost importance for socialization. Feelings tend to influence cognition or thoughts, thoughts influence feelings, and both determine behavior.

At times, we know that emotions may not attain a homeostatic balance and because of this dysfunction aggression and violence may ensue. Also, as a consequence of a dysfunctional emotional life we often observe a state of immaturity.

A thirty-four year old black male came to my attention when he entered a plea of not guilty by reason of mental disease or defect following a charge of attempted possession of a controlled substance. He appeared to be slow in his ambulation and somewhat bewildered. There was no eye contact and he often stared into space. His attitude was somewhat passive, his affect was flattened and he showed no spontaneity in his speech, and when he answered my questions his speech was delivered in a slow manner. Nevertheless, he was friendly and cooperative. The defendant claimed to have served in the United States Army for a period of seven and one-half years, receiving an honorable discharge. He had been addicted to cocaine and alcohol since age eighteen. He claimed to have had psychotic episodes previous to his arrest that required several hospitalizations in psychiatric settings. In fact, the records showed that the defendant had been hospitalized thirty-four times over the previous ten years and had usually been diagnosed as schizophrenia with drug addiction. At the time of the examination, he voiced paranoid fears and claimed to have been hearing voices for fifteen years. He expressed the wish to kill himself so that he would no longer suffer from the disparaging remarks that people made about him. He stated that on the evening of the offense, while going to buy some beer, he had seen two men in the hallway of his apartment building and had asked them for a dime bag of crack. "I only had $6, and it is strange that I would ask for that because I know it costs more. I just wanted some beer to put me to sleep." He was found to be suffering from a personality disorder of an inadequate type and alcohol and cocaine dependence.

These emotionally immature people show a lack of dependability, an incapacity to adjust to the rules of social life and to the mores of society. They lack the capacity to recognize their own limitations or to learn from past experiences and do not relate to others in a civilized way. This is the characteristic behavior of children. Indeed, immature behavior is often seen in adolescent rebellion, in the psychopath's disregard for others, and obviously in the many maladjusted individuals that we call mentally ill. Immaturity, with its egocentricity, impulsivity, defensive projections and the incapacity to properly relate to others, is a basic part of the dysfunctional personality of the aggressive and violent person. "A hostile person expects others to be hostile and behaves in ways which elicit the expected reaction."[105] p.235

Hostile impulses are also facilitated in their aggressive expression by situational factors, by the use of alcohol to excess, and the use of the illicit drugs, especially cocaine, that are flooding our streets at present. Guns have become the weapon of choice because of their easy availability, but are certainly not the only arms used in committing violent actions. In my professional experience, I have encountered many offenders who have expressed their destructive hostility using knives or simply the strength of their own hands.

At times violent behavior is the expression of a serious personality disturbance or a mental disease from which an individual suffers. Blackburn states that correlational studies also indicate that aggressiveness is associated with a broad personality dimension of unsocialized aggression or psychopathy of a type that includes impulsivity and extrapunitive hostility.[105] Here, I refer to the delusional paranoid disorder, to the agitated depressive persons who suddenly may turn their hostility outwardly, and to some of the various forms of schizophrenia, ranging from catatonic excitement to the bizarre paranoid type.

A thirty-nine year old, black male, poured gasoline over a woman and attempted to set her on fire after he had apparently stalked her on a city street and city bus previous to his act. He was carrying what appeared to the victim to be a lunch bucket. While standing in line in a university waiting to buy a bus ticket and attempting to get change from her purse, the victim felt someone pouring liquid all over her. She was totally soaked, both front and back. She turned around and realized that the stalker was behind her about four feet away and trying to light matches. She tried to run from him but he followed her and sought to enter the bathroom where she had gone in her attempt to hide from him. While caught with his arms in the door, the assaulter appeared to be trying to strike some matches. She screamed from the bathroom, ran up the stairs and met a friend to whom she told her story in a frantic way. The culprit was apprehended by four students but not without his putting up a struggle. By the time the victim arrived at an emergency hospital her skin had been burned by the gasoline. Previous to his apprehension the offender had succeeded in throwing a match at the victim and at another person who had been in line with her and who was also soaked with gasoline. A forensic psychiatric examination determined that the offender had been suffering from paranoid schizophrenia for many years and had been using cocaine and alcohol as well. He claimed that the attack was provoked by "voices" telling him that he had something to do. He was found to be legally insane and sent to a mental health institute.

Feldman states, "There seems to be no special link between crime and mental disorder in general. With respect to specific disorders, only the paranoid sub-group of the schizophrenias seems clearly connected, specifically to violent crime; and even within this segment most sufferers are not violent, . . . "[110]

A forty-seven year old, black male was apprehended and charged with first degree intentional homicide. When arrested two blocks from the scene of the crime he was covered with blood. Upon apprehension he stated that he had been released from jail the same night, at 12:01 A.M., and since he had no place to live, he had gone to the house of an old friend, the victim, who had helped him in the past. He said that his friend took him in and allowed him to stay for the night. They talked for a while and then both of them fell asleep. The offender stated that he slept for a few hours and when he woke up he began thinking about how badly he had been treated in prison. He claimed to have been in a state of despair. He remembered walking into the kitchen, seeing a knife and taking the knife, but claimed that he did not remember anything else except running out of the apartment. However, he remembered dropping the knife in a back alley. A witness stated that she was awakened by the arguing between the two men, walked into the living room and observed the defendant on top of his friend. When the defendant stood up, his face and neck were covered with blood. He turned to the young witness saying, "Don't worry about him. Now he is alright." The defendant was found to be suffering from paranoid schizophrenia of a litigious type. He was intelligent and articulate. He committed suicide by hanging while awaiting trial.

A 1983 study by Monahan and Steadman[111] reported a weak relationship between psychiatric disorders and antisocial violent behavior. On the contrary, in a study of 1200 randomly selected residents of a large Canadian city, Bland and Orn[112] reported a psychiatric diagnosis rate of 54.4 percent in violent people, especially antisocial personality disorder with alcohol dependence. Recurrent depression rated at 80–93 percent in the same group, together with a 50 percent rate in those persons who had previously attempted suicide. The study found a strong link between depression and violence and mental illness and the arrest rate. Certainly depression and other forms of mental illness could lead to social and family violence and consequently to incarceration.

Henn, Herjanic, and Vanderpearl[113] assessed 2,000 persons arrested for murder in St. Louis between 1964 and 1973 and found that schizophrenia was diagnosed in (0.98%) of cases; affective disorder in (0.4%); and organic brain disorder in (0.5%) of the offenders. Häfner and Böker[114] studied 533 cases of murder, attempted murder and manslaughter in the Federal Republic of Germany between 1955 and 1964. The mentally disordered accounted for slightly less than 3 percent (2.9%) of convictions for serious violence and for more than 5 percent (5.6%) of murder victims.

Steadman, Fabrisek, Dvorkin and Holohean[115] collected data from a random sample of 3,332 inmates in the general prison population (9.4%) and 352 inmates in prison mental health units in the state of New York.

Their study found that 8 percent of the state's prison inmates had severe psychiatric disabilities that warranted mental health intervention and another 16 percent had marked mental disabilities requiring periodic services.

Sivetz, Saline, Stough and Brewer[116] investigated the prevalence of mental disorders among 190 male prison inmates (aged 15+ years) using a needs assessment survey for prison populations and found that 19.5 percent suffered from psychiatric disorders requiring treatment, and an additional 8.9 percent needed further evaluation for possible psychiatric problems. Taylor and Gunn[117] found that out of 107 men charged with or convicted of homicide more than 1/3 showed symptoms of mental disorder: schizophrenia (9.3%); affective psychosis (1.9%) mixed disorder (20%). Taylor,[118] in a study of life sentenced prisoners in London, most of them murderers, found that 9 percent showed symptoms of schizophrenia, 13 percent were depressed, and 33 percent were diagnosed with personality disorder.

Using nursing, physical and psychiatric evaluations, and diagnoses made according to the *Diagnostic and Statistical Manual of Mental Disorders (DSM-III-R)*, Strick[119] examined the characteristics of 81 female offenders admitted to a female forensics unit over a three year period. His study revealed that 79 percent of the subjects were psychotic on admission, and combinations of more than one personality disorder were found in 61 percent of subjects diagnosed with Axis II disorders.

In 1990, Snow and Briar[120] reported that in research conducted in a Pacific Northwest urban jail, of the 1565 cases reviewed, 332, or 21 percent, were designated as mentally disordered. Of this group, they found that 74.3 percent were substance abusers; 36.7 percent were mentally ill; 3.9 percent also developmentally or physically disabled; and 14.5 percent were both mentally ill and substance abusers.

Lindqvist and Allebeck[121] found that violent offending in discharged schizophrenic patients was four times more frequent than expected (7% of the sample). Blackburn[105] reported that, "The role of mentally disordered homicides per head of population appeared to be relatively constant across countries and over time, at about 0.10 per 100,000."p.270 Häfner and Böker[114] stated that five out of 10,000 schizophrenics are likely to become violent (.005%), and among the affective disordered and mentally retarded 0.006% are likely to become violent. Hodgins[122] stated that mental retardation was associated with a risk for violence, but to small proportion.

Tammany and Evans[123] tested 766 male felons with the 16 Personality Factor Test (PF which provides scores for sixteen primary factors and four second-order factors) and with the Multidimensional Aptitude Battery Test (which measures the intellectual functioning). They found that the four groups of felons examined, (murderers, kidnappers and assaulters; sexual offenders of juvenile victims; possessors and dealers of drugs; arsonists and burglars) demonstrated "relatively few personality and intellectual differences."p.911 They stated, "It seems that while the MMPI is useful in identifying the presence of severe pathology, such pathology is not present in most inmates."p.907 The authors cited Cattell, Eber, and Tatsuoka[124] who described 891 inmates studied with the 16PF as being "unconventional, low in ego strength, unable to handle impulses, and . . . having a disregard for rules and obligations."p.907

Tammany and Evans also report that DeWolfe and Ryan[125] described the offenders' WAIS-type Performance IQ as exceeding their Verbal IQs. In addition, they state that Holland and collaborators[126] found a negative correlation between IQ scores and the seriousness of violent offense in a sample of violent offenders.

The relationship between major mental disorders, substance abuse, and violent criminal behavior is intriguing. It has been my experience that the mentally ill often use alcohol/illicit drugs in an attempt to medicate themselves, especially with alcohol, while, at the same time, they are non-compliant with their prescribed medication which they usually refuse because of side effects.

> This thirty-eight year old, white male was charged with attempted first degree intentional homicide. The complainant stated that from his apartment situated on the third floor he had heard a man shouting for help. He flew down the stairs to the first floor from where the voice was coming and he saw the defendant, a hunting knife in his right hand, plunge the knife into another man's body three times. His intervention put a stop to the stabbing. The defendant was found to be suffering from a long standing schizophrenic illness, medicated with alcohol, and at the time of the offense had been drinking "a lot of beer." He was reacting to his fixed delusional belief that the victim was trying to influence his life with religious thoughts. The victim survived. The defendant was found to be mentally ill and was committed to a mental institution.

There is evidence to support the thesis that schizophrenics and bipolar sufferers, especially manics, have a higher rate of use or abuse of psychoactive substances, inclusive of alcohol, when compared to persons not classified among the sufferers of major mental disorders.[127,128,129]

Hodgins,[130] questions, "Is the increased vulnerability for substance abuse related to the major disorder, to the personality disorder, or to both, or is it independent of the two? Is criminality related to the major disorder, the personality disorder, alcohol- and drug-use disorder, any combination of these disorders or to none of them?"[p.71]

Is substance abuse a manifestation of an antisocial personality disorder which is prevalent among offenders with major mental illness? This is a frequent occurrence in my experience, as stated previously, and also in the experience of others.[131,132,133] A mental disorder among violent offenders and their co-occurring substance abuse may create diagnostic perplexity. Incipient schizophrenia often heralds itself with a pan-anxiety and in response to this the young schizophrenic may resort to substance abuse to quiet the auditory hallucinations which may promote his or her criminal offense. Many young adult offenders carry a dual diagnosis of schizophrenia and bipolar illness and drug-alcohol dependence. The substance abuse often began at a very early age (12–13 years) and continued uninterruptedly for many years with all the manifestations of drug or alcohol psychotic behavior. Initially, many of these offenders were classified as schizophrenia or manic-depressive psychosis, and the diagnosis, which may have been incorrect, then follows these persons throughout their lives. The question then arises, should these people be classified with a diagnosis of mental illness and drug or alcohol abuse, or just as a personality disorder with the substance abuse? Diagnostics must consider the evolution of a person's psychotic behavior in order to avoid the continuation of the above mentioned possibility of an initially incorrect diagnosis.

In Hodgins's Swedish study[122] comprising 7,362 men and 7,039 women, it was found that almost half (48.7%) of the male offenders with a major mental disorder and slightly more than 40 percent (42.9%) of the female offenders with a major mental disorder had secondary diagnostic labeling of alcohol and drug abuse. "Among both men and women, more of those with a major mental disorder, and those with an intellectual handicap committed violent offenses and theft."[p.481] The above study places the dual diagnosis category, mental illness plus substance abuse, at an approximately 50 percent occurrence rate among offenders. "Men with a major mental disorder were 2½ times more likely than men with no disorder or handicap to be registered for a criminal offense. Among women, the risk for those with a major mental disorder was five times higher than for women with no disorder or handicap."[p.481] The study appears to agree with previous reports that psychiatric patients suffering from major mental illnesses behave more aggressively than non-psychiatric patients.[134,135,136]

Hodgins[122] lists various hypotheses that have been proposed regarding the relationship between the major mental disorders, substance abuse, and criminality: substance abuse as an aspect of antisocial personality in adolescents who later develop bipolar illness; substance abuse as concomitant to the antisocial personality disorder often found among offenders suffering from major mental disorders; substance abuse as a coping mechanism in pan-anxiety, as in incipient schizophrenia; and that substance abuse has nothing to do with criminality, as in the case of a patient reacting in a violent manner to auditory or visual hallucinations. However, he concludes that "these hypotheses are not mutually exclusive, and they could all be correct, applying to different sub-groups of patients, or they could all be wrong. However, to my knowledge they have not yet been tested."[p.71]

Blackburn found that "extreme assaultives were significantly more controlled, inhibited and defensive of psychological tests than moderate assaultives, and were significantly less likely to have a prior criminal record or to be diagnosed as psychopathic personality."[105 pp.238–239] In another study of 56 murderers, also by Blackburn, "almost half" showed those characteristics. He reports a study of Lang and collaborators stating that murderers differed from assaulters because of a lack of or less frequent criminal offenses prior to the murder and because of a lower score on psychological tests for hostility.

A longitudinal Swedish study of 644 schizophrenics revealed that the relative risk of a criminal offense among these persons was 1.2 for the men and 2.2 for the women when compared with the general Swedish population. The report also stated that the schizophrenics had committed four times as many violent offenses as the general population.[121]

Another earlier Swedish study[137] considered the relationship between criminal homicide, alcohol intoxication, alcohol abuse and mental disease and found that forty of the sixty-four offenders under consideration "had within the past 5 years been subjected to psychiatric care, 10 of these solely for treatment of alcoholism."[p.26] The author of the study also stated that twenty of the offenders were mentally ill and fifteen of them were remanded to a psychiatric hospital for care after trial. "Another 14 offenders were mentally diseased *and* abusers, alcoholics or personality disordered. Fifteen of the 19 sober offenders were mentally diseased."p.27 Only three of the sixty-four offenders were classified among the neurotic disorders.

> A twenty-three year old male was charged with two counts of armed robbery after participating in a supermarket hold up with a friend, obtaining $22 which he then used to purchase cocaine. At the time he was charged, he pleaded not guilty by reason of mental disease or defect. The defendant was friendly, anxious, and cautious, but was in good contact and fully cooperative with the examination. His affect was minimally depressed. He stated that he had been prescribed an oral antipsychotic for daily use because of insistent and persistent voices telling him to commit suicide. He voiced previous suicidal attempts and claimed that he once attempted suicide by drinking gasoline. He recounted a history of drug use (marijuana, cocaine, and amphetamines) and also a history of seizures that required Phenobarbital and Dilantin for several years. He was found to have been legally sane at the time of the offense.

Abram and Teplin[129] found that among the detainees suffering from a severe lifetime mental disorder, 80 percent met the criteria for two or three of the other disorders (alcohol dependence, drug dependence or antisocial personality disorder), while slightly more than 6 percent (6.4%) did not meet the criteria for any of the three co-disorders. However, "among subjects with a current severe disorder, only 10 percent had no codisorders, and 59 percent met criteria for two or three of the codisorders."p.1038 They further reported that "the rate of codisorders among [their] sample of severely ill jail detainees was also considerably higher than rates found in patient population."p.1041 The occurrence of alcohol-drug abuse in mentally ill jail detainees was found in misdemeanants and felons alike, and concluded that "the predominance of severely ill jail detainees with co-occurring disorders may reflect their inherent criminality."p.1042 They pointed out that, contrary to the "pure schizophrenic" the schizophrenic "contaminated" by alcohol and/or drug use and abuse may be more likely to commit a crime.

Even though statistical studies generally support a lifetime substance abuse (alcohol or illicit drugs) among young adult chronic mental patients ranging from 38 percent to 83 percent, and of current usage ranging from 30 percent to 56 percent, as reported in the above study of Abram and Teplin,[129] there are studies which do not support this association. In fact, several studies have reported schizophrenics to be less likely than other diagnostic groups to have substance abuse disorders.[138,139]

Abram and Teplin report that one study[140] found an interesting association between major affective disorders and substance abuse. "The co-occurrence of alcoholism among veterans with major affective disorders is higher than for schizophrenics and, depending on the definition of alcoholism, has been found to be as high as 63 percent."[p.1041] This may be due to the fact that the manic agitated individual often uses alcohol as a sedative.

The study by Abram and Teplin[129] and that reported above seem to contradict the commonly held notion that patients suffering from major mental illness are no more likely to commit violent and non-violent crimes than the general population. The question, then, is what kind of crimes are committed by the mentally ill and what is their frequency? Are they more represented among the group of felonies or the misdemeanors? Are those who commit these crimes really suffering from a bona fide mental illness or is their behavior the outcome of a chronic psychotic-like behavior due to their long-standing addiction to alcohol or drugs?

In 1991, in an attempt to objectify the relationship between mental illness and criminal behavior, together with collaborators, I conducted a statistical survey of 272 defendants who came to my personal attention over a period of three years for competency evaluation after having been charged with misdemeanors or felonies: 67.28 percent were charged with a misdemeanor and 32.72 percent were charged with a felony.[131] Of this sample, 53.31 percent were black males, 30.51 percent were white males, 5.15 percent were Hispanic males, 5.15 percent were white females, 5.15 percent were black females, and .74 percent were Hispanic females. The average age of the defendant was 31.5 years old. Slightly more than 71 percent (71.32%) were found to be competent and the remaining number (28.68%) were found to be not competent.

As can be seen in Table 3.1, fifteen *Diagnostic and Statistical Manual-Third Edition-Revised* (*DSM-III-R*) diagnostic types accounted for the sample of 272 defendants. The inmates were diagnosed as suffering primarily from chronic schizophrenia, or a mental disturbance of a disruptive, occasionally psychotic type—antisocial personality disorder with polysubstance dependence. Dysthymia, passive aggressive personality disorder and bipolar disorders were also represented in the group of defendants in this study. Only two cases of dissociative disorder, N.O.S., Ganser syndrome type, were diagnosed, not supporting the assertion by Bliss and Larson[141] that antisocial criminal behavior may be the result of "spontaneous self-hypnotic dissociative states" or "multiples." Their conclusions were based on a highly select and small group of sexual offenders and probably would not apply to the vast number of habitual offenders. Collins and Bailey[142] report a relationship between violent crime and PTSD in a prison sample of 1,140 males, the majority not associated with personality disorder. In our study, we found 12 cases of PTSD (4.41%), mostly misdemeanants who were found to be competent to stand trial.

Both our study and the above mentioned one of Snow and Briar revealed similar percentages of mental illness/schizophrenia (36.7% mentally ill in Snow and Briar's study and 37.87% schizophrenia in our study). The major difference was in their reported substance abuser group, 74.3 percent, compared to our study's combined 31.25 percent including antisocial personality disorder with polysubstance dependence, found to be 23.53 percent, and cocaine induced organic mental disorders of 7.72 percent. The demographic attributes of the mentally disordered in both studies were quite similar, with the exception of a higher percentage of black inmates in our study (53.7% vs. 35%).

Our above study, even though not relating specifically to the number and type of the psychiatric population in the jails or prisons of the United States, which ranges from 15 percent to 30 percent depending on the statistics reported,[111,143,144,145] is, nonetheless, a differential rundown of the psychopathology that may be encountered among the detainees in correctional institutions.

Phillips, Wolf, and Coons[146] stated that " . . . schizophrenic patients are not to any appreciable extent responsible for the high level of violence in our society." In fact, mental illness is not a frequent source of violent criminal behavior except for those occasional bizarre violent offenses perpetrated by schizophrenics, either acute or chronic, and by the interesting group of the paranoid delusional personality disorders.

"Although there appears to be an increased risk in schizophrenics, particularly in paranoid schizophrenia, it must be reiterated that only a small minority of patients in the category are violent, and that the disorder itself is rarely sufficient to account for violent acts in instances when they do occur"[105 p.274] Unfortunately, many of these people medicate themselves with illicit drugs or alcohol in an attempt to escape the sad realities of their existence, and they thus compound their already bizarre social behavior.

A twenty-seven year old, well-developed and well-nourished black male pleaded not guilty by reason of mental disease or defect to charges of arson to a building. He was coherent, relevant and logical in his thinking

TABLE 3.1

DIAGNOSIS BY TYPE OF OFFENSE AND BY FINDING FROM COMPETNECY EVALUATION

DSM-III-R-Diagnosis	Sample Size n.	Percent of Total Sample	Type of Offense		Finding from Competency Evaluation	
			Misdemeanor %	Felony %	Competent %	Non-Competent %
1.Schizophrenia (295.xx)	103	37.87	83.50	16.50	57.28	42.72
2.Antisocial Personality Disorder with Polysubstance Abuse (304.90)	64	23.53	35.94	64.06	98.44	1.56
3.Antisocial Personality (301.70) [including 4 malingerers (465.200) and 1 pedophile (302.20)]	22	8.09	45.45	54.55	90.91	9.09
4.Paranoid personality Disorder (301.00)	3	1.10	100.00	0.00	100.00	0.00
5.Psychotic Dsorders Not Otherwise Specified - Atypical Psychosis (298.90)	4	1.47	50.00	50.00	0.00	100.00
6.Cocaine-Induced Organic Mental Disorder [cocaine intoxication (305.60) and cocaine withdrawl (292.99)]	21	7.72	80.95	19.05	23.81	76.19
7.Post Traumatic Stress Disorder (309.89)	12	4.41	75.00	25.00	75.00	25.00

TABLE 3.1 (continued)

8.Delusional (paranoid) Disorder (297.10)	5	1.84	60.00	40.00	80.00	20.00
9.Bipolar Disorders – Mixed (296.6x)	14	5.15	78.57	21.43	78.57	21.43
10.Dysthymia (300.40)	6	2.21	83.33	1.67	100.00	0.00
11.Dissociative Disorder Not Otherwise Specified (300.15) – Ganser Syndrome	2	.74	.00	100.00	0.00	100.00
12.Pervasive Developmental Disorder Not Otherwise Specified (299.80)	3	1.10	66.67	33.33	66.67	33.33
13.Passive Aggressive Personality Disorder (301.84)	9	3.31	88.89	11.11	100.00	0.00
14.Borderline Personality Disorder (301.83)	3	1.10	100.00	0.00	66.67	33.33
15.Primary Degenerative Dementia of the Alzheimer Type –Senile	1	.37	100.00	0.00	100.00	0.00

although his affect was blunted. He was generally cooperative but at times became loud and angry and was reported to be unpredictable in his behavior. He had previous police records for assault and battery and for sexual assault and endangering life. He had been hospitalized ten years earlier at the local community mental health complex because of psychotic symptomatology with visual and auditory hallucinations. He drank to tacitate his "voices," and related that prior to the offense he had been sitting on his front porch drinking with his brother. "I went into the house and continued to drink. Then, I smoked cocaine in the bathroom because I didn't want them to know. I was gone, because I had just done a dime bag of crack cocaine. I was drinking and the next thing I knew the DA wanted to talk with me. My brother said I went off. I didn't know what I was saying. I'm afraid of the people around me. When I'm not on medication I hear voices telling me that they might do something to me." The defendant was diagnosed as schizophrenia, paranoid type, by history, alcohol dependence, and cocaine dependence, but was found to have been legally sane at the time of the offense.

Recidivism of violent behavior is a frequent occurrence. However, Quinsey[147] and collaborators found higher violent recidivism in released maximum security patients with a diagnosis of personality disorder than in those with a diagnosis of psychosis.

Even though a direct relationship between mental illness and violent behavior may be questionable, there is no doubt that the mentally ill, with few exceptions, are usually aware of their actions and therefore responsible for them.

The following case illustrates the concomitance of antisocial confused, destructive behavior in a person with an organic psychosis.

A thirty-eight year old white male came to my attention because, having been charged with arson to a building, his attorney requested a forensic psychiatric examination to assess his possible criminal responsibility. On apprehension by the police the defendant had appeared confused and clearly delusional. However, from the history obtained, his delusional behavior seemed to be part of an organic involvement of his brain. This defendant, at age thirty-two and at the acme of his career as the manager of a restaurant, had had a myocardial infarction for which he had received proper and efficacious care. At age thirty-five he had suffered two strokes which had left him paralyzed on the right side and unable to speak clearly. He became depressed and in need of psychiatric therapy which he received. On examination, he continued to have difficulty in speaking and some of his words were unintelligible. He was repetitive, perseverative, and showed loss of memory. His affect was inappropriate and emotionally he was occasionally jocular. He continued to be paretic in his right upper and lower extremities. At times during the conversation he became confused. His delusions were quite interesting. While at home, he stated, he felt the presence in his room of someone whom he later identified as the devil. He believed that the devil, after placing his hand on his right shoulder, was requesting to have sex with him. The defendant became frightened and suddenly decided to place an empty coffee can in the middle of his living room with a rock-music tape and a rag soaked with alcohol inside of it. He then lit it with a match. He thought that the devil was part of the music and that in so doing he would get rid of him. The bizarre delusional ideas and the neurological brain deficit most probably led to this man's antisocial confused behavior. He was found to be suffering from an organic psychotic reaction, adjudicated not guilty, and directed to a state mental institution for treatment.

There can be no more eloquent words to end this chapter than those of Dostoyevski:

It is clear that evil is buried more deeply in humanity than the cure-all socialists think, that evil cannot be avoided in any organization of society, that a man's soul will remain the same, that it is from a man's soul alone that abnormality and sin arise, and that, finally, the laws that govern man's spirit are still so unknown, so uncertain and so mysterious that there are not and cannot be any physicians or even judges to give a definitive cure or decision, but that there is only He who says, Vengeance is mine, I will repay.

Chapter Four

THE SOCIOLOGY OF VIOLENCE

In any society, social conflicts are present at different periods, and at times are disruptive of social order. It seems reasonable to assume that these conflicts are an expression of dissatisfaction with the status quo or a call for help. Most probably they serve a useful purpose, not only for the resolution of the conflicts themselves, but as a sign of healthy progress toward better social integration. An analogy can be made between conflicts in society and the anxiety at an individual level. As the purpose of anxiety for individuals is to make them aware that there is some dysfunction within their own psychobiological selves, so social conflicts, to a certain extent, are a manifestation of a malfunctioning society which seeks correction.

While we are all aware that violent behavior has reached high levels, most of us are also aware that the majority of people in our society are not prone to violence. They are, instead, passive bystanders or victims — either intended or random — of the violent person. This is of interest for those people who see socio-economic deprivation in the cause of aggression as being a form of human adaptation. Even though allowing that a society without conflict may be utopian, one should not disregard the fact that the degree of social dysfunction and violent behavior in our society has reached such high levels that it is disruptive of social order. Violence is creating a defensive behavior in its members which at times culminates in social isolation of the individual.

A discussion of the sociological factors at the roots of violence requires a definition of society and its meaning for the majority of people.

Edward Shils[148] defines it as one that "presupposes the existence of families, neighborhoods and cities, churches and sects, states and provinces, schools and universities, firms, farms, industrial plants, and cooperative societies, all interpenetrating each other and performing an exchange in services with each other within a common, bounded territory and possessing a common, all-inclusive system of authority which makes and enforces rules and suppresses or adjudicates conflicts."[p.54] Baumeister,[149] on the other hand, defined society very succinctly as "a large set of interconnected human beings, and culture as the set of ideas, practices and institutions that they share." There is no doubt that people, both in small and large groups, are able to live together because they share a similar culture allowing for better integration and functioning. Baumeister also stated that "... culture and society form a system that is set up to perpetuate itself and to maintain a certain level of efficiency, internal harmony and flexibility."p.8

No one would disagree that the economic and moral standards, and the political conditions of a society greatly contribute to the level of criminal behavior present in it. The post-war transition of the fifties witnessed the beginning of a crescendo of social violence, possibly expressing the personal insecurity of people who felt themselves to be caught in the web of a new adaptational period. In the sixties, the advent of new social philosophies created societal unrest that became fertile ground for individual violence against persons. That was the time when civil rights debates and demonstrations, supported by phenomenological schools of thought, and by an insecure economy, clearly demonstrated and emphasized that society is the cradle of human behavior.

In sociology, as in other sciences, various theories have been proposed in the attempt to explain violent behavior. Theories are the resultant of hypotheses which have been validated. Various theories have been advanced to explain violence. One of these proposed theories of social violence is the differential association theory of Sutherland,[150] which essentially states that criminal behavior is learned in the interaction with other persons during the process of communication. Another is that expressed by Sheldon and Eleanor Glueck[151] during the fifties, which associated community disorganization with delinquency rates. They stated that conditions of social disorganization generate variables in personality type, among which the delinquent personality is meaningfully linked to that disorganization. Inkeles[152] believed that these ideas were the further development of a theory proposed by C.R. Shaw,[153] in 1931, in his work *Delinquency Areas,* and also remindful of Durkheim's theory of anomie.[154]

During the fifties and sixties the attention of sociologists and criminologists studying delinquency and crimes of violence directed itself specifically towards sociological variables such as the family, schools and teachers, peer groups, neighborhoods and gangs. This was the time when Wolfgang and Ferracuti[155] wrote their seminal research work on the subculture of violence. In this work the authors speculate that the black experience has promoted the development of a subculture of violence in inner city ghetto areas. Membership in the subculture demands the use of physical force as a solution for everyday encounters.

Further impetus in directing the researchers attention to the influence that social structures might have on promoting crime and violence came from an influential group of people who belonged to the challenging phenomenological schools of thought and whose main exponents were Reusch, Laing, Cooper, Foucault, and the Jean-Jacques Rousseau of the sixties—Marcuse. The European existential philosophical schools, with Sartre, Strauss, and Heidegger, also influenced the course of American and European sociology, participating in the search for the possible social causes of human violent behavior, and violent behavior was thought to be, at times, the expression of an existential vacuum.[156]

These new approaches brought about an active revision of society, its structures, and its laws, at times in such an abrupt fashion that it seemed to be untimely and revolutionary. It was proposed, and strongly advocated, that the primary source of delinquent behavior and of humankind's violence was not to be found in the family and the individual, but primarily in society, with its often unfair, discriminatory and repressive way of dealing with people. In the social conflict view, violence is a function of conflict between the haves and the have-nots. The capitalist system produces violence through its stress of values of materialism and competition.

The advocates of a more permissive society viewed the individual as having been originally a *tabula rasa* at the mercy of society, and on which society would make its own imprimatur. Western societies were almost flooded by a wave of mass demonstrations against those persons in authority thought to be responsible for social decision making and oblivious to the needs and rights of the people. Both as a result of popular sentiment and political influence, social policies which provided economic, educational, and social opportunities were enacted to deal with the anomie, expressed at times as violence, in lower socioeconomic level populations.

Mention should be made of the ecological theories of Shaw and McKay[157] who proposed a cultural transmission of antisocial behavior. At times I wonder whether these ideas, as well as those of Marcuse, have influenced society in a malignant way. Many people credit poverty and poor standards of education as causative factors in social violence and view the family and social institutions as primarily repressive of the individual's freedom and rights.

Human thinking has been capable of creating revolutionary ideas which have actually revised views of what is society, and the sixties and seventies were no different. They were a steady indictment of society and its systems, an attack on the authority of parents and other authority figures, such as teachers, the police, legislators, judges, the military. Material possessions began to be disregarded. People became demotivated and the use of illicit drugs appeared on the social scene. Slowly, one of the attributes that made American society so appealing to Tocqueville, the desire for achievement, until then thought to be a positive trait, was looked upon as causing evil. What until then had been considered to be good became synonymous with bad, or at least became questionable. Upholding a virtuous life lost its attraction for many of the young persons. Drug cultures and subcultures, hippies and punks, alternated on the social scene. The appearance of myriad angry people in every walk of life testified to a transitional decline of civilization where civility had lost its place. Their behavior was motivated by anger, a type of anger that came from feelings of abandonment and neglect, an anger that was often of a personal nature and motivated by a human quest for acknowledgement and the fear of being clay in the manipulative hands of an authoritarian and outdated social system. A period of progressive social confusion ensued, in which delinquency, crimes of violence and drug cultures soon reached new peaks, progressing to the present day social situation in which homicide and other crimes of aggression against persons have reached record highs when compared to other Western industrialized societies or to America itself as it was twenty years earlier.

All of this was occurring while both the American and European continents were moving into a new and promising technological era. One could certainly argue that the restless violence of those days may have been due to an unconscious premonition of modern humans that evolving technology with its inanimate computerized machines might eventually extrude them from the labor scene like a useless foreign object. This required adaptation to a new way of life and to their status quo. This was, obviously at an unconscious level, felt as a threat, and one from which they felt they could not defend themselves. Social unrest, group or collective, in fact, is often the outcome of intense frustration. There is no doubt that transitional social periods, even those aimed at improving human conditions, at times create not only contradictions but temporary suffering for the people involved. Ogbrun[158] discussed the phenomenon of cultural lag in which a people's values and beliefs do not change as quickly as technological changes in a society. Dysfunction in a range of social settings (e.g., family, community, organizations) is the result.

Merton,[159] in his inquiry into the delinquency of adolescents, proposed the strain theory, the idea that struggle and frustration in a growing person, caught between what he or she aspires to—often prompted by social customs and stimulated by the various media—and the concomitant lack of a suitable means to achieve it, may create his or her delinquent behavior. The strain theory reflects the upsurge of a budding consumerism and the widespread social attitude that equates the worth of a person with what he or she possesses. Especially during the past several decades, many people have equated these material possessions with social respectability.

In some sub-cultures, where the conventional ethic of success shared by the majority of people is thought to be unachievable—or actually is unachievable—social respectability was found, instead, in toughness of behavior, the immediate gratification of one's desires, and, often, macho violence and delinquency. This view is supported by those who state that disadvantaged adolescents commit crimes in order to obtain whatever material goods they want, and that in doing so, they are able to overcome the realistic sense of economic failure intrinsic to their way of life.

Even though the above sociological interpretations are attempts to understand deviant, delinquent and violent behavior, and are as well the indictment of at times unjust social structures, at the same time, they may resound as a justification for those persons who are seemingly unwilling to direct their energies towards the betterment of themselves and towards more worthwhile and advantageous aims. Within such a social climate of widespread aggressive tendencies and de facto aggression the American child has been growing into adulthood. It is no wonder there is so much violence among our adolescents!

However difficult the separation of the sociological from the psychological in any given culture, I feel that it is important for a better appreciation of human aggression and violence to discuss the child's early stages of development. The old Latin axiom, *in puer est homo,* should be considered a pearl of bio-sociological wisdom and tradition. It is commonly felt that a basic bond of love between the child and its parents will be conducive to a psychologically integrated and emotionally stable individual who is able to relate to fellow human beings in a socially respectable, human way. It is also a common observation that a nurturing relationship with loving maternal and paternal figures, consistent in its manifestations, will, generally, condition the child to emotional and behavioral stability and that the existence of a good bond between parents and children will eventually promote in the growing child social concern and adequate social competency as well as a better capacity to control his or her inborn tendency to increasing impulsivity and aggressivity and the desire for immediate gratification.

It is within the boundaries of the child-parent relationship, the first microcosmal inter-relationship, usually occurring in that primary social agency that we call the family, that the child grows into acceptable, mature social behavior in accordance with the expectations of his parents and the dictates of society at large. It is within the dyadic relationship between *gemeinshaft* and *gesellshaft* and their continuous interplay that the child shapes his social self and hopefully achieves the integration of his psychological self and his social persona. How difficult it is to strike a relative happy medium in this undisputed important child-parent relationship is well known to any insightful person.

A poor relationship between child and parent may generate a dissatisfied, rebellious youngster and future adult who may easily become delinquent and violent due to his previously unattended and ungratified emotional needs. It seems that any disruption of the psycho-social bond between parent and child will create distress in the child, lack of assurance, or demanding behavior. The above may eventuate in problems of socialization, in problems in relating to others, and at times in deviant behavior characterized by a future inability to form lasting and meaningful relationships, an inability to obey rules, a lack of empathy towards others, impulsivity and aggressivity.

However, even if at times the growing individual does not have a good relationship with his or her parental figures, or even when parents may not be present, society offers many opportunities for identification with virtuous people who could serve as role models for the development of a well-balanced, mature social being—teachers, religious figures, and others.

As we will see later, connected with the problem of violent behavior is the presence of what can be called moral and social conscience. It is during early childhood that the youngster develops first, its super ego, and then, what is called conscience. Conscience, if viewed as a learned behavior acquired through conditioning and reinforcement during the developmental stages of childhood, has all the attributes of a socially determined development. The development of this controlling conscience is very important for rational, human and humane living, and should be recognized as the most important and useful attribute of a well socialized person.

Personal conscience is obviously strictly connected with what we call social conscience and the lack of development of this social conscience should be looked upon also as a failure of society. The lack of morals within a family, the lack of values, and the lack of the conditioning effect of a good adult role model, are not conducive to the development of a personal moral conscience, and, of consequence, of a good social conscience, and this lack often leads to deviant behavior. In fact, the remorseless, unfeeling psychopath frequently recognized among the anti-social violent or non-violent criminals lacks a social conscience.

A good moral personal conscience and a social conscience, with flexible, adaptive overtones, are sociological assets, but what can be said of the development of a too strict moral personal conscience and social conscience? The development of such a type of conscience, in addition to creating an incapacitated obsessive-compulsive individual, continuously prey to doubts and indecision, may form an individual unable to react to assault or attack who becomes easy prey to victimization.

Without discussing here either the Freudian libidinal drives at the basis of a child's development,[91] or Kolberg's stages of moral development,[160] it is important to restate that the process of socialization in a child's life is primarily the outcome of the interactive conditioning between the child and its family—parents and siblings—during which the child adapts to family values, ideas and expectations, and makes them an integral part of itself, a self that will move on to the larger social arena and hopefully become a socially mature adult. It is for this reason that one should also look at a person's development as a social development, a progressive social adaptation of the budding psycho-biological self to a well established organized society through the mediation of a family with its moral and social ethical values—values that are gradually instilled in the child-adolescent, future adult. One should not dismiss that in this process of socialization and acculturation the personality makeup, cultural and life experiences of the parents and their attitudes towards their children, and their expectations for them and from them, are of great importance.

The interaction between children and parents is at times a very difficult one, and the type of relationship they establish may be somewhat
unpredictable because of their individual, and often different, personalities,
and because of the many contingencies of life. A child should know what
to expect when he or she does or does not obey rules and regulations. A
child who is the object of inconsistent and noncontingent parental behavior,
feels more free and is more prone to use violence in his or her daily
encounters.

McCord's[161] analysis of a longitudinal study of a group of children,
the youngest of whom was age eleven, spanning the period from 1937 to
1955, pointed out that the combined effect of warmth and consistent
discipline on the part of the parents was a powerful determinant of
acceptable behavior of the child even into adulthood. West and Farrington,[162] instead, followed 411 boys, randomly chosen, for a period of
seventeen years, starting at age eight. They concluded that delinquent
boys usually came from homes where parents were cruel, neglectful, or
even passive.

Certainly, from a sociological point of view, it is not hard to understand that children who were born into families where there is a low
income, parental criminality, poor child rearing practices, large number
of siblings, low IQ in the child or in the parents, and especially a lack of
affective bonds between the child and its parents, and a lack of supervision and interaction between parents and children, may show propensities for criminal behavior.

In further discussing sociological theories, that of Durkheim[154] is
relevant to the question of violence. In writing about the importance of
sociological factors as the basis of crime and delinquency, he viewed
antisocial behavior as strictly an epiphenomenon of a particular society
at a particular historical time. Today, we live in a society where norms
are frequently questioned and at times are barely respected, and that
almost deserves his attribute "anomic." His thoughts, even though purely
sociological, are certainly enlightening.

Merton, also, believed that society is immersed in a hypocritical state
of anomie. He blamed all types of rebellion on society's structures and
explained rebellion as a rejection of mainstream societal values, encouraging the substitution of those values with new ones.

Reik[163] viewed criminality and violence as a social protest and believed
that the remorseful criminal wanted to be caught and punished and
inadvertently left incriminating evidence behind at the time of his

illegal act. He theorized that the criminal desired, through his incrimination, to punish the punishing society.

In assessing crime and violence, one should take into consideration specific socio-demographic variables. These parameters vary from time to time in their representative quantity. Variables that have been taken into consideration in the assessment of criminal offenses and violence thus far, have been race, age, sex, education, I.Q., housing, employment, economic situation, and drug and alcohol abuse. Even though these variables fluctuate from time to time, during the past two decades they have remained quite steady.

An appreciation of the violent state of our nation can be obtained by reviewing a survey done by the Bureau of Justice Statistics[164] that comprised 13,714 violent offenders representative of the seventy-five most populace counties of the nation. Of defendants taken into consideration in the survey, approximately 30 percent of offenders in the categories of murder, rape, robbery and assault had felony convictions prior to that for which they were incarcerated, the highest number being the 40 percent reported in cases of robbery. Indeed, the survey revealed that of 517 offenders who were charged with murder, only 35 percent were reported as having had a prior felony conviction. Of the 719 cases of rape reported, 23 percent had a prior felony conviction. Four thousand five hundred and sixty-one cases of robbery were reported with 42 percent of the defendants showing a prior conviction for felony. Six thousand five hundred and nine cases of criminal assault were reported; of the defendants charged, 29 percent had a prior conviction for felony.

Another recent large survey reported by the United States Department of Justice in 1993,[165] described the major characteristics of felony defendants in large urban counties in the United States. About 86 percent of all defendants were male, including 95 percent of the defendants under age eighteen. Fifty-four percent of all defendants were black, 44 percent were white and about 2 percent were members of other racial groups. A slight majority of the defendants in each group under age thirty-five were black, including 60 percent of those under age eighteen. Defendants aged thirty-five and older were evenly distributed between black and white. Men comprised the largest percentage among defendants charged with rape (98 percent), burglary (94 percent), robbery (93 percent) or murder (92 percent). About one in six defendants was charged with drug offenses or non-burglary property offenses. A majority of the defendants charged with a violent offense (61 percent) or a drug offense

(57 percent) was black, while the majority of public order offenders (57 percent) was white. For specific offenses, blacks comprised the highest percentage among those convicted of robbery (73 percent) while the highest percentage of white offenders was among defendants charged with driving related offenses (84 percent).

The average age of the defendants in the above survey was twenty-eight years with 63 percent of all defendants, and a majority within each of the four major crime categories, under age thirty. About five percent of all defendants were under age eighteen and twenty-two percent were under age twenty-one. Only ten percent of the defendants were age forty or older. More than half of the murder defendants (60%) and robbery defendants (53%) were under age twenty-five, and about a third were under age twenty-one. About one in nine murder and robbery defendants was under age eighteen. Defendants charged with driving-related offenses (23%) or rape (18%) were the most likely to be forty or older.

And finally, the report stated that a violent offense was the most serious charge for about 25 percent of the defendants. Nearly half of these defendants were charged with aggravated assault, and a third were charged with robbery. Those charged with murder or rape each comprised about 5 percent of all defendants charged with a violent offense.

From a sociological point of view, these national surveys of violent offenses reveal that the violent offender is usually young and his age ranges from sixteen to thirty-four years, even though recently violent crimes have been increasingly committed by juveniles younger than sixteen, at times even as young as twelve and thirteen. It has been my experience with the many offenders that I have seen that the highest level of formal education in these offenders ranges from the ninth to the eleventh grade, with an occasional high school graduate and a rare college graduate. Some of these felons later obtain a high school equivalent diploma, often during a period of incarceration.

In my experience, most of the very large number of violent young inmates that I have had the opportunity to examine are at a level of education that is far below that of the formal education they received and that is normally expected of their age group. Even though many of them seem to be rather street-wise, the intelligence quotient of these people appears to be at the low average level.

The number of black prisoners is apparently higher than that of white prisoners, although this may be somewhat inaccurate due to the fact that black defendants are often unable to post bail or bond. Nonetheless, the number is higher than that of white defendants relative to the black and white population in the United States.

Male defendants are much higher in number than female defendants. The majority of violent offenders has been unemployed in a steady way, holding only occasional menial jobs. Most of the defendants draw either welfare support or supplemental security income (SSI), generally due to a long standing incapacity to function independently due to drug and alcohol addiction. There is also a sizable group of defendants receiving benefits who have a dual diagnosis, i.e., mental illness coupled with drug or alcohol addiction.

Many of these defendants, regardless of ethnicity, live in inadequate and unhealthy conditions prior to their incarceration, as I was able to observe during trips throughout inner-city neighborhoods. This has been confirmed to me by a large percentage of a group of six hundred inmates who came to my professional attention during the past six years for evaluation of legal competency to stand trial. I have also noticed a high degree of recidivism, poor paternal contact, the absence of any well defined religious affiliation, occasional gang membership, and frequent gun possession and use in the majority of the inmates, especially those charged with major crimes.

If one looks at the statistics of offenses against persons or property in the United States during the past two decades, it can easily be seen that crime of all kinds is soaring in our cities; and when murder, aggravated assault, battery and rape are taken into consideration the high number of these offenses is appalling, and it is obvious that it represents a rapidly progressing menace against the members of our society.

The scale of justice has on its balance plates the two important values of rights and duties. When there is a lack of balance between the two there is a dysfunction and at present this dysfunction is highly visible in our society. Daily living is fraught with fears, not only in large metropolitan areas but even in small towns and rural areas. People have assumed coping mechanisms which, though meant to establish some equilibrium, often bring about even more dysfunction in their lives.

The cases reported below are representative of a large number of patients seen by me in my psychiatric practice, and illustrate the aforementioned coping mechanisms. They are part of that silent majority of our citizens who are daily victims of our chaotic, violence-prone social living, but they do not always reflect the vast group of the heinous social aggressive crimes that usually make the front page of our newspapers.

A forty-five year old homemaker, resident in a large metropolitan city, presented herself with problems of anxiety, irritability and agoraphobia. Her mood had been depressed for the previous year and she had lost interest in normal social interaction and refrained from going to the movies or theater which she previously enjoyed. During psychotherapy, the patient revealed that her progressive social isolation and anxious depressed mood were due to her fear of being attacked in the streets following a purse snatching of which she had been the victim. At that time she had become panicky, fell to the ground, broke a few ribs, and fractured her right forearm. After a successful course of psychotherapy, she still remained rather cautious and continued to avoid crowded city places.

A twenty-six year old white male professional consulted me because of marital difficulties. In discussing his social life, he stated that during the previous three years he had increasingly isolated himself from social interactions. This was due to his fear of exposing himself to assault while in the streets during the evening. During one of the interviews he stated, "I always have a $20 bill in my pocket ready for someone who might attack me. They only want money for drugs. So far I have been successful in avoiding a confrontation."

While the above cases are in the category of the social-defensive mode type of behavior, the following is an example of what I call the aggressive-defensive mode:

S.M. is a forty year old white male living in the so-called inner core. He consulted me because of increased anxiety, depression, restlessness and irritability. His history revealed that two years previously he had purchased a gun and he always carried it with him because of his fear of being attacked by city gangs while going to work on the bus. He had been mugged once and importuned several times. One night he fired his gun at a homeless beggar who insistently tried to manhandle him and he seriously wounded him. He felt guilty and became increasingly depressed.

A final example belongs to the social apathy mode of behavior:

A sixty year old white housewife who had become increasingly withdrawn was brought by her husband and children for consultation because they suspected that she was suffering from either depression or an organic illness of the brain. She was moderately depressed and voiced her fear of possible street aggression and attributed her behavior to that fear. "The only way I can protect myself is by going out the least amount of time necessary—actually only during certain hours of the day. I feel unprotected."

Siegel,[166] in 1986, attempting to clarify the relationship between social crime and mental disorder, concluded that jail and prison inmates are mostly persons of a lower social class. In his opinion and contrary to many other reports, the rate of mental disorders among inmate population does not exceed the rate of mental disorders among groups of a comparable social class in the general community. However, the presence of such a type of population among the jail inmates, either of a lower social class or afflicted by mental illness, could be explained on the basis that these groups usually comprise those persons who, once apprehended, are unable to avoid detention through circuitous maneuvering. Some of these people are also known to conduct themselves in such a way as to be apprehended, preferring jail to their unpleasant and difficult living conditions, and, at times, to escape psychiatrization.[131] This is particularly true of misdemeanants.

Factors leading to deviance are instrumental co-factors in the manifestations of emotional and mental illness. At times it is difficult to differentiate what is psychological from what is sociological. There is no doubt, however, that the streets are flooded with illicit drugs of all types, making some sections of society look like an experimental biochemical research laboratory; the easy accessibility of weapons has reached the point that it has led to a declaration of war on crime by the government; the frequent presence in many streets and public buildings of unkempt, homeless people and the obviously deranged mentally ill have all combined to make our cities the unfortunate breeding ground for aggressive behavior. This presence of the mentally ill is, unfortunately, the heritage of selfish and uncaring attitudes under the guise of the benevolent decisions of deinstitutionalization which were mostly inspired by economical and political factors.

Durkheim[154] wrote extensively about the role of the moral community, a community which would provide social integration, bonding its members to the group. The increase in crime throughout the United States is certainly an expression of a lack of this moral bonding among its members and of the escalation of selfishness and the decline of altruism. Many people are tense and insecure, families have disintegrated, and moral values are often absent.

Some of the findings of a survey of state prison inmates by the Bureau of Justice Statistics[165] in 1991 support the contention that either crime is destroying, slowly but surely, the moral fabric of our society, or that the decay of the moral fabric of society is breeding an incessant wave of crime. A vicious circle! Thirty-two percent of prison inmates sentenced for a violent offense had victimized relatives, intimates, or persons whom they knew well. Nearly 25 percent of white inmates imprisoned for homicide had killed a relative or intimate. Among inmates sentenced for a violent offense, women (48 percent) were nearly twice as likely as men (24 percent) to have committed homicide. Nearly half of these women had murdered a relative or intimate. Among inmates in prison for assault, 44 percent of men, compared to 30 percent of the women, had victimized a stranger. Further, 21 percent of violent male prisoners had committed rape or other sexual assault. While 38 percent of the sex offenders had assaulted a relative or intimate, more than 80 percent of both men and women convicted of robbery had victimized a stranger or a person known only by sight.

In comparing the 1991 offense distribution of inmates with that of 1986, it appears that the percentage of inmates sentenced to life in prison or to death was unchanged. It is shocking to realize that almost 75,000 inmates were serving a sentence for murder in 1991. Of this estimated number, 45 percent had received a sentence to a term averaging thirty-two years, 41 percent received a life sentence, 11 percent received a life sentence plus years, and 3 percent had been sentenced to death. Black, white or Hispanic inmates were about equally likely to be serving a death sentence or to have been sentenced to life imprisonment. Of the estimated 60,000 inmates with a life sentence, most (96 percent) were men age thirty-five or older, 46 percent were black, 37 percent were white, 14 percent Hispanic, and 2 percent were of other races.

Thirty-six percent of violent inmates had carried or used a weapon when they committed the offense of which they had been found guilty. However, weapon use did not vary significantly between the sexes or between racial or ethnic groups. Fewer than 1 percent of all inmates (2,100) had been armed with a military weapon, such as an Uzi, AKA-47, AR-15, or M-16. Also, 61 percent of violent inmates stated that they, or their victims, were under the influence of alcohol or drugs at the time of the offense.

The above survey of state prison inmates certainly is sociologically useful because it shows the characteristics of those inmates who have been involved in violent criminal actions. The characteristics of their family environment, ethnic origin, race, their use of drugs and alcohol, and their gang membership are also evident. Their relationship to their victims is also noted, as well as the means by which the crimes were committed.

A survey of one hundred inmates in a county house of correction conducted in 1991, revealed that the inmates themselves attributed their fall into criminal behavior to a breakup in their families and a lack of male leadership in their lives. It showed that a lack of love and nurturing prevented younger criminals from developing any sense of values, and also indicated that without first learning to love parents and siblings, children, when referring to young violent criminals, could never learn to love their friends or neighbors. Some of the inmates also believed that the younger criminals display a penchant for violence that has not been seen in the past.[167] The same group of inmates also cited as causative of crimes of violence against persons, especially in the younger population, a lack of positive role models, substandard education, a breakdown in morality, and drug addiction. Even though blaming violent behavior on the abuse of drugs is like mistaking the fever for the infection, the relationship between drug use and crime is well accepted.

Inmates surveyed by the Bureau of Justice Statistics in 1991[165] reported an increased use of cocaine or crack but a decrease in the use of marijuana when compared to 1986. It appears, also, that recidivism, regardless of the type of security section in which the inmates found themselves, either maximum security or minimum security, is reported as being in the eighty percent range.

The upsurge of gang membership in our society deserves a few words. Gang membership is intended as a formal type of membership requiring initiation to specific rules. Also, a gang has a leader or group of members whose orders must be followed. At times the members of a gang use similar clothing, symbols, tattoos, or special language. The gang usually has a group name and the participants are usually from the same neighborhood, street or school. Each gang usually has its own turf or territory. The aforementioned survey of prison inmates done by the Bureau of Justice Statistics[165] reports that 6 percent of inmates belong to a gang before entering a prison. This phenomenon of gangs in our city streets is increasing and is very alarming.

A great deal of what is apparently random and motiveless crime, such as frightening drive-by shootings, finds a lack of jobs, poor education, dysfunctional homes, and escapism into drugs and alcohol as co-factors in the existential confusion of many of these young violent offenders who, fearful and frustrated, come from dysfunctional homes or no home at all. Almost as a reaction formation, they have assumed a defiant macho attitude while, apparently emotionally detached, they carry out their murderous actions. As previously stated, it has been speculated that their antisocial behavior is a conscious or subconscious act against a system that they feel to be uncaring and oppressive, and that is, in their eyes, emarginating them from the mainstream of society. But their violence is directed primarily towards their own neighborhoods which supposedly are also suffering the consequences of similar alleged socio-racial aggression. Could this be a form of socially assisted suicide?

Crime in the United States is rampant and victimization is at record levels. We must ask ourselves what is wrong with our society. Even though containing more or less those components included in Shils'[148] definition of society, it does not function the way one would expect it to, and we must realize that some of the institutions he mentions no longer hold the same value as in the past in the mind of the average person. The role of teachers, for example, and the importance of their teaching has been undermined during the past decades. They are often no longer viewed as possessors of knowledge and have at times lost that enthusiasm that attracts and motivates students to listen attentively and to learn in an orderly classroom. Truancy, illiteracy and illegitimacy are frequent occurrences. Some adolescents live a life that is socially unacceptable and morally questionable.

Religious values also, even though still shared by society at large, are of little or no consequence in the lives of those numerous people who either do not attend religious services as they used to do, or who no longer place the same trust in their religious leaders. Indeed, it is difficult to envision how social and moral values may continue to be present within a progressively disintegrating family and society.

Even though there is a society, with all its props, it is often a non-functioning or poorly functioning one, and it seems devoid of real participation of its members, who are playing a role without any great enthusiasm and reaping neither satisfaction nor pleasure. It is a vicious circle that will be interrupted only when humankind's fascination with social disorder will be halted by the moral pain and physical suffering which it inflicts upon itself and when society's members, often lonely and dehumanized creatures, cry out for moral order and for more pre-dictability in their daily lives.

As fever is an expression of an infection in the human body, so is crime a reflection of the decline of the moral fabric of our society. Social chaos, with its confusion of identity and sudden eruptive street and home violence, is what we may be reaping from the abandonment of many of our cities and the increased emphasis placed on rights to the detriment of duty.

Chapter Five

STATISTICAL STUDIES

One of society's tendencies at present is the objectification of any assertion that is made. So to say that aggression, violence and crime are at high levels in society is not satisfying to the majority of us, even though we are witness to the daily escalation of aggressiveness in our streets and our homes. The best way to objectify our perception is through a statistical analysis, and, in the case of violent behavior, this is of the utmost importance: a good assessment of the rate of violence is essential in order to create preventive and controlling programs. Crime statistics do not assess human suffering and are usually viewed as cold data; however, they aid in better understanding the problem and give an indication of the state of the nation. I would like to stress the word *indication,* because, except for data on homicide, which obviously reflects a rate very close to reality, many other crimes, including violent ones, are underreported. The question of why some types of violent crimes, such as rape, aggravated assault and robbery, go unreported is important and calls for an explanation.

A woman who is the victim of rape often does not report the offense of which she was a victim for fear of retaliation or of social and court exposure, or frustration with a lengthy police investigation. An added factor may be found in the slowness of the judicial process. But perhaps the most important factor is the ever present, conscious or subconscious, concern about the possibility of questionable innuendos regarding her conduct prior to the victimization, and whether it led, in any way to that victimization.

The same underreporting may occur in cases of aggravated assault, especially when the assault takes place in the home. These assaults may involve people who know one another or who are strangers and are usually the consequence of sudden violent, emotional, explosive behavior. Often, illicit drug or alcohol use or abuse is thought to be a contributory factor.

Underreporting is also a frequent occurrence in cases of robbery, which is obviously a form of violence against someone else's property. The victim may willfully choose not to report the offense to the police, again because of lengthy investigative procedures and the slowness with which justice is, at times, delivered due to myriad bureaucratic factors or a plethora of court cases. This supports my assertion that statistics, except for those regarding homicide, while helpful, may not reflect the actual number of offenses that are perpetrated in society—day-in and day-out. They are essential, nonetheless, to illustrate the cancerous presence of social aggression.

Social aggression is ubiquitous and often present among family members as a strong disruptive force. Indeed, it has invaded the sacrality of the home and statistics tell us that violence is frequent between husbands and wives, children and parents, brothers and sisters, and among neighbors. People are not only harmed by strangers, but are victimized by the ones they love, and in their own homes. Children who are raised in violent households may learn and incorporate into their behavior what they witness within their family.

The learning of violence, however, is not limited by the boundaries of a household but goes beyond them into the streets, which, unfortunately, have become the theater wherein humans act out their inhuman tendencies; where disagreements are no longer talked out, nor argued out, or even settled by a fist fight. People's capacity for dialogue has given way to forceful demonstrations of bravado attitudes that often end in destructive behavior.

Newspaper headlines throughout the country testify to this destructive conduct: Washington-9 People Died over Weekend; Houston-9 People Killed from Friday Night to Sunday Morning; New York-5 Young Robbers in Brooklyn Took the Cash, Then Killed 3 Anyway, Police Say; Philadelphia-6 Bloody Weekends Boost Toll of Killings; Milwaukee-81-Year Old Robbed, Attacked in Mall Lot; Boston-3 murdered; New York-3 Shot; Baltimore-2 Killed; Neptune Beach-2 Kmarts, 2 bombs, 1 blast; Irving-Bystander Killed in Mall Shooting.

Gun possession and its use by delinquent persons, either juveniles or adults, has reached high levels, and violence has reached epidemic proportions. There is a high correlation between the possession of guns and illegal drug trafficking. The percentage of juveniles, either prison inmates or students, who have dealt with drugs is also very high: 78 percent for the prison inmates and 18 percent for the students. Firearms, too easily accessible, have become an artificial extension of the human hand. Indeed, all too often, the hand of both rebellious youngsters and callous criminals is used not to make a fist with which to fight, but to hold, and to use, a gun to commit a violent crime. A 1990 report from a commission established by the American Medical Association and State Boards of Education stated, "On the average day, 135,000 students bring guns to school." We are told that guns kill fourteen children a day and that in one given year violent acts killed 50,000 people. "By comparison, [the AIDS epidemic] took 30,000 lives and drunk driving another 18,000," during the same year.[168]

Even though "handguns and semi-automatic rifles are still for most drug dealers the weapons of choice"[169] there is growing concern about the use of hand grenades, dynamite or dynamite-like explosives in drug gang wars. The statement, "It is to Los Angeles, which had more automatic weapons victims than Beirut last year [1989] that the U.S. army sends its physicians for combat training, at Martin Luther King, Jr./Drew Medical Center,"[170] portrays the state of crime in many of our cities. It must also be noted that, "Guns cause hundreds of millions of dollars of injuries and the costs . . . are borne by society."[171] Already in 1986, Siegel[166] had estimated the cost to the victims of all crimes as being in the range of many billions of dollars.

Killers, often under the influence of illicit drugs, have become more vicious, often firing weapons after trivial provocation. Many homicides are a part of domestic violence, others occur in street brawls, during the commission of another crime, or in drive-by shootings. They usually involve people who are acquainted with one another, gang members, people who were engaged in the same criminal behavior, or people who used drugs or alcohol together. People have assumed different modes of behavior in trying to cope with this rampant crime. A defensive reaction is no longer enough, and some people have adopted an aggressive-defensive attitude, while a few have become apathetic, indifferent, almost like automatons.

Murder is the most catastrophic violent crime from a personal and community point of view, and sociologically the most revealing of the moral decline of a nation. In 1992, there were 23,760 murders in the United States, fewer than in 1991 (24,700), but more than in 1988, 1989 and 1990 (20,680, 21,500 and 23,400 respectively). At the same time, the number of rapes at a national level has increased progressively from a reported 92,490 in 1988 to 109,060 in 1992. Robbery, burglary and larceny have also steadily increased during the same period.[172]

Even though crime is rampant in metropolitan cities not only in the United States but throughout the world, the number of violent crimes commited in the United States is certainly much greater than that in other countries. A comparison of London and New York, largely similar in terms of population (by 1990 the population of New York had reached 7,322,564[173] while that of London is reported as 6,765,000[174]), shows that in 1987, recorded crimes of violence in metropolitan London rose by 11 percent over those reported in 1986, and again by 26 percent in 1988.[175] The majority of crimes were so-called "minor offenses." In 1987, 194 murders were committed in London; eight times that number were committed in New York during the same period. Again in London, in 1988, there were 1,600 armed robberies, while in the same year in New York that number was ten times as large. In some districts of London an increasing number of racial attacks, street robberies, muggings, and domestic violence have been reported,[176] and major American cities are all disrupted by these same crimes.

Violent crime is found both in poverty and in affluence, but most of the killing is done by young males—sixteen to thirty-four years of age—frequently illicit drug users, especially crack cocaine, and coming from disadvantaged areas where moral fabric is often lacking. Most frequently, a firearm is the weapon used in murder, followed by knives, cutting tools or heavy instruments. Body force and strangulation are also reported as causes of homicide. It has been suggested that the viewing of violent films on television or at the movies may be one of the contributory causes of violence in our society. "It is estimated that by the age of 16 the average TV viewer might have witnessed nearly 11,000 screen deaths. This must have an impact on his/her perspective on violence," states one report.[176 p.425] Another states that "by the age of 18 the average American child will have seen 200,000 violent acts on television, including 40,000 murders. . . . [and] exposure to televised violence is one of the causes of aggressive behavior, crime and violence . . . [affecting] people of all ages, of both genders, at all socio-economic levels and all levels of intelligence."[177] Since the arts often shape our behavior and attitudes, the assault of brutal imagery may prompt some people already predisposed to outbursts of aggression to commit a criminal offense and threatens to desensitize all of us to violence.

The seminal study on the subculture of violence of Wolfgang and Ferracuti[155] in 1967, even though historically important, only partially reflects the present-day widespread state of violence in society. Indeed, since 1967, victimization has increased at a rapid pace throughout the United States, and ghettos, still in existence, have grown in number with their boundaries increasingly poorly defined. Psychoactive substance use and abuse has inundated mainstream society, almost to an epidemic degree, becoming a *trait-d'union* between cultures and subcultures. This widespread illicit drug use and abuse, together with that of alcohol, is frequently responsible for unleashing humankind's primitive instincts. It is no longer a question of cultures or subcultures; violence has infiltrated all levels and all groups of society.

Fears and the uncertainty about the future have taken hold of many people and have probably unleashed their deepest destructive emotions. Large strata of the population seem to have been desensitized to crime and/or have assumed an attitude of passivity and resignation regarding it.

Daily living in major cities in the United States has become uneasy and constricted due to the frightening rise in the crime rate. Bureau of Justice statistics from 1984[178] and 1985[179] reported staggering numbers of yearly, serious victimizations in the United States. The number of total offenses in 1984 had reached 11,881,800. More than 2,000,000 of these were considered to be serious offenses, and the above was probably grossly underreported. In 1989, New York, with a population of 7,369,454, had reported 1,905 murders; Chicago, with a population of 2,988,260, reported 742 murders; Washington, D.C., with a population of 604,000, reported 434 murders; Dallas, with a population of 996,320, reported 351 murders; Milwaukee, with a population of 689,800, reported 112 murders; and San Francisco, with a population of 750,964, reported 73 murders.

During 1989 the number of murders in the United States rose to 19,600. By the end of 1990, that number had risen to 23,200, higher than the previous peak reached in 1980 of 23,040.[180] That is 9.2 murders/100,000 population, more than seven times the rate in England or Japan.[181] In 1990, New York City reported an average of six murders a day, an increase of 18 percent over 1989, while Los Angeles reported 983 murders during that same period of time, a 12 percent increase.

In 1992, together with collaborators, I reported an analysis of the murder rates from the F.B.I.'s Uniform Crime Report for the years 1965, 1971, 1974, 1975, 1979, 1980, 1984, 1989 and 1990, in a comparison of eight major American cities.[182] We chose murder rates because of the seriousness of the crime and its apparent rapid increase.

As can be seen, Table 5.1 shows the murder rates of eight major U.S.

cities for ten measurement year periods over a 24 year time span. Two population estimates for each city were included; one estimate for 1965, and the other estimate for 1989 (because these were the only convenient population estimates available to us at the time of the study).

The data in Table 5.1 illustrate the awesome increase in murders from 1965 to 1990. Even though five of the eight major cities listed showed a decline in their population from 1965 to 1989 (a 24 year time span), all five of these cities (i.e. New York, Chicago, Detroit, Philadelphia, and Milwaukee) demonstrated large increases in their murder rates during that sametime period. For example, the range of population decrease for these five cities from 1965 to 1989 was from −5 percent for New York City to −38 percent for Detroit, while the range for the murder rate increase in the same five cities was +88 percent for Chicago to +315 percent for Milwaukee.

All eight of the major cities showed increased murder rates from 1965 to 1989 regardless of whether their populations were increasing or decreasing, and the range of the murder rate increases over this twenty-four year time span was from 28 percent for San Francisco to 315 percent for Milwaukee. Seven of the eight cities listed demonstrated from over two to over a four-fold increase in their murder rate from 1965 to 1989. It can also be seen that the murder rate for seven of the eight cities declined dramatically from 1980 to 1984, slightly declined or increased in 1985, and markedly increased in 1986 again.

As can be seen in Table 5.2, in 1992, New York City reported a population of 7,375,097, a slight increase of 5,552 from 1989. The number of murders reported, interestingly enough, dropped from 2,245 in 1990, to 1,995 in 1992. The difference is quite substantial—250 fewer crimes per 100,000 population, reverting almost to the 1989 level. During the same period, the population of Los Angeles increased by 173,906 persons from 1989, reaching 3,615,355. The number of murders in 1992 increased 111 units from the 983 units of 1990, with 1,094 homicides reported. That increased number of offenses appears to be in accordance with the increase in its population during 1989–1992. Chicago, on the other hand, with a population of 2,988,260 in 1989, had 850 murders in 1990; even though its population declined to 2,832,901 persons in 1992, it showed an increase in the number of reported homicides to 939 during the same period. It can be seen that while the number of murders committed in Los Angeles and Chicago increased considerably during the years 1990–1992, those in New York City dropped, in spite of the fact that the city showed a statistically insignificant population change.

Detroit shows a 1992 population of 1,044,128 people and reported 595 homicides. In comparing these numbers with those reported in Table 1 the change is seen to be statistically unimportant: 1,039,599 inhabitants in 1989 and 624 reported murders for the same period. Here we see a decline comparing the data to 1989–1990 in both population and murder rates which is statistically insignificant.

Philadelphia, as seen in Table 5.1, with a 1989 population of 1,652,188 reported 475 murders. In 1992, both parameters of population and reported homicides decreased, the population of Philadelphia declining by 48,550 units with a reduction in the number of murders to 425 units. The city of San Francisco had a reported population of 750,964 in 1989 and 750,885 in 1992, which can be considered stable. The city reported 117 murders in 1992, an increase from 101 in 1990. Lastly, Milwaukee, with a reported population of 643,017 in 1992 compared to 600,868 in 1989, reported 146 murders in 1992, a decrease from the 165 reported in 1990. During the same year, 1992, Atlanta, Dallas and Miami, all three southern cities, ranked high in their homicide rates, while Phoenix, Boston, Seattle and San Diego had the lowest rates during the same year.[183]

A comparative analysis of the previously mentioned report regarding the eight major American cities relative to the period 1965 to 1990 was done with the above data relative to 1992. The statistical analyses (a Chi-Square Test of Independence) of city by year (1990, 1992) on the murder rate showed that there was an association between city and year (Chi-Square = $40 - 2707 > 14.067$, 7 d.f., $a = .05$), however the magnitude of the relationship or correlation between year and city was very small (Phi = .0584). Similarly, even though there was a statistically significant association between city and year when looking at population (Chi-Square = $8323.4023 > 14.067$, 7d.f., $a = .09$), the magnitude or correlational relationship between city and year on population size was very small (Phi = .02).

After another set of analyses using a different statistical method was done, it was found that there were no significant differences in murder rates between 1990 and 1992 (T = $.0913 < 2.145$, 14 d.f., $a = .05$, 2-tail) and population rates between 1989 and 1992 (T = $.0076 < 2.145$ d.f., $a = .05$, 2-tail). These results support the main finding from the first set of results, which lead to the conclusion that, overall, there were no statistically significant changes in the murder rate from 1990 to 1992 or in the population rate from 1989 to 1992. In other words, the murder rate

TABLE 5.1
MURDERS COMMITTED IN EIGHT MAJOR CITES IN THE UNITED STATES
BY YEAR †

City a.% Increase (+) or Decrease (-) From Prior Year b.1965 to 1989 Comparison	Two Population Estimates		Murder Rates By Years									
	1965	1989	1965	1971	1974	1975	1979	1980	1984	1985	1989	1990
New York City	7,781,984	7,369,545	631	1117	1554	1645	1733	1814	1450	1384	1905	2245
a.		-5%		+77%	+39%	+6%	+5%	+5%	-20%	-5%	+38%	+18%
b.											+202%	
Los Angeles	2,479,015	3,441,449	249	395	481	555	786	1011	759	777	877	983
a.		+39%		+59%	+22%	+15%	+42%	+29%	-25%	+2%	+13%	+12%
b.											+252%	
Chicago	3,550,404	2,988,260	395	810	970	818	856	863	741	666	742	850
a.		-16%		+105%	+20%	-16%	+5%	+1%	-14%	-10%	+11%	+15%
b.											+88%	
Detroit	1,670,144	1,039,599	188	495	714	628	452	549	514	635	624	582
a.		-38%		+163%	+44%	-12%	-28%	+21%	-6%	+24%	-2%	-7%
b.											+232%	
Houston	938,219	1,713,499	139	289	330	347	--	--	473	457	459	568
a.		+83%		+108%	+14%	+5%	--	--	+36%	-3%	±0%	+24%
b.											+230%	
Philadelphia	2,002,512	1,652,188	205	352	444	435	385	437	264	273	475	503
a.		-17%		+72%	+26%	-2%	-11%	+14%	-40%	+3%	+74%	+6%
b.											+132%	

TABLE 5.1 (Cont'd)

City												
San Francisco	740,316	750,964	57	108	139	138	112	110	73	85	73	101
a.		+1%		+89%	+29%	-1%	-19%	-2%	-34%	+16%	-14%	+38%
b.											+28%	
Milwaukee	741,324	600,898	27	50	62	69	63	74	44	68	112	165
a.		-19%		+85%	+24%	+11%	-9%	+17%	-41%	+55%	+65%	+47%
b.											+315%	

Footnotes to Table 1

† Data for this table were partially obtained from the Federal Bureau of Investigation <u>Uniform Crime Report</u>, years 1965, 1971, 1975, 1979, 1980, 1984, 1985 and 1989. The 1990 data were also obtained from the <u>Milwaukee Journal</u>, April 29, 1991, Latest Edition.

A dash (--) denotes incomplete or unavailable data.

Reprinted with permission of The Guilford Press.

TABLE 5.2

<u>Homicides Committed in Eight Major Cities in the United States</u>		
<u>1992</u>		
<u>City</u>	<u>Population</u>	<u>Number of Murders</u>
New York City	7,375,097	1,995
Los Angeles	3,615,355	1,094
Chicago	2,832,901	939
Detroit	1,044,128	595
Houston	1,695,239	465
Philadelphia	1,603,638	425
San Francisco	750,885	117
Milwaukee	643,017	146

Data for this table were obtained from the Federal Bureau of Investigation Uniform Crime Report, 1993.

appears to be staying about the same regardless of minor population fluctuations in the eight U.S. cities we sampled.

The population census, especially in large cities, may not be reported precisely because of people's frequent migration and abscondance. But the murder rates are close to reality — a cadaver is incontrovertible objective evidence. While the attempt to objectify murder data within a given population has to be taken with a grain of salt, the undeniable and shocking fact is that the number of murders in our cities is generally on the increase.

A very interesting phenomenon as far as the homicide rate is concerned is offered by a comparison of the rate of murder in San Francisco and that in Washington, D.C. San Francisco, with a population of 750,885 people in 1992, reported only 117 murders during the period, while Washington, D.C. with a population of 589,000, reported 443 murders. If we also introduce the city of Milwaukee, a sizeable Midwestern city with a population of 643,017 in 1992 and a murder rate of 146, we will have to ask why there is such a difference in these crime rates.

Is the above due to ecological and economical factors, variables such as poor and overcrowded housing conditions, unemployment, low educational levels, whose negative influence is facilitated by the use of illicit drugs, especially crack cocaine? Or is it due to gang association and fighting, the availability of guns, or the disintegration of the family unit?

In 1992, I published, together with several collaborators, a statistical analysis of the crime rate in Milwaukee from 1965 to 1990, comprising twenty-five years of reported violent crimes against persons.[167] I chose Milwaukee not only because of my association with the criminal justice system in that city, but because it was my perception that the crime rate, even in this conservative Midwestern city, was rapidly increasing. Crimes against persons were classified under the headings of homicide, rape, robbery and assault. The study confirmed the impression that violent crime has increased in the city of Milwaukee during the past twenty-five years.

All four categories of violent crime demonstrated very statistically significant differences in crime rate changes from 1965 to 1990, as can be seen in Table 5.3. Throughout the 25-year span measured, the murder rate in Milwaukee increased 511 percent, the number of rapes jumped 1,712 percent, the frequency of robberies rose dramatically by an appalling 1,990 percent, and the number of assaults rose by 217 percent. This very dramatic increase in violent crime in Milwaukee is even more significant when one considers that the population decreased by 15 percent during that same time period. Table 5.3 also shows that from 1982 to 1984, three out of the four crime categories (homicide, robbery, and assault), experienced a significant decrease. Even the number of rapes markedly declined in the year 1982. However, by 1985, the four categories of violent crime, most notably homicide and rape, again showed increasing trends. It was theorized that increased use of crack cocaine may have contributed to the soaring crime rate.

In 1992, the adjustment index crimes against persons for the city of Milwaukee are reported as follows: homicide-146; rape-523; robbery-4,334; and assault 1,329.[184] A comparison of these 1992 figures with the last entry in our statistics for 1990 shows a diminution of − 10.4 percent in the murder rate, an increase of +4.2 percent in the rape rate, of +1.9 percent in robbery and +1.4 percent in the assault rates. The fluctuations in plus or minus are probably of minor importance as crime predictors if one considers that in 1991, only one year earlier, the number of murders was 163, while the other categories showed minimal differences.

Of interest for the discussion is Table 5.4, which compares the homicide rate in Milwaukee with that of six American cities whose population differs plus or minus ten percent from that of Milwaukee according to the 1990 census. It can be seen from Table 5.4 that Washington, D.C., had a significantly higher homicide rate than Milwaukee, (79.4/100,000 compared to 26.0/100,000); while Boston had a significantly lower rate (19.7/100,000) than both cities, particularly Washington. It appears that the murder rate is quite stable and the fluctuations seen may be due either to a minimal decline in the frequency of aggression manifested by people against people, or may be the consequence of a more positive action against crime that has been taken by both police and communities at large.

Demographic factors reflect primarily the socio-economic aspects of the communities of residence, and the rate of violent crimes against persons differs considerably in different areas of a city. Henry and Short,[185] in 1954, theorized that there is a linkage between aggressive behavior, and specifically between homicide and suicide, and economic fluctuations at a personal and national level. The existence of low socio-economic conditions among offenders was also studied by Wolfgang, Gillies and Hansen.[186] However, even though a large percentage of offenders, regardless of race, belong to the lower socioeconomic class, that does not justify the assumption that this is the cause of crime: the

The Faces of Violence

TABLE 5.3

MILWAUKEE CRIME REPORTS YEARS 1965, 1971, 1974, 1975, 1979 and 1980-1990

CRIMES REPORTED TO POLICE AND PERCENT CHANGE FROM PREVIOUS YEAR

VIOLENT INDEX CRIMES AGAINST PERSONS †

Year	Homicide*		Rape*		Robbery*		Assault*	
	Number	%change	Number	&Change	Number	%Change	Number	% Change
1965	27		33		214		477	
1971	50	+85%	93	+182%	649	+203%	720	+51%
1974	62	+24%	196	+111%	1647	+154%	827	+15%
1975	69	+11%	146	-26%	1968	+19%	1020	+23%
1979	63	-9%	283	+94%	1592	-19%	1101	+8%
1980	74	+18%	213	-25%	1796	+13%	1227	+11%
1981	76	+3%	296	+39%	1894	+6%	1272	+4%
1982	70	-8%	200	-32%	2218	+17%	1272	±0%
1983	54	-23%	243	+22%	2297	+4%	1251	-2%
1984	48	-11%	310	+28%	2118	-8%	1274	2%
1985	73	+52%	426	+37%	2271	+7%	1519	+19%
1986	85	+16%	520	+22%	2427	+7%	3450	+127%
1987	95	+12%	487	-6%	2178	-10%	3524	+2%
1988	86	-10%	492	+1%	2302	+6%	2450	-30%
1989	116	+35%	618	+26%	2602	+13%	1233	-50%
1990	165	+42%	598	-3%	4472	+72%	1513	+23%
Change From 1965 to 1990		+511%		+1712%		+1990%		+217%

Population Change
from 1965 (741,324)
      to
1990 (628,088) -15%

Footnotes to Table 5.3

* Goodness-of-Fit Chi-square significance level, p < .001.

† Data for this table were obtained from the "City of Milwaukee 1990 Crime Report," page 4, and from the Federal Bureau of Investigation, <u>Uniform Crime Report</u>, years 1965, 1971, 1975 and 1979.

†† Some of the homicide data on Milwaukee from years 1980 to 1990 varies slightly from the data published in a prior article by these authors, possibly because of different sources who obtained data at different times which may have affected the data's completeness.

Reprinted with permission of The Guilford Press.

TABLE 5.4

HOMICIDES AND RATES PER 100,000 POPULATION*				
<u>1991 No.</u>		<u>Rate</u>	1992 No.	<u>Rate</u>
Washington DC	482	79.4	445	73.3
Memphis TN	169	27.7	176	28.8
Milwaukee	163	26.0	146	23.2
Jacksonville FL	128	19.0	121	18.0
Columbus OH	138	21.8	113	17.8
Boston MA	113	19.7	73	12.7

Cities within 10% of Milwaukee's population according to 1990 Census. <u>City of Milwaukee 1992 Public Safety Report</u>.

majority of indigent or economically marginal people do not commit crimes of violence. I certainly agree with Gottlieb and collaborators who stated that most people, no matter how poor, never kill.[186] However, even though a low socio-economic status per se does not drive people to commit a crime, at times, it may drive a person to use drugs in order to escape what is felt to be a social status of impotent indigence. The use of drugs may then secondarily contribute to criminal behavior. In fact, alcohol and drug intoxication, especially crack cocaine, are strong co-factors in the national murder rate.

A Danish study[186] found that "homicide defendants seemed to deviate more than other inmates [taken as a comparison by the authors] in terms of psychopathology as indicated by their higher rates of previous psychiatric admission and suicide attempts." The authors concluded that potential links between social difficulties, special circumstantial conditions, and homicidal behavior, are influenced by the psychopathology of the actor-offender.

The results of their study of 71 male, non-psychotic defendants charged with homicide in Copenhagen between 1959 and 1983, showed that 19 of the 71 defendants came from broken homes and that during the first fourteen years of life had moved at least to three different foster homes. Forty-eight percent (34/71) of the same group of defendants charged with homicide showed difficulty in learning, and 56 percent (39/71) showed maladaptive or dysfunctional conduct. The defendants' housing conditions prior to the homicides rated far below average. Fifty-two of 71 defendants had a previous criminal record, and 19 of the 52 had previously been in prison. Twenty out of 71 had attempted suicide prior to the homicide. In their study, no defendant was found to suffer from a psychotic condition. Most of the defendants, however, carried a diagnosis of antisocial personality disorder or borderline personality disorder as described in *DSM-III-R*.

Their group of 71 homicide defendants had a much higher rate of drug and alcohol abuse than that of the general inmate population, 65 percent and 42 percent respectively. They also scored higher in previous suicidal attempts, 29 percent versus an average of 6 percent in the general prison population.

The above study also took into consideration the households of the general population and of the defendants considered. It found that while single-person households in the general population increased in Denmark from 7 percent in 1969 to 13 percent in 1983, the percentage of defendants living alone increased from 24 percent (10/41) to 43 percent (13/30) within a twenty year period. They also documented that out of 1,651 male prisoners in 1961, only six percent carried a sentence for violent crime against persons, while in 1979, among a prison population of 2,645 males, 20 percent were sentenced for crimes of violence. The study also pointed out a high degree of social maladjustment in most of the homicide offenders. They concluded that on the whole they found the socioeconomic background of homicide defendants and prison inmates to be poor when compared to that of the general population.[186]

The above findings of Gottlieb and collaborators are similar to our American statistics, as are those in the study of the Canadians Langevin and Handy[187] which considered a cohort of 1,418 inmates convicted for homicide. Fifty percent were found to have a low educational level, poor occupational record, poor job skills, and to have lived in single-person households. Gillies[188] after reviewing homicides in West Scotland from 1953 to 1974, concluded that the increase in violent crime is due to those same factors that are today commonly identified as the main variables in crimes, such as crowded urban living, lack of space-territoriality, gang warfare, low economic conditions due to a lack of jobs or underpaid jobs, low education levels, and drug and alcohol use and abuse.

It is evident from statistical tabulations that from 1985 to 1990 black males have been the victims of homicide in an alarming crescendo. The highest rate is in the age bracket from twenty to twenty-four years (from 63.5% in 1985 to 140.7% in 1990).[189] Even though statistical data confirm the highest rate of violent victimization to be between ages twenty and twenty-four, it is extending in the fifteen to thirty-four year age group at an increasing rate. The victims and their killers are almost always of similar age groups.

Based on 1980 and 1990 census reports, the United States Justice Department reports that with the exception of Boston, which showed a decrease of − 18.7 percent (11,904 in 1983 to 12,562 in 1993), the crime rate per 100,000 residents has risen in those cities reported. The increase ranges from +6.5 percent in San Francisco (8,734 in 1983 to 9,302 in 1993) to +51.9% in Jacksonville, Florida (7,039 in 1983 to 10,690 in 1993). It must be noted that Boston did not include arson in its 1993 statistics.[173]

In 1990, the city of Milwaukee reported 4,146 robberies, 1,468 aggravated assaults, 495 forcible rapes and 155 murders. By 1991, with the exception of aggravated assaults, which showed a slight decline to 1,311 cases, the number of cases had increased to 4,252 robberies (+2.6%), 506 forcible rapes (+2.2%), and 163 murders (+5.2%). In 1992, the number of robberies reported was 4,895, aggravated assaults were 1,517, rapes were 726 and reported homicides were one hundred and fifty-three. The statistics for 1993 show that there were 4,528 robberies, 1,495 aggravated assaults, 561 rapes, and 164 homicides. These statistics seem to confirm recent reports that the rate of crime is declining while the rate of murder continues to increase.[184] It can be assumed that these statistics from Milwaukee reflect those of the nation.

Out of 12,354 agencies with an estimated population of 222,105,000, the number of major offenses known to police in the United States in 1991 and their rate of increase from 1990 is reported as follows:[190] (1) Murder, 19,782 (+4.7); (2) Forcible rape, 93,084 (+0.9%); (3) Robbery, 636, 185 (+7.0%); (4) Burglary, 2,763,79 (+1.9%).

In 1991, the total number of homicides in the United States is reported as 24,703, of which 15,511 (66.3%) were firearm related; 12,408 (53.1%) were handgun related; and there were 806 (3.4%) rifle related homicides.

The highest number of homicides in 1991 was registered in California (3,859), followed by Texas (2,652), New York (2,571), Illinois (1,300), Florida (1,248), Michigan (1,009), Georgia (849), Ohio (783), and Pennsylvania (758).

The Uniform Crime Report for 1992 on a national basis lists the number of aggravated assaults as 1,126,970; robbery is given as 672,480; forcible rape is reported as 109,060; and the number of murders is reported as 23,760. These statistics, excepting those for murder, may not reflect the reality of the crime situation because of underreporting. However, it may be that even the number of murders is higher than that reported since some of the thousands of people reported to be missing each year may be the victims of unknown killers.

The State of Wisconsin[191] reports 348 adult arrests for murder in 1993, 947 for robbery, 642 for forcible rape, 246 for forcible rape, and eight for manslaughter. During the same year, the juvenile arrests were 105 for murder, 559 for robbery, 230 for battery, and sixty-one for forcible rape. The total arrests for felonies and misdemeanors for juveniles in 1993 was 16,885. During that period, 242 juveniles were waived to adult court.

In a study of 800 offenders examined by me for competency or for criminal responsibility in the period from 1988 to 1994, and comprising 50 percent felons, 10 percent of them charged with first degree intentional homicide or manslaughter, I found the following demographic data basically similar to other reported studies: The age range of the defendants at the time of the offense was between eighteen and thirty-two, with a median age of twenty-five. Their I.Q. usually fell within a low average or borderline level and they generally acquired only a tenth or eleventh grade education, very rarely obtaining a high school diploma. Their knowledge level was lower than that officially expected for their age group, but they were generally street-wise. Their work record was very poor, and at times non-existent, and almost all of them were on public assistance. They had a history of continuous alcohol and drug addiction, usually starting at age twelve or thirteen. They often had contact with mental health or drug rehabilitation centers. They had a police record for misdemeanors, escalating into felonies of increasing gravity, and had several incarcerations and were frequently recidivistic. Their mobility was of a medium degree and they lived in poor housing conditions. They were raised in a dysfunctional family or foster family. They were mostly male, single, with several children, however from different women.

Among the many variables considered so far one should also include religious affiliation. Among a group of 272 defendants, 60 percent accused of violence against people and 40 percent of violence against property, only 10 percent reported to me that they had a religious affiliation.

Statistical predictors may be able to predict those who have a high likelihood for violent behavior so that preventive efforts may be focused on these people Nevertheless, any statistical analysis, being a collection of cold data, can only serve to compute numbers and rates, but will fail to explain the riddle of why people kill one another. We can debate the importance of demographic variables but the increasing lack of socio-moral values in our communities is too evident to be denied. I feel that those many factors usually taken into consideration in the attempt to explain the possible causes of crime probably fail to give us a conclusive answer to the problem of violence because that answer lies within the individual.

Chapter Six

THE PHENOMENON OF
THE ANTISOCIAL PERSONALITY
AND THE PRISON

S emantics, the study of meanings, can be helpful in understanding hostile emotions in their various manifestations. Within the definitions of aggression as a forceful action or procedure (as an unprovoked attack) especially when intended to dominate or master, and violence as an exertion of physical force so as to injure or abuse, or as an intense, turbulent or furious and often destructive action or force,[192] one already sees their dynamic meanings. However, for a more a meaningful appreciation of the above words, critical for this discussion, one must return to their etymology.

The word aggression, deriving from the Latin *ad-gredior*, actually conveys the act of moving towards or approaching the other; violence, on the other hand, from the Latin *vis*, meaning force, carries within itself the force that one applies against someone while moving towards that person during an attack. Obviously, the Latin *vis and violare* "to violate" further qualify the forceful act as an infringement upon, or abuse of, the rights of another person, and have to do primarily with violence to persons. In psychiatry, we think of aggression and violence as the personal expressions of uncontrolled hostility, either as a personality trait or as a pattern of a well defined personality structure. In such cases, aggression retains its basic meaning of acting out a feeling that may be harmful to another person.

The personality structure is, obviously, of great importance in a discussion of the antisocial personality disorder. The change in terminology to "antisocial personality disorder" from the former "psychopath" places emphasis on the stressful effect of internal or external factors on the person, and shifts attention from character to personality. Character conveys a more dynamic meaning than personality and seemingly represents the personality in action.

103

Physical appearance has been described in literary works from the time of Homer to that of present day writers as an indication of the virtue, or lack of it, in the bearer of this or that particular physique or facial feature. Facial expression and facial mimicry, and especially the play of one's eyes, are often revealing of one's emotions, and the dramatization of it has been part of theatrical production since the early periods of the Greek tragedies and comedies. In fact, people's outward appearance and behavior, attracting or distancing as they may be, are part of their character and often tell a great deal about them. To this effect, Macdonald,[193] in his book, *The Murderer and His Victim,* a clear, concise and scholarly disquisition on crime and criminality by a forensic expert with a humanistic tradition, repeats the story of Socrates, who, when told by a Greek physiognomist that his facial features bespoke a person who was "brutal, sensuous and inclined to drunkenness," admitted that, even though that was, indeed, his natural disposition but that he had overcome it.p.27

The criminologic study of man, or criminal anthropology, began in 1809 with the observations of Gall, whose craniological measurements laid the foundations for the pseudo-science of phrenology. Even though at present we look upon the observations of this Viennese doctor as an extravagance, and occasionally with ambivalent thoughts, we cannot deny that his rudimentary, unscientific examinations were an expression of the eternal dilemma that confronts, and still puzzles, many scholars: is the physical appearance and demeanor of a person helpful in our appreciation of his behavior?

In the latter part of the nineteenth century, Cesare Lombroso, psychiatrist and anthropologist, who was first Chairman of the Department of Legal Medicine and Public Hygiene of Psychiatry and later of Criminal Anthropology in Turin, Italy, became interested in the peculiar physical characteristics of criminals, believing that murderers had some physical degenerative traits that were usually associated with their tendencies to destructiveness and combativeness.[31, 193, 194] These persons, he maintained, had "enormous jaws, strong canines, prominent zigomae and strongly developed orbital arches.... [The] span of the arms ... often exceeds the height.... The eyes ... are cold, glassy, immovable and blood shot; the nose ... always voluminous."[193] p.28 He wrote the first edition of L'Uomo Delinquente in Rapporto all'Antropologia, alla Giurisprudenza e alle Discipline Economiche in 1876, in which he developed the theory of the born criminal.

Even though Lombroso believed that criminality was an inborn characteristic, he thought that the criminal could be rehabilitated to some extent. Hooton, a follower of Lombroso, also believed that murderers are "taller, [and] larger in chest" when compared to other criminals.[193] p.28 These Lombrosian criminals, in addition to these supposed peculiar physical signs of degeneracy, "talked like savages," and showed violent passions, lack of foresight and frequency of tattooing. Lombroso's conclusions, based on his personal observation of almost 6,000 criminals, may have been influenced by Darwin's theories, reflecting the expression of an incomplete evolution in some individuals, a fixation to earlier stages of development (genotypic development) or simple quirks of mutation.

Bromberg[32] reports that prior to Lombroso, the presence of degenerative traits, physical or behavioral, had been noted by Morel, in France. In 1857, he had reported his findings of the association of a variety of degenerative malformations present in those of his patients diagnosed as suffering from mental deficiencies or moral depravity. However, Göring, in a painstaking study published in 1913 in England, regarding 3,000 English criminals followed by him for an eight year period, dispelled the clouds of the atavistic theories of both Lombroso and Morel, and their followers, Brace in New York and Boies in France, when he wrote that he had found no signs of physical degeneracy in any of the subjects he had studied. Nonetheless, I cannot deny that when confronted with myriad criminals, as I am in my criminological psychiatric practice, I have often noted certain particular physical features which are similar to those previously described as degeneracy traits. However, in all fairness, I must admit that similar traits are also observed in the general population.

While we should not, perhaps, dismiss *tout-court* the clinical observations of the early founders of criminology, this attitudinal approach should not go to the detriment of the consideration of the psychological and environmental factors at the basis of crime. For years, psychopathic criminals have been diagnosed by psychiatrists the world over only on the basis of their offensive actions and they have been viewed in a descriptive and non-dynamic fashion from a psychiatric point of view. In Europe, as well as in the United States, the prognosis of the psychopath was considered to be hopeless. At present, those persons diagnosed as suffering from an antisocial personality disorder continue to be viewed as being remorseless and unable to learn from experience, just as the previous psychopath was seen. Psychodynamically, their behavior is seen as primarily a reaction to social factors rather than to their inner conflicts. However, Blackburn and Maybury[195] subscribe to both. In a 1985 study they stated that "the psychopathy dimension corresponds to a dimension of hostility that, together with an independent dimension of dominance-submission, forms the basic element of the interpersonal system of personality description. . . . "p.510 How did this nosographic transition come about? Is their antisocial behavior due to organic factors or to maladaptive behavior to the environment?

There is no doubt that for many years after the historical period which called them constitutional psychopathic inferiors, who, when chronically manifesting their condition, become persons classifiable as suffering from a constitutional psychopathic state,[196] the approach to the psychopathic patient was solely behavioral, and they were considered to be just maladjusted persons. Then, in 1953, new diagnostic labeling eliminated the psychopathic inferior and, in an all embracing rehabilitative hope, the sociopathic personality disorder came to light.

Noyes and Kolb,[197] in 1958, categorized under the sociopathic personality disorder those people previously recognized as psychopaths, who were considered unable to make "acceptable and successful adjustments to the prevailing social and cultural milieu,"p.545 and whose characteristics were emotional immaturity, impulsivity, absence of rational behavior, lack of conscience, affectionless, narcissistic feelings, lack of remorse, not showing foresight and unable to profit from experience. At that time, the personality in the group of the sociopathic disorders whose characteristics stood out most clearly was thought to be the antisocial type. The sociopaths, like the Lombrosian born criminals, were reported as showing a blunting of their moral and ethical selves, a superficiality of interpersonal contact, as lacking ambition, unable to show affection or real love, consideration for others, prone to lying and swindling and with a chaotic sexuality.

Cleckley,[198] in a deeper analysis of criminality, distinguished between the psychopathic criminal and the ordinary criminal and wrote that the psychopath differs from the ordinary criminal among other things in that, "often his antisocial acts are quite incomprehensible and are not done for any material gain. . . . [He] usually does not commit murder or other offenses that demand major prison sentences."p.293 In addition, psychopathic criminals often seem to ignore the consequences of their brutal acts, and "they carry out an antisocial act and even repeat it many times,"p.293 even though knowing that they may be apprehended. He further thought that they did not appear to be "purposive . . . in comparison"p.292 to the ordinary criminal, and that their acting out did not usually derive from tremendous, intense passion, but from a "relatively weak emotion breaking through even weaker restraints."p.294

Cleckley reported that in 1931, Eugen Kahn, after studying what he termed the psychopathic personality, described sixteen different clinical types. Could they be considered the forerunners of the present classifications of the Personality Disorder found in DSM–IV? Unable to present distinctive evidence of the sixteen types he had described, Kahn limited himself to stating the following: "By psychopathic personalities we understand those discordant personalities which on the causal side are characterized by quantitative peculiarities in the impulse, temperament, and character strata and . . . impaired by quantitative deviations in the ego and foreign valuation."p.556–557

A 1985 study of 60 male patients detained in a maximum security psychiatric hospital because of dangerous, violent behavior or criminal tendencies, strongly supported, in spite of the small sample, the usefulness of identifying psychopaths within the framework of an interpersonal descriptive system. The study proposed that " . . . Cleckley's criteria of psychopathy represent one axis [of a circumflex] system, hostility vs. warmth [and] that these criteria alone are not sufficient to identify a homogeneous group of deviant persons."[199] p.375 The authors of the study further stated that the assessment could be more complete and valid if the behavioral dimension of impulsive aggression and sociability were added to the second rating scale, the Blackburn Scale, in addition to the scales for Cleckley's variables.

Hare and McPherson,[200] in an interesting study published in 1984, stated that there was evidence to support the fact that in addition to being more numerous, "the crimes and behavior of psychopaths are also more violent and aggressive than are those of other criminals." They report that McCord and McCord, in 1964, portrayed the psychopath as impulsive and aggressive, needing and craving exciting and thrill seeking behavior. They also reported that Buss, in 1966, believed the psychopath to be unreliable, given to pathological lying, lacking remorse, unable to delay gratification, prone to lose control, and antisocial in his behavior. Proneness to boredom, low frustration tolerance, easy irritability, attempted suicide, and belligerent behavior, even while in prison, higher in frequency than in nonpsychopathic or mixed groups of inmates, were also part of the psychopathic personality described by him. Their conclusion was that there is a strong relationship between psychopathy and violence prior to age thirty or thirty-five.

In a 1988 review and critique of the psychopathic personality concept, Blackburn[195] concluded that the current concept of psychopathic personality or antisocial personality remains a "mythical entity" as described by Karpman in 1948. He believes that this diagnostic category includes a large number of different and deviant personalities and that "given the lack of demonstrable scientific or clinical utility of the concept, it should be discarded."[p.511] However, Blackburn stated that socially deviant behavior remains related to personality characteristics.

Serin,[201] in his 1991 paper on psychopaths and violence in criminals, reported that Williamson, Hare and Won made a distinction between the criminal psychopath and the criminal non-psychopath. They claimed that the criminal psychopath is more likely "to have committed serious violent assault and property crimes but that non-psychopathic criminals were more likely to have committed murders."[p.424] The rationale for the above assertion is understandable if one considers that the acts of violence, among which murder is the most extreme expression, are usually the outcome of explosive emotional outbursts and unrestrained aggression. Serin further reports the results of the study of a random sampling of eighty-seven male inmates. The subjects were extensively interviewed concerning their demographic variables and especially about psychopathy, child abuse, and prior violent behavior. They were challenged emotionally through hypothetical vignettes to measure their hostility, anger, frustration. A computerized analysis of various psychological tests aimed at checking aggressiveness, impulsiveness, anger, hostility, aggressiveness and traumatic aggressions experienced in childhood or in adulthood, revealed that violent psychopaths exhibited more impulsive tendencies, more aggressivity and reported more instrumental aggression on the Eysenck and Eysenck Impulsiveness Scale than non-psychopathic violent inmates. Also, violent psychopaths were more likely to be convicted of violent crimes, to use a weapon, to make threats. His analysis confirmed that violent psychopaths have histories of impulsive and violent crimes that go beyond the usual age bracket assumed by textbooks, "well into their 40s."[201 p.430]

All the above studies and observations from Lombroso to Hare and McPherson basically agree that the psychopath is endowed with a personality that is very distinct from any other type, that he is a recidivist in his delinquent and violent behavior, and that he seems to be utterly defiant of rules, laws and mores, usually pursuing a self-incriminating, impulsive, reckless and often non-sensical type of behavior.

As I stated earlier, I feel that character connotes the personality in action; therefore, before taking into consideration present day views of the antisocial personality, I would like to touch upon the concept and development of character. In Engel's[202] description of the formation of character, he states that it is during the latency period, from about age six to approximately age twelve, that the child begins to relate to people outside his family, within the cultural milieu in which he lives. The child, while beginning to control its developing sexual self and its aggressivity, becomes more intellectually and socially mature and this process leads to the formation of character structure. Engel describes the process, by stating: "As the child assumes more an more responsibility for his own behavior and learns what is expected of him, the various patterns of ego defense concerned with impulse control tend to become crystallized in characteristic ways for each child. He now begins to show habitual patterns of reacting to external as well as to internal demands. These patterns in the aggregate make up what is generally known as character."p.133

According to this theory, the child first forms object relations and identifies with his parents, and then moves towards the outside world and the emancipation of the self and a better delineation of his character. There, he will be helped by teachers, peers, or others who have become important role models; at times, these may even be casual acquaintances or movie or television characters. In normal development, the child, through his new relationships, and while continuing his education, will usually be able to make the social adjustment that his family and peer groups expect of him, learning how to interact with others, both people he knows and those he does not, and his socialization and maturation is furthered.

The importance of the formation of an individual's character was stressed by Plato in the *Republic,*[203] where he emphasized that efforts should be made first to consciously try to form a person's character, rather than stressing ludic accomplishments, and, in advocating upright-ness, he suggested that, ideally, character training should even precede intellectual training. Indeed, he believed that right opinion leading to right habits and dispositions should first be implanted by non-intellectual training, and then it would be safe, at a much later age, to introduce people to philosophy, so that they might acquire the necessary knowledge of Good in order to determine which opinions are right. This has been partially the conditioning that parents have exercised on their children for centuries, generally with good results on the children's moral character formation.

While Plato stressed the formation of good character and right opinion already from childhood, Aristotle believed that, "... character produces plans that express an overall unity of ends of life. Such planning is carried out by the deliberative capacities and a capacity to make reason choices or *prohaireseis*. These choices involve the assessment of actions as they cohere within some overall system of good living ..."[204] p.58 Further expanding on his ideas, he added that in order to have "rationality" one must think of oneself as connected with the future. He maintained that making reasoned choices would give the individual a sense of self and purpose and would enable him to acquire practical wisdom or *paronesis*. The above qualities are not part of the personality or character of a psychopath.

There is an obvious difference between the way in which Plato and Aristotle looked at character. Plato thought of it as the outcome of conditioning first and of intellectual knowledge later, while in Aristotle's view the opposite is true. Even though these two views are still being debated in society's dilemma on how to raise children, it is probable that they are not mutually exclusive. Aristotle also clearly stated that "the ability to plan, schedule, and integrate will be pointless in a life devoted to the cravings of the moment,"p.109 and he seemed to be skeptical that the vicious individual would have the capacity to change.[204] Indeed, he believed that the vicious person does not have the ability to study and see human goodness. He thought that passion would yield to force rather than reason. "Such a person does not listen to arguments that dissuade him, nor understand them if he does."p.113

I believe that it is very difficult to find any better description of the antisocial personality disorder (psychopathic personality) than the above stated one by Aristotle. The lack of character is evident in the antisocial personality in his interpersonal relationships throughout his life. In my experience with many adult criminals, and increasingly with late adolescents, I have been confronted with the stark reality that their antisocial behavior has a tendency to escalate. This usually starts in the early teens, if not before, and moves from the oppositional defiant disorder to the conduct disorder, and around the early twenties explodes into a full blown antisocial personality disorder. The iter from hyperactivity disorder to conduct and psychopathic behavior is well exemplified by the following case:

> A nineteen year-old black male was charged with disorderly conduct because he had been playing with a BB gun and aiming it at traffic. On examination he appeared to be restless, and exhibited an overplay of his facial mimicry, as well as a defiant attitude. He claimed that he did not graduate from high school because he found it boring. He had experimented with drugs and alcohol but only sporadically. At age twelve and again at age sixteen he had been hospitalized at the local children's treatment center because of his hyperactive behavior and had been prescribed Ritalin. He had recently been placed on an antidepressant and he believed that this was helping him. His thinking was scattered with a great deal of tangentiality. He was able to give a good account of the offense he was charged with and demonstrated that it was the result of impulsive childish behavior, incongruous with the situation. His attitude, however, was the bravado, uncooperative, and defiant one of a young psychopath. He had a history of attention deficit disorder but at the time of the examination his conduct disorder was a precursor of an antisocial personality disorder.

It is legitimate to presume that an individual whose psychiatric-legal history reveals personality traits such as an unstable disposition; impulsivity, and proneness to act out against others in a disruptive, destructive way; lack of inhibitions; deeply repressed hostile feeling; depression or dysthymia; delusions of persecution; previous institutionalization, either in a mental hospital or a prison; previous threats to kill; loss of consensual view of reality; or an inability to cope with anger and hostile impulses, or historical, genetic, or neurophysiological factors might have a higher propensity to act out in a violent way against others.[205]

The case below clearly demonstrates such a progression.

> A twenty-six year old black male pleaded not guilty by reason of mental disease or defect to charges of burglary. At the time of his forensic examination he was coherent and relevant, friendly and cooperative, and eye contact was present. His ideas progressed logically and his affect was appropriate to the situation. The young man reported a history of oppositional conduct as a child and truancy at school as an adolescent. He also had a history of drug addiction (marijuana, cocaine, and heroin) since age fifteen and admitted to numerous previous criminal charges for burglary. He had often been on probation. He stated that at the time of the crime he had attempted to escape apprehension, running away when the police came. "I had been doing drugs—all kinds of drugs, and also alcohol. I was high. During that time I forgot a lot of things, like I put things in the refrigerator that didn't belong there." The defendant was

diagnosed as antisocial personality disorder and polysubstance dependence. He was found to have been legally sane at the time of the offense.

At present, in order to properly diagnose the antisocial personality disorder in young adults, there should be evidence that its manifestations have been present for months, possibly a year, and that they are not a fleeting episode of that antisociality which, instead, should be ascribed to the developmental curiosity, gregariousness, and group identification which most children experience during their maturational process. Also, one should establish whether there is the presence of a constellation of disturbing traits in the young person's behavior. Problems usually start with the child actively defying the requests of his parents or parent substitutes. He or she is often resentful, spiteful or vindictive, loses his or her temper easily and has a bent towards destroying the possessions of others. The above behavior is usually contained within the family or group of close acquaintances, but as soon as puberty is reached this behavior manifests itself outside the home—in the streets and in those places where he or she associates with his peer group. A conduct disorder ensues, more virulent in its manifestation than that exhibited in childhood, and more disruptive of home and community living. He continues to lie, and he may begin stealing in a progressively escalating manner. He may enjoy setting fires, running away from home, skipping school, engaging in fist fights, using weapons, giving in to the use of illicit drugs—marijuana, cocaine, LSD, phyencyclidine, amphetamines and barbiturates. He may threaten others and destroy their property.

A twenty-five year old black male was held in jail because of a burglary that he had committed. He had a history of truancy and fighting while in school and had dropped out of school during the ninth grade. His use of drugs, joy-riding, and truancy led to a period of detention in a juvenile correctional institution. He had been placed on probation because of a charge of burglary a few years previous to his detention. His attitude at the time of examination was uncooperative and defiant. At first he disclaimed any responsibility for the offense he was charged with through evasiveness and denial but he then admitted to it and stated that he was high on drugs and alcohol at the time. He had broken into an office and stolen a telephone and an answering machine and stated that he had needed the money "for dope." His antisocial behavior led to incarceration.

This escalating antisocial behavior is observed not only in the school or on the street, but also in many so-called dysfunctional homes. It is usually the pedigree of many young adults who are called sociopathic and antisocial, and who are the frequent guests of our jails and prisons.

They have graduated, by then, to the antisocial manifestations which include burglary, aggravated assault, rape, first or second degree murder. They have reached the final stage of that course of life that began with a solitary or group type of rebellion, defiant of family rules and parental or parent-substitute authority. Impulsivity, often accompanied by alcohol imbibition, is frequently observed in these persons. The following case testifies to this type of impulsive, explosive behavior.

A twenty-one year old black male charged with two counts of battery pleaded not guilty by reason of mental illness or defect. On examination he was pleasant, cooperative, coherent and relevant. His ideas progressed logically and his affect was appropriate to the situation. He was free from psychotic thinking or behavior. His sensorium was clear. He denied drug use but admitted to weekend alcohol abuse. He stated that throughout his high school years he was transferred to different schools because of his tendency to fight, which he described as explosive in type. Specifically asked about the events preceding, during and following the offense, he stated that after coming back to his girlfriend's house at 2 A.M. from a nearby tavern he wanted to sleep his alcohol off. However, the girlfriend and her cousin began to argue with him because they had seen him in the tavern with another girl. They poured hot water on him and started biting him while he was trying to sleep. The defendant remembered hitting the girl, swinging her back and forth, banging her head against the wall, hitting her about the face, knocking her down, and stomping on her stomach. He also remembered hitting the other girl. He had a good recollection of the events and admitted the charges. He claimed that his offensive, explosive behavior had gotten worse after he had been hit with a baseball bat at age seventeen. At that time he had sustained a subdural hematoma, apparently not requiring surgical intervention. He was, however, hospitalized for three months, and necessitated physiotherapy for left hemiplegia. Tests for organicity (Gestalt picture drawing, three word recollection after three minuets, and 100-7) testing were within normal limits at the time of the forensic examination. He was diagnosed as antisocial personality disorder, alcohol dependence, and intermittent explosive disorder. He was found to have been legally sane at the time of his offense.

The determination of impulsivity is normally based on police reports describing the characteristics of the index crime. A recent article categorized the offense as being impulsive if "a) the victim was previously unknown to the offender, b) no provocation or only minor verbal altercation was evident, c) the offense was not premeditated, d) the offense was not motivated by financial gain."[206] In trying to determine in their study violent recidivism in killers or attempted killers the authors concluded that violent recidivism was usually associated with impulsivity and with a diagnosis of antisocial personality or conduct disorders. The younger age group (26.7 ± 9.6 years) achieved lower scores in the WAIS IQ (mean scores of 92.9 ± 13.6). Their parents were classified as alcoholists. Individuals with passive aggressive personality or with a paranoid personality were reported as less prone to violent recidivism.

However, if the rebellious adolescent clashes with a well defined and structured family with parents who are interested in their welfare, ready to listen, advise, reward or punish, or with a community that does not tolerate or easily justify under the banner of psychosocial deprivation their grossly disruptive behavior or does not misinterpret it as necessary for the useful self-expression of growing towards maturation, he will usually not proceed to a sociopathic adult level of behavior with its tendency to callous chronicity.

When Wolfgang and Ferracuti[155] described the subculture of violence they conveyed and supported the idea that antisocial or delinquent behavior should be looked upon as learned in a mini-culture that is often quite different from the main one, and at times in contrast with it. In some subcultures machismo and defiant behavior may be acceptable, for example. The subculture they described referred to that in which violence itself has assumed a major value. Subcultures, however, are not devoid of values or good behavior. Even though some of the members may be rebellious and defiant, being participants in the group of subculture of violence, they still have a code of ethics among themselves, often reflecting those of the main culture. It appears that they cannot escape the basic human tendency to form groups and to create codes of behavior of their own, just as in the principle culture that they defy!

Culture is "the integrated pattern of human knowledge, belief and behavior that depends upon man's capacity for learning and transmitting knowledge to succeeding generations;" or, more dynamically, it is "the act of developing the intellectual or moral faculties especially by education."[192] p.314 Subculture, on the other hand, means "an ethnic, regional, economic or social group exhibiting characteristic patterns of behavior sufficient to distinguish it from others within an embracing culture or society."p.1173

Aided by the above definitions one may be led to question whether the present day random, purposeless, explosive violence can be considered a part of a subculture, and whether it is correct and appropriate to use the term sub-culture in describing it. It is my opinion, indeed, that a subculture, even one of violence, should have a certain idiosyncratic but nevertheless fairly well defined purposeful structure. I do not perceive that in today's violence in those at-risk zones that are mercilessly destroying themselves. There are no clearly defined characteristics at the basis of the myriad aggressive, motiveless crimes that are perpetrated daily, and I believe it would be more appropriate to view this violence as interactional in type—violence often perpetrated by people onto people they don't even know and for reasons unknown to either of them. There is no reflective capacity and certainly not any subcultural purposeful aim in this violent behavior. This is the violence committed by childish, immature persons, unable to live in a civil manner with others within the boundaries of their subculture. This is the plain, uninhibited expression of destructive anger of the disappointment with a life that is not life, a disregard for its sacredness.

A nineteen year old black male charged with the first degree intentional homicide of a seventeen year old girl pleaded not guilty by reason of mental disease or defect. During the forensic examination he was friendly, cooperative, and in good contact. His speech was coherent and relevant and his ideas progressed logically. He was free from psychotic thinking or hallucinatory experiences. The affect was appropriate. He claimed to be remorseful for his action but added that he had not killed the girl, that his friend had done it. He stated that the day of the offense he had been drinking with a group of friends. This drinking continued until late in the evening because he had argued with his girlfriend who thought he was going out with another girl. He was angry at her and decided to have "some fun." He went to the nearby apartment of a friend who dealt in cocaine and was helping him sell it. While there he had sex with his young victim. The encounter was interrupted by his agitated friend who told him that someone wanted to buy some "dope" and he had to leave. On the way out, the defendant realized that he did not have his wallet which contained $500. He returned to the apartment and accused the victim of having stolen it. While they were arguing, he left the room and returned shortly afterwards with a loaded shotgun, with which, he stated, he wanted to frighten the girl. He continued to argue with her but was held back by his friends. She suddenly tried to run away and he claimed that as he tried to free himself from his friends the gun, which was aimed at her legs, went off. She began screaming and at that point, his friend began shooting and the girl fell. The defendant claimed that he then gave his gun to another girl and started jumping around repeating, "Man, I'm in trouble." Then, since everyone said to take the body out of the house they took her out to the porch. At that point, his friend shot her in the head at close range, stating that she was still moving. The two young men then went home where they were arrested five hours later. The defendant claimed that he had been drunk at the time of the offense. He was diagnosed as antisocial personality disorder and polysubstance dependence (alcohol, marijuana, and cocaine). He was found to have been legally sane at the time of the offense.

These crimes are not part of a subculture! It is my feeling that describing these violence prone people as belonging to a subculture of violence does a disservice to those people who actually do belong to a subculture. It certainly diverts our attention from the widespread violence present in all of our communities and throughout the world, and, in the process, scapegoats certain groups of people.

The social panorama confronting us today is that of motiveless crime so rampant in our society, be it vandalism, burglary, assault, drive-by shootings, rape and murder, and is a sign of socio-moral dysfunction and of the decline of personal responsibility. The ease with which antisocial people give vent to their instinctual hostility and aggression is astonishing and is performed in an almost ludic way with emotional indifference and lackadaisical attitudes. These antisocial violent acts are part of a meaningless and unstructured type of behavior. A quasi detached, indifferent attitude is typical of present day violent offenders, not only when committing their offenses but also visible upon apprehension by the police. This is not only due to drugs and alcohol, the use of which is often a routine part of their life, but is due to their apathy and disregard for life and are reminiscent of the "cool-cat" ideology.

In this regard, I would like to share with the reader my feeling of puzzlement when viewing the behavior of many of these violent offenders when they enter the jail or during their permanence there. It seems, from their lack of gross emotional display and their silent, distant and cool behavior that they accept jail not as a consequence of an offensive act, but as an integral part in a drama, which, in their case, is the drama of their life. There is no surprise, no anguish, no sadness on their faces. They silently move through the routine of incarcerations as if they were going to an expected and familiar place. This perception of jail by the violent antisocial defenders has reached absurd proportions. Today, time spent in jail or prison is almost a pedigree, something one can use to threaten people, because it means that the one who has been in jail knows the ropes and, since he has nothing to lose, he may hurt or kill in a much more thoughtless way outside of the jail.

Some people have said that our society seems to lack rites of passage.

For many of these offenders, unfortunately, it appears that one of their rites of passage is a forced period of time spent in a jail or in a prison. The view of these young people, strong and well-developed, handcuffed or chained to one another as they are transferred within the jail is remindful of scenes from movies that portray a crowd of slaves taken to the plantation for work! But today this crowd is made up not only of blacks, but of whites, Hispanics, and Asians. Could this apparent indifference and detached behavior and air of resignation be only an expression of silent defiance? One young prisoner told me, "Some young brothers seem like they don't care if they go to prison . . . They think it is macho, that it gives them more power out on the street." Another, a younger offender, added, "I wasn't too worried about going to jail because my uncle came back all built up. I kind of wanted the experience. He told me it was smooth in there, that doing time was a piece of cake."

Could there be a better explanation? In the jail, many of these offenders find a substitute for their unhealthy, crowded homes, better nourishment, a more stimulating life; a place where they encounter many familiar faces, an educational arena, and personal and medical attention. It takes them away, at least for a period, from illicit drug and alcohol use and abuse. From a sociological point of view, the jail, today, is not an extension of their neighborhood but it appears that the neighborhood, the streets and the jails are all one, and that the jail, all considered, for many of these offenders, is a better place than the other two.

Why is there such a pragmatic philosophy in many present day criminals? Jails and prisons have acquired a new significance for millions of poor blacks, Hispanics or white persons, having been divested of the negative connotations they once had as the place where one guilty of an offense against another would be sent to pay for his crime by having his liberty restricted and by being punished by the rigors of discipline; and where, it was hoped, reflection would bring about the realization of having done wrong, and remorse for his wrong deeds would ensue, possibly leading to a desire to start a different and more honest life.

In analyzing the psycho-sociological dynamics of this apparently compliant attitude towards imprisonment, we come across a simple logical sequence of events that may explain our wonder. If we assume, hypothetically, that there is someone who, as part of a family, lives in a decent home, has a job, and for some reason particular to his psychic self breaks the law by assaulting, maiming or killing someone else, and because of that is sentenced to jail, away from his family, his group and his decent life, and in an environment that is worse than that in which he lived prior to incarceration, we can assume that he would envision that incarceration as something negative, reacting to it with despair, and living the time of incarceration as a debasing, depressing period. He would certainly look forward to returning home following his sentence, perhaps feeling regretful for what he had done, and with intentions of keeping away from any possible trouble in the future.

This, one would have to agree, is the most common reaction to the deprivation of human liberty by incarceration, whatever the crime may have been. No person who enjoys a good family life, has a satisfactory job and good social relationships would be insensitive to a jail sentence. This, however, is not the case for those many aggressive criminals who are poor, uneducated, jobless, often untrainable, with families that are almost non-existent, whose lack of a paternal presence has created resentment towards authority figures, and who see no future for themselves in a technological and highly sophisticated work force. When they feel helpless, useless, jobless, and placed outside of the mainstream of society by means of a demoralizing, demotivating social support system, they do not care about either their present or their future, and they develop hostile feelings towards authority figures and towards society in general.

These offenders express their destructive hostility by rebelling, mostly within the boundaries of their ghetto; they kill one another because of boredom or anger, for kicks or as a larger manifestation of a social protest. For many of them going to jail is an escape from their unbearable social conditions. The time there may become a learning period— many have studied for and received their high school equivalency diploma while in jail or prison. They are an object of much attention by a comprehensive management of care and they may also achieve, unconsciously, a coveted revenge towards a society that they feel to be emarginating and castrating them. Many rehabilitative programs are quite active and at times they may help the offenders find an answer to their personal despair and to gain a more objective view of themselves and of society. Unfortunately, in spite of all these good efforts, once they are freed, they usually return to their dreary lives, to homes that are inadequate, where their future is uncertain, where their life has assumed defensive tones and where death through drugs or guns may be just around the corner, if not in their own homes. A vicious circle is then established—from nothing to something and again to nothing. This vicious circle can only be broken if the families of these offenders are reintegrated with the presence of parental figures, with training for jobs, and by eliminating the possibility of reaching out for the spurious Nirvana of illicit drugs or the use of guns—guns which seem to have become an extension of their hands.

The same resigned attitude mentioned above is shared by many of those who visit these antisocial offenders in the jails or prisons, at times interrupted by their friendly chatting with one another in the waiting rooms, their laughter and teasing, as if the place and their visit were not compenetrated by sorrow and shame, but only the expression of a happy communal affair, intruded upon at times by the crying of a new born infant or the sound of innocent children racing through the corridors. This is part of a stark social reality that makes some children believe that a period in jail is almost a mandatory step in growing up, and view it as a school, a place to finally get some attention, and a place to make new friends. And this reality makes other children believe that they will not live to be adults!

The sacred and the profane, the church and the justice system, both aware of the aggressive, violent bent of man, have long worked together and cooperated to suppress, divert, or punish the violence in people. The common sense of early civilizations recognized the naturalness of retaliatory action, but, in order to avoid social slaughter, they devised the diversion of sacrificing a weaker member of the tribe or, later, an animal, with similar weak characteristics, in order to pacify the clan of the victim and avoid any chain reaction blood shed.

As time went on, societies legislated different kinds of reparation for violent crime; but even incarceration and execution can be considered forms of violence. For centuries, judicial systems have attempted to dispense justice, even though not always in an objective and unquestionable way. Today, society is overwhelmed by an unleashed wave of crime, and finds itself unable to keep pace with the discharge of what was once viewed as beneficial retaliatory punishment. Myriad rules, almost annulling punishment under the guise of understanding, have greatly diminished the true essence of the system, the distribution of a just revenge, and deterrence of violence. Thus, when the restraining social rituals and taboos are shattered, man is left to himself, to contend with his anger and his violent behavior. What does this violence mean? It is arguable that the killings in our streets may serve a hidden purpose. In addition to being the expression of some individual's uncontained violence, they may feed the hostile feelings in all of us, discharging our inner tensions, and diverting our hostilities through a process of ambivalent identification with the killer whom we officially despise, and the silent acceptance of the myriad victims, as if they were the victims of a ritualistic sacrifice to the god of violence. Is that the reason for so much voiced leniency towards the criminals, and the indictment of society, of us all, for this destructive behavior?

We can wonder whether this could be an explanation for the apparent indifference of a large strata of our society to the increasingly appalling number of murders in our inner city homes and streets. These victims may be viewed as the weaker, the sicker, and the least productive members of our society. As such, they fit quite well into the role of victims of a ritual sacrifice.

Chapter Seven

SERIAL KILLERS AND MURDER-SUICIDE

This chapter will discuss not the common forms of murder and aggravated assault that are tearing apart our communities and are, at the same time, an expression of the decay of the fabric of our society and of the social bonds that hold it together, but the shocking, destructive hostility of a serial killer, a camouflaged monster, who has puzzled and frightened us with his heinous, meticulous programmed killing of members of society. The realization that a human being is capable of being so destructively sadistic towards another human being is something that sickens all of us. His actions are considered to be so appalling that people have frequently defined him as a monster. Ethologists tell us that animal predatory aggression is not usually directed against its own species, but is aimed at a weaker, at times defenseless, different species. An animal usually aggresses his own species for territorial or group dominance instinctual factors. On the contrary, humans show little reluctance to use their physical strength or the cunningness of their minds in order to further their own interests, and easily, and often with pleasure, inflict pain, injury, mutilation and death upon their fellow humans.[1]

In my estimation, the American term serial killer conveys the concept and dynamics of this behavioral-psychological monstrosity better than the term multiple killer. The term multiple killer, I believe, should refer to that individual who murders disparate numbers of persons who usually lack those similarities generally found in the victims of many serial killings. European criminologists, in classifying the serial killer as a multiple killer, seem to take into greater consideration the number of murders committed by the killer, rather than the common typology of the victim.

European criminology includes under the classification of multiple killer two types of murderers: the paranoid schizophrenics and the sexual sadists. In both of these sub-classifications, the killers, regardless of the presence or lack of manifestations of illness, are considered to be seriously ill individuals, with primitive, ambivalent and unconscious destructive conflicts and motivations.

Frequently, the serial killers show obsessive compulsive characteristics as part of their urge to kill. This was quite evident in the sexual-serial killer, Jeffrey Dahmer, whom I had the opportunity to examine.

Holmes and DeBurger,[207] writing on serial murder, express their view that the social-cultural context in which the killer and victims live may serve as a co-factor in the genesis of serial murder. They refer to the excessive violence in mass media entertainment in the United States as well as to the anonymity and dehumanization of urban society. They also stress the great mobility of Americans and are of the opinion that all of the above factors may play a significant role in unleashing the homicidal fury of a serial killer, and they also stated that "normal socialization is unfortunately saturated with norms, values, beliefs and behavioral models that carry strong potential for normalizing violence in interpersonal relationships."p.45

Obviously, contradictions are present in any society. In the American society, the culture is basically patterned along Calvinistic norms of work, family, duty, and respect for religious doctrines and obedience to God's dictates. At the same time, people are exposed to all types of pornography, violent movies and indecent talk shows. This often occurs in the privacy of the home, at times during moments of relaxation when one is more receptive to audio-visual messages that often negatively influence morals and behavior. Children and adolescents are also exposed to the above, often unsupervised by their parents. People are subjected to double messages, and they may be conditioned to direct their normal or exuberant aggressivity into an abnormal or criminal type of conduct. "Serial murder has been viewed as the ultimate criminal violence for several reasons directly related to the social and cultural context. Foremost is the fact that it represents the antithesis of those benevolent aspects of culture that are worth valuing."[207] p.45

Following an examination of data relative to 110 serial killers, their personality was analyzed by the Federal Bureau of Investigation, Science and Behavioral Section.[208] The FBI lists four major types of serial murder: the visionary type; the mission oriented type; the hedonistic type; the power control oriented type.

The visionary type of serial murderer includes those serial killers who are perpetrators of homicides in response to hearing "voices" or seeing "visions." These murderers are usually under the influence of what are called command hallucinations, and the hallucinated voice is usually the voice of God, directing them to do the killing. As part of the visual hallucinations, some of these murderers are driven by a strange sensation that they identify as the presence of a power entity or a demon within themselves. It is obvious that most serial killers of this type are suffering from a bona fide mental illness which is usually a paranoid type of schizophrenia or a paranoid delusional disorder. In the first type, the killing is usually poorly organized and bizarre, while in the second type it may be carried out in a rather well planned fashion.

The mission oriented type of killers, as is obvious from the name, claim to have a mission, and the mission is usually a firm belief that they must rid the world of persons they consider to be undesirable. These are usually prostitutes, homeless vagabonds or drug dealers. This type of serial killer does not usually suffer from a psychosis, but at times their belief may be supported by some paranoid misperceptions. They feel no remorse for their actions because they believe they are accomplishing a useful and desirable task for the welfare of society.

The hedonistic killers are those who derive pleasure from the murderous action. It is the actual act of killing that gives them this pleasurable feeling, similar to the quasi emotional orgasm the gambler derives from betting and waiting for the results.

The power control oriented type, as the name indicates, is one of those serial killers whose main aim is to exercise full control over another person, and to have the ultimate power to decide that person's fate.

I agree with Holmes and DeBurger[207] when they state that rape, sodomy and destruction of sexual anatomy, are not erotic, but are expressions of power and control over the victim. This is what I thought of Dahmer's behavior, and what he also stated himself. This type of serial killer views his victims as objects. This is the type that is frequently associated with the lust killer, whose primary focus is centered around sexual gratification.

In considering the lust serial killers, those perpetrators of rape, sodomy and sexual mutilation, the FBI Behavioral Science Unit classifies them as belonging either to a disorganized asocial type or to an organized non-social type. The first type of lust killer may be psychotic, while the organized non-social type is not, even though his way of deriving sexual gratification is utterly bizarre and obviously far from any normal sexual pattern of behavior. The lust killer is a person who, because of deep, unconscious or subconscious conflicts, attempts to temporarily resolve the anxiety produced by those conflicts by his obsessive compulsive, occasionally ritualistic, lustful destruction of another person's life, deriving in so doing not only a sense of power but a sense of sexual gratification.

I believe that Dahmer, for instance, fits the typology of the organized non-social type of the lust-serial killer.[209] Indeed, he was "methodical and cunning...fully cognizant of the criminality of his act and its impact on society."[p.129] He wants the excitement derived from the publicity about the bodies of discovery."[p.131]

In a psychoanalytic interpretation, one would think that the struggle in the serial killer is usually between the Id and the Superego, or, as described also, the victory of tension over control within the killer. There is no doubt that the behavior of serial killers is a barbaric one, and we have no difficulty in accepting their own assertions that in the midst of the killing it was almost as if their personality had been taken over by the beast and that they were witnessing their actions but unable to stop themselves. Actually, the above assertions testify to the intensity of their violent hostility, which the killers feel as ego-dystonic, as if their destructive fury was the action of someone else. It has been claimed that the homicidal acts of the serial killers/sexual killers, represent, at times, a mixture of symbolic elements of destructiveness and reconciliation. Their destructive murderous acts are seen as a reintegrative attempt to restore the homeostasis of the psyche of the killer.

Fantasies usually play a large role in the criminal conduct of the lust killers, and they often spend a great deal of time imagining how they will go about their criminal actions. In fact they almost follow a preparatory pattern: first, they think about the crime; they search for the victim; they commit the killing; and lastly, they attempt to dispose of the victim's remains. The disposal of the remains in the case of the serial killer Dahmer, for example, was so well programmed that it proved incontrovertibly his legal responsibility for the crimes he committed.

During the eighteenth century, the erotic and licentious writings of the libertine Marquis de Sade shocked the world with their descriptions of cruel violence and unbound perverted lust. Sade, who believed that instincts are the motivating force in life, and that pleasure is the most important goal one should aim for, wrote his books about debauchery and acts of sexual violence while in jail for crimes of poisoning and sodomy and died in a lunatic asylum.[210] Years later, in 1869, von Krafft-Ebing[211] coined the term sadism and the term acquired the meaning of a sexual perversion in which the pervert forced upon the subject of his sexual attraction physical or moral suffering, deriving sexual pleasure from his actions. It has been thought that the sadist may suffer from an arrest of his psycho-sexual development, possibly at the anal stage (called the anal-sadistic stage), or from a neurotic regression to that level. Freud's[91] thinking at first viewed sadistic drives as primary instincts camouflaged by the drive to dominate, but he later came to believe that sadism is the excessive outward manifestation of the death instinct. The gratuitous cruelty of sadism is possible because of insufficient control by the basic mechanism of defense. One may wonder whether the behavior of the sadistic, power and control driven serial killers reflects, in their often bestial dismemberment of their victims, the conduct of a curious child in the demolition of its toys.

How does the case of the serial killer, Jeffrey Dahmer, fit the typology of the serial sadistic killer, and what does he have in common with previous serial killers? Since Jack the Ripper made the world shudder in 1888 with his sadistic sexual murders, a great number of sadistic sexual killers have appeared on the international scene: the German Ludwig Tessnow from Osnabruck and Rugan (1898–1901); Bela Kiss in Hungary in 1916; George J. Smith in England, and Henry Desire' Landru in France, in 1921; Earle Nelson in the United States in 1926, Albert Fish in New York in 1928; Peter Kurten, the Düsseldorf Ripper, in 1929; the "Mad Butcher" of Kingsbury Run in Cleveland between 1935 and 1938, William Heiren in Chicago in 1946, Rudolf Pleil in 1958, Richard Speck in Chicago in 1966, Albert DeSalvo, 1962–1964—the "Boston Strangler," Ed Kemper and Dean Corll in 1973, in Texas, and Joachin Kroll, 1976. Closer to us were David Berkovitz, "The Son of Sam" in New York in 1977; Kenneth Branch, "The Hillside Strangler" in 1978 in Los Angeles; Peter Sutcliffe, "The Yorkshire Ripper," in England; Theodore Bundy, in 1975, and the recently executed John Wayne Gacy, in Chicago; and finally, Joel Rifkin in New York, in 1994.[212]

Among the most notorious serial killers, and belonging to the group of sadistic killers, Bruno Ludtke of Germany holds the world record of known sex murders, having confessed to eighty-five murders between 1927 and 1944. He claimed that he had taken slices of flesh from the buttocks or thighs of fourteen of his victims and had later eaten them. The young Chicagoan, William Heirens, eighteen years old, raped and murdered his victims by strangling, then cut up their bodies and disposed of the parts in a manhole. All of the above serial killers admitted to not being able to control themselves and to being prey to an obsessive-compulsive force. Heirens, indeed, called for help, asking to be caught because he could not control himself and was afraid he would kill again.[212]

Many of the victims of the above killers, both male and female, were impaled after death.

The American killer, Ed Kemper, (1973) was quite close to Jeffrey Dahmer in his conduct. He raped the bodies in his mother's house after killing them, dissected the bodies, and seemingly enjoyed having sex with a headless body. Some of his homicides had necrophilic elements.

Mutilation of the bodies with dismemberment, surgical dissection, and decapitation were a frequent occurrence in the victims of serial killers like Ted Bundy, Jack the Ripper, Fritz Haarmann, "The Butcher" of post-war Hannover, Germany. Haarmann, a homosexual, butcher by trade, killed fifty young male vagrants by biting through their windpipes. He later sold their bodies for meat. George Grossman, during the period 1914–1921, in Berlin, butchered girls into neat sections. In France, in 1921, Henry Desiré Landru murdered ten women and burned their bodies piecemeal in a stove. Peter Kurtenthe, the so-called Dusseldorf Ripper, killed nine victims in 1929. He stated that he had committed his first murder as a child and that he could only achieve sexual orgasm through strangling or stabbing. In the United States, Earle Nelson was hanged in 1927 for the rape and strangulation of twenty-two women during 1926. The United States also witnessed the case of the "Mad Butcher of Kingsbury Run," in Cleveland, Ohio. From 1935 to 1938, he dismembered twelve bodies whose heads were never found.

The sadism of Neville Heath, the murderer of two girls in 1946 Britain, is "not simply a matter of sexual desire, but of the need for ego-assertion," a reaction to the humiliations inherent in the life of an unsuccessful man.[212p.617]

Rudolf Pleil, in 1958, killed fifty women and was proud of his "excellence." Richard Speck is well known for his murder of eight young nurses in Chicago in 1966. All of their bodies were found naked, slashed and stabbed. Alberto De Salvo, the Boston Strangler, murdered thirteen women between 1962 and 1964. They were left in obscene positions, with brush handles inserted in the vagina, and the genitals facing the door. Later, he claimed to have raped two hundred women between January and October 1964.

All of the above serial killers achieved an orgasmic release through the heinous mutilation of their victims' bodies. Sheer sexual lust, coupled with their basic hostility and their desire for control, were at the basis of their crimes. Often, the crimes they perpetrated showed a good deal of methodical programming. Victims, at times, as in the Dahmer case, were arranged in obscene sexual postures and photographed as mementos. They were often dismembered and at times their flesh was eaten by the sadist killer, as in the cases of Karl Denke, Albert Fish and Joachin Kroll. Denke, the landlord of a house in Munsterberger, killed more than a dozen vagrants, both men and women, and ate portions of their bodies which he kept pickled in brine. In 1928, in New York, Fish, a kindly looking old man, tortured a large number of children and killed them by strangling them and then ate parts of their bodies in a stew. Kroll and Dean Corll, in 1973, in Texas, raped, tortured and murdered thirty-one boys.[212]

In 1974, Paul John Knowles, went on a rampage during which he murdered and raped nineteen women in four months. In 1976 and 1977, in New York, David Berkowitz, the above mentioned Son of Sam, killed young women and courting couples; seven killings were attributed to him. Kenneth Bianchi, the Hillside Strangler, who later claimed to have a dual personality, committed seven murders in Los Angeles between 1977 and 1978; all his victims were women. In 1978, twenty-eight bodies of young men were found in the Chicago house of the recently executed John Wayne Gacy, and he admitted to having killed another five victims. Apparently he killed the young men in the course of sadistic homosexual rape. Peter Sutcliffe, the thirty-five year old Yorkshire Ripper, in England, committed thirteen mutilation murders of women. He stated that he derived sexual gratification from stabbing.

Ted Bundy committed his vicious murders between 1974 and 1978. He was charged with the killing of nineteen young co-eds, often of the same body type and of a similar appearance. He committed these homicides during moments of narcissistic grandiosity. He later claimed to have killed more than three hundred women.

This long list of sexual serial killers testifies to the vastitude of the presence of this social evil. Unfortunately, these are only representative of the recorded cases. It is logical to think that their actual number was larger and that their presence in our society may be more numerous than we think. Indeed, the majority of these murderers do not show any peculiar or questionable behavior, which makes their detection very difficult.

Abrahamson,[213] in 1973, expressed the opinion that the so-called multiple killer is a very ill person. Often, multiple killers are paranoid schizophrenics, and their killing is of a random, inexplicable and bizarre type. However, that is not usually the case of the sexual serial killer of the organized lust murderer type to which category most of the infamous and notorious killers belong.

The following case report of Jeffrey Dahmer is typical of the organized lust murderer.

The homicides of Mr. Dahmer, which had occurred between 1988 and 1991, were discovered during the summer of 1991. When the case was brought to court, he pled not guilty by reason of mental illness or insanity to the fifteen counts of first-degree homicide with which he had been charged; he was not charged with an additional homicide to which he had confessed because of lack of evidence and, in addition, he confessed to a previous murder in 1978. Because of the type of plea, I was appointed by the Circuit Court of Milwaukee County to conduct an expert forensic psychiatric examination of him.

In accordance with Wisconsin law, this psychiatric and forensic examination of the defendant was to determine whether or not, at the time of each and every offense, he had possessed substantial mental capacity to distinguish right from wrong, refrain from doing wrong, appreciate the nature and quality of his actions, and conform with the requirements of the law. I examined Mr. Dahmer on several different occasions for a total of thirteen hours. In addition, a complete battery of psychological tests were performed, including a Wechsler *Adult Intelligence Scale-Revised (WAIS-R)*, a Minnesota Multiphasic Personality Inventory (MMPI), and a Rorschach test.

At the time of my examinations, the defendant was thirty-one years old. He is a white male, with a light complexion, tall, well developed, and well nourished. His hair was brownish-blond and his face was unshaven during most of the interviews. His posture was erect, his ambulation normal and, on observation, he evidenced no presence of any neurological deficits, unusual facial mimicry, tics, or mannerisms. He sat up straight in his chair, a bit tense only during the first part of the first interview, and his attitude was one of cooperativeness and friendliness. Calm and free from any emotional lability, his speech was clear and understandable. His answers or statements were coherent, relevant, and logical. He did not show any circumstantial, tangential, or disorganized thinking, or delusional or hallucinatory ideas. He generally provided direct and full answers to questions posed to him and he appeared to have a high level of intelligence. He showed reflective capacity and unimpaired and rational thinking, and he assumed complete responsibility for all of the murders he was charged with. He was emotionally tranquil and at ease as he unburdened himself of many memories pertinent to his offenses.

Mr. Dahmer recounted a number of changes of residence during his childhood for family reasons. He described himself as having been a loner during childhood and adolescence, surrounded by arguing parents at home and "arrogant jerks" in school. He thought his schoolmates picked on him and he felt unable to express his anger openly for fear of retaliation. He felt angry at his parents who frequently argued during a long pre-divorce period. When he was not sulking, he would often express his resentment by destructive activity in his backyard.

He became interested in taxonomy and had a collection of insects. He also exhibited an interest in anatomy by dissecting small animals and using formaldehyde to preserve them. He claimed that when he was fifteen or sixteen years old he had a compulsive interest in dissecting animals that he found dead on the road: "I did it four or five times. I was going to keep their bones and make a statue out of them like a taxidermist, but I never got to it. [They] were mostly dogs or foxes."[214] He also stated that during that period he was doing some dissection in biology class at school as a part of his curriculum, and he remembered taking home from school the head of a pig and keeping the skull. He stated that he graduated from high school at the age of 18 with a C grade average.

During his early adolescence he was involved in homosexual experimentation on a few occasions and also in streaking (running naked). At age thirteen he began to drink alcohol, alone and with friends. However, most of his heavy drinking and marijuana smoking (three or four joints daily) started at age seventeen. He had experienced some drunkenness and hangovers, and several times he had passed out. He had a poor self-concept during childhood and adolescence. As previously stated, he was a loner and felt picked on by other boys but claimed that he never got into fights. He stated that he had never enjoyed sports, always thinking that the other guys were better than he. He was envious of them and stated that at times felt so angry that he had thoughts of killing them. He stated that he masturbated daily while looking at pictures of "good-looking guys in magazines—trim with good muscle tone, youngish, not older than thirty."[214] He stated that he admired their physical appearance and when he imagined himself in bed with them it was always as a male, never a female. He stated that he had no racial preferences in his fantasies.

During his actual homosexual encounters, he stated that he had assumed an active role. He enjoyed sodomizing people but abhorred the idea of being sodomized. He had never had any heterosexual experiences. At that time, he was disturbed about his increased weight — 190 pounds — following his continous use of marijuana. He was shy and somewhat uncomfortable when having to start new relationships. He felt attracted to men and helpless and frustrated in his desire to change his sexual orientation and his social timidity; he was basically withdrawn and sad. He said that his father's strict demands and his mother's unpredictable and argumentative behavior, both toward his father and toward him, angered him. He was subject to violent fits of anger and occasional rage, and was prone to lying and deceit at home for which he was reprimanded. He became angry when he was found to be lying, but eventually would admit to his wrongdoing. He denied sibling rivalry with his younger brother.

He claimed that while at college he had felt directionless and without clear ideas. His drinking increased, and he did not feel that he fit into any particular group. After a semester, at his father's suggestion, he joined the army, and he seemed to be proud of having gone through basic training. He became a medic and after two weeks he was transferred overseas. He had been taught basic CPR, how to set bones and stop bleeding, medication dispensing, and so on. At that time, he was drinking heavily — a six- or twelve-pack of beer at night, and, at times, brandy, wine, or liqueurs. He was involved in a few fights and yelling matches. His sexual activity was limited to looking at pornographic magazines and masturbation; he disclaimed any romantic or non-romantic homosexual relations at that time, stating that he was afraid of engaging in any such relations while in the army.

Back in the United States and discharged from the army honorably, after a brief period with his father, he moved to Milwaukee to live with his grandmother, hoping that by living with her his heavy drinking might diminish. At first, he limited his drinking mostly to weekends, but eventually he began to drink more. He would go to local taverns and would often get drunk, returning home at 2 or 3 A.M., or, occasionally, staying out all night. On three occasions he was arrested for drunkenness and jailed overnight.

He was fired from his job at the city's blood plasma bank after one year because of poor performance. He had been ambivalent about the job, and, ironically, he stated that he did not like to stick people with needles. He did temporary odd jobs until he was hired by a local company where he worked for seven consecutive years.

Mr. Dahmer claimed that during the time he resided at his grandmother's he began to go church with her and he tried to stop drinking and to stop his homosexual behavior, attempting to turn his life around. He claimed that he didn't drink for two years until one day, while in a public library quietly reading a book, one of the other library patrons handed him a note, inviting him to have sex with him downstairs in the library bathroom. Even though he had dismissed the offer, he claimed that the episode changed his life for the worse.

While still living at his grandmother's house, he started drinking heavily again, going to porno book stores, gay bars, and bath houses. At the bath houses he started his homosexual behavior again and, wanting to be in control of the relationship, he began to give his occasional sexual partners drinks containing dissolved sleeping pills. In 1989, he was charged with and convicted of second degree sexual assault for enticing a child for immoral purposes and placed on probation for five years, during which period he had to report to the state correctional service.

In 1989, he moved to his own apartment in the inner city because, he stated, he wanted a place of his own which was close to work and had low rent. He stated that he did not want his drinking behavior to upset his grandmother any longer and, at the same time, wanted to be free of her supervision. But even more central to this move was the fact that by that time he had been turned out of the bath houses because some of the patrons reported their suspicions of having been intoxicated and taken advantage of sexually by him.

When questioned specifically about the offenses he was charged with, Mr. Dahmer explained in a calm and spontaneous fashion that the fifteen charges did not include a white male victim that he killed after a rendezvous in a city hotel, nor that of a young man, his own age, whom he had killed at the age of eighteen in another city. He added that when he had been about fifteen years old and was out for a walk about five miles from his home, he had seen a young man about eighteen years old. He stated that he had liked him and had the idea of sawing a baseball bat in two so that it would be small enough to carry on his bike. He said that he had the idea of hitting him on the head with the bat and then having sex with him.

While discussing each murder he continued to be coherent, relevant, and logical. In a calm, controlled way, as if he were at a recital, he went into the specific details about the enticement and sexual seductions of his victims, love-making, use of drugged drinks, his killing them by knifing or strangling, his photographing the dead persons or parts of the dead bodies, and his disposal of the dead bodies, whether by crushing bones, by cutting, dismembering, disemboweling them, or boiling the flesh, and his attempts to preserve them. It was evident that on each and every occasion his murderous actions were born out of a calm, calculated, prearranged plan. He described how he obtained all the necessary items for such heinous crimes and how he decided to secure his apartment with a high-quality security system.

Repressed hostility, frustrated desire, and an intense fear of rejection by his peers were freely voiced by him upon specific questioning. His loneliness was also exemplified by his remarks that he didn't want to lose his victims and would like to have kept them with him. He stated that he wanted to keep some memorials of them. He also stated that at times he had continued to lie next to a dead body kissing it. He claimed that the motivation for his actions was neither love nor hate, but was, instead, lust. He described his maneuvering to keep some of the victims in a zombie-like state and to eventually make fetishes out of their body parts. Symbolic memorabilia such as parts of the victims' bodies, isolated bones, or entire skeletons and skulls testify to his fetishism. Sexual sadism seemed to be at the base of his wanting to keep his victims half-alive by drilling holes into their skulls and injecting muriatic acid into their brains. Anthropophagy, as stated by him, possibly climaxed some of the murderous scenes.

He clearly stated that he always wished to have control over events and his fantasies were linked to power, sex, and money. He believed that he had made his fantasies more powerful than his real life and he admitted to getting a partial thrill from the killing. He apparently used to drink while performing his criminal acts but was always aware of what he was doing. He emphasized that lust and power were at the basis of his actions and demonstrated no remorse for what he had done.

Dahmer, in addition to being a simple sadist, as his aggressivity and cruelty testify, can be further classified as a sexual sadist because of his motivating drives for lust and power, as he himself stated. His sexual sadistic involvement with his victims was often paraphilic in nature. He also showed ananchastic features. His heinous behavior was not the outcome of a psychotic decompensation but rather the programmed manifestation of a meticulous erotomanic action of which he was always aware, as he stated to me. Indeed, in his tendency to act on weekends, he showed calculated planning, with risk avoidance. The media interpretation that his behavior was racially oriented concerned and frightened him because he was in a jail/prison environment surrounded by many black inmates and most of his victims had been black.

The destructive hostility of this serial killer needs no comment. It was heinous repetitive behavior, programmed and methodically carried out by a person who was suffering from a deep disturbance of his inner persona, without the overt manifestations of a distorted psychotic mind: a man who was found to be legally sane. One explanation for his abhorrent conduct is that he was driven by compulsive hostile aggressivity, and that his violence was so profound as to kill, cut, dismember and dissect in an obsessive, sadistic way, the body that attracted and repelled him at the same time—a body that he wanted to torture and destroy because he felt that by doing so he would be able to get rid of his inner torture and unwanted attraction; a body that he really did not love, contrary to what he wanted to believe or, once apprehended, wanted to make others believe, since it would have been easy for him to continue a living relationship with his victims; a body, parts of which he claimed to have eaten, possibly, I would say, as expression of his biting hostility or his desire to incorporate and make his own their attractive qualities, and perhaps part of a superstitious, atavistic belief remindful of tribal anthropophagy. His hostility-out was the counterpart of his hostility-in. His actions may have, in some way, saved him from committing suicide. And even his sadism was the exercising of power and violence upon another for the assertion and preservation of his Self. He joins a long list of sexual murderers previously reported. He shares with them not only a deep violent destructive hostility, but also boredom, loneliness, fear of rejection and an ambivalent craving for human closeness, as described by Wilson.[212] Needless to say, tests for organic pathology were negative.

He was diagnosed and reported to the Court by me as suffering from a mixed personality disorder with sadistic, obsessive, fetishistic, antisocial, necrophilic features, typical of what has been called the organized nonsocial, lust murderer.[209] He had entered a plea of not guilty by reason of insanity. The verdict of the jury found him legally sane on all fifteen murder counts and the Court sentenced him to fifteen consecutive terms of life in prison—one for each count of murder that he had been charged with—without the possibility for parole.

Levin and Fox were of the opinion that serial killers belong to the group of psychopathic personalities, who lack self-control and have an intense drive to dominate others.[215] However, this is not always the case. Both Jeffrey Dahmer and Theodore Bundy were described by many as being just like the well behaved, next-door neighbor—charming and helpful. In the specific case of Ted Bundy, he had worked efficiently in a social agency while a pre-law student and was involved in community activities.

Lunde[216] stated that frequently the serial killer commits his acts without being intoxicated either by drugs or alcohol, and his victim is usually only a casual acquaintance who assumes a psychological, symbolic value. This casualness of the acquaintanceship with the victim, who usually fits a particular typology, is a fact shared by many serial killers. Contrary to Lunde's assertion, these murderers often use alcohol in a moderate amount in order to acquire more self assurance when searching for their prey, as Dahmer used to do, and continue their drinking, as he did, throughout their macabre crimes.

Serial killers usually follow a pattern in their killing that is centered around a specific type of victim and the way in which the crime is committed. There may be similarities, for example, in the method of the killing, or in the place or time. Motivation is often similar, as can be seen particularly in the vision oriented type of killer. Hickey, in his *Serial Murderers and Their Victims,* states the following: "Of greatest importance from a research perspective is the linkage of common factors among the victims. . . . Communality among those murdered may include several factors any of which can prove iuristic in better understanding victimization."[217]

It is believed that it would be helpful in the detection of suspected serial killers to know the communality in the both the crimes committed and in the victims.[218] This communality also facilitates the making of an identikit of the killer. Bennett[219] suggested that in the case of Jeffrey Dahmer, he had "carefully selected most of his victims on the basis of their external phenotype . . . [and that] similarity in cranial, facial architecture strongly influenced his choice of victims."[p.1227] Even though Bennett's analysis is rather intriguing, one should not forget that his victims not only "just happened to fit the body type he fantasized about . . . very pretty men, almost boyish, willowy and effeminate,"[219 p.1228] as he had also clearly stated to me, but that he also took advantage of the easy availability of such a type of prey in the places that he frequented. Nonetheless, it is quite possible that, at least subconsciously, he was also attracted by the phenotypic type represented by his victims, which again would support the theory of the commonality of physical characteristics of the victims in serial killings, especially in those in which lust is involved.

In considering the possible psychodynamics of a sexual serial killer, one should take into consideration the interplay of many factors, such as the fear of losing self-esteem, narcissistic aspirations and narcissistic wounding, homosexuality, paranoid ideation, the malignant narcissism of Kernberg,[220] the pathological grandiose self of Klein[99] and Mahler,[98] any or all of which are often found in the killers during a psychological investigative analysis. All of the above contribute to the formation of a dysfunctional personality in the serial killer, bringing about sexual confusion, poor male identification, hostility, aggression and obsessive-compulsive patterns of behavior, and, occasionally, a reaction formation of superiority to their deep inferiority feelings.

Serial killers share certain characteristics, such as impulsivity, lack of remorse and disregard for the welfare of others, all of which are also found in the person with a sociopathic type of personality with antisocial behavior. Abrahamsen[221] stated that a serial killer's mind, which he called the "murdering mind," incorporates a persistent motivation to kill and a basic tendency to an absence of guilt and a warped capacity for love.

The description and dynamics of the lust killer or sexual sadistic killer are the same as those of the larger group of serial killers. As previously stated, the classification of the FBI subdivides the serial lust killer into the disorganized asocial and the organized non-social murderer. The disorganized asocial murderer is usually below average in intelligence, is socially inadequate, an unskilled worker, sexually incompetent, has a low birth order status, and was harshly disciplined as a child by a father who was an unstable provider. He claims to be rather anxious during the perpetration of the crimes, uses alcohol to a minimum and reacts strongly to even minimal environmental stress. He usually lives alone, and lives and works near the crime scene. He has minimal interest in the news media and his behavior is often erratic.

The organized asocial murderer, instead, is of average to above average intelligence, is socially competent, usually a skilled worker, sexually competent, has a high birth order status, his father had a stable job, the childhood discipline was inconsistent. The mood of this type of murderer is usually well controlled during the offense even though he uses alcohol before or during the crime. In addition, he shows interest in criminal reportage of the media and at times shows a high degree of mobility in his life.[207]

Jeffrey Dahmer, the Milwaukee serial killer, well sums up most of the characteristics of this latter group of antisocial people. He was rather personable in his appearance and behavior. He seemed to be shy and minimally tense, rather well organized in his thinking, without any presence of tangential thinking, blocking or vagueness. He appeared to be even in his affect, minimally reserved, and easily explained to me his desire for lust and power which drove him in an obsessive compulsive way to perpetrate his sadistic murders on young acquaintances that he had enticed with promises of money and a pretense of some photographic posing. He appeared to be very narcissistic, self-assured and very much troubled by his ambivalence about his homosexuality, which consisted primarily in his desire to sodomize others. He was programmed in his actions, very meticulous and cautious, and was cold blooded in his victimization. He had no remorse, even though he proffered some words to that effect. He attempted to emphasize the bizarreness of his behavior, terrorized by a possible transfer during his incarceration to a high security correctional institution where he feared that he might be attacked by the black inmates. He disclaimed racial intention publicly, in court, and recognized, at least in public and again in court, the heinousness of his crimes, and stated that he deserved the death penalty for his actions. However, his verbalization appeared to me to be rather self-serving.

Since in a court of law facts count more than fancies, the wisdom of the jury found him responsible for his actions and he was sentenced to a minimum of ninety-nine years in prison with no possibility of parole. As the reader has seen, Jeffrey Dahmer is one of the most recent in a long list of serial killers who have been apprehended by the police, tried and sentenced in a court of law.

As mentioned previously, it is probable that many other serial killers have never been apprehended and many more will continue to prey on and to destroy their victims. Our lives are becoming more chaotic and our communities are becoming increasingly dehumanized, and this type of social setting is unfortunately a good breeding ground for predators, and a difficult one for their detection and apprehension. Let us hope that our families will become better nurturing grounds, better educational arenas, better role models for the children and thus, to some extent, perhaps aid in the prevention of this most dreadful and unconscionable social crime.

A comparison can be made between serial killers and events which we define as mass murder-suicide that have recently been increasing at an alarming rate. This comparison will complete the descriptive analysis of the serial killer. The mass murder-suicide often occurs in public places and ends in the suicide of the killer at the scene of the crime. In reviewing several cases, I was struck by the different personality characteristics of the perpetrator of mass murder-suicide and the serial killer, especially the non-social organized one. While the serial killer is a calm, cold, calculating person who shows little or no evidence of excessive anxiety, the mass murderer who commits suicide is, instead, a vivacious reactor, prone to anxiety and depression, and often loosely associated in his thinking, especially at the time of his destructive action. The serial killer is a highly programmed person, who is able to keep his personal conscious and subconscious conflicts under control within his rigid personality structure. The mass murder-suicider, on the other hand, shows fragile psychological defenses, an unstable ego and an unrestrained impulsivity. Jeffrey Dahmer fits the characteristics of the serial killer, while Dion Terres, who killed two people in a McDonald's restaurant before committing suicide, clearly represented the personality in action of a mass murder-suicider.

> He was a thirty-three year old, white male, borderline in his previous behavior, who opened fire in a McDonald's restaurant killing two patrons, wounding a third and immediately afterwards turning the gun on himself. He was killed instantaneously by a self-inflicted wound that lacerated his skull and brain from front to back. The day previous to his act he made a videotape of a good-bye soliloquy while walking through his apartment, reminiscing about the traumatic events of his life and ruminating aloud about his conflicts with himself and with society, his hatred towards parents and relatives and his desire to kill himself and others. During his videotaped soliloquy he showed depression, ambivalence, and magical thinking.

Ambivalence and conflicting feelings and attitudes towards others, may be present in both types of murderer. However, it is more likely to be spontaneously expressed by the mass murder-suicider. The identikit of the mass murder-suicider, besides showing him to be a very angry and impulsive individual of relatively young age, also portrays him as depressed, prone to self-pity, with feelings of hopelessness, revenge and obvious paranoia.

In addition to the above very striking types of crime mention must be made of the sad altruistic elderly murder-suicide and the jealous paranoia murder-suicide. The first, mainly reflects an individual's inability to endure the suffering—physical or emotional—of a loved one and the calm determination to end it all. The latter type, instead, is the outcome of the feelings of the intensely troubled mind of a person who feels rejected, frustrated and desperate in his or her most important relationship. These murderers may show either impulsivity of behavior or well calculated programming of their actions.

A thirty-two year old, 6'2" tall, black male, somewhat overweight, was charged with first degree intentional homicide. The historical events state that one morning he took a sawed off shotgun with only four cartridges and drove to his estranged girlfriend's place of work—an official building— with the intent to frighten her back into their relationship. He was ambivalent about her, felt the loss, and was tortured by jealousy. He had been doing cocaine the night before the occurrence. When he arrived at his estranged girlfriend's office she became frightened, ran away, and hid in a vault, refusing to talk to him. Holding those present at gunpoint, the young man took her out of the vault, walked her to a nearby lounge, assaulted her verbally, and asked her for reassuring, loving words. He did not believe her when she stated that she had been faithful to him. He forced her into fellatio and masturbation and then fired two shots at her. When the police arrived *en masse* he fired his gun one time at them, proceeding to go towards them with the hope of being killed by them. He was wounded badly when the police fired at him but survived. At the time of my examination of him he claimed that he had wanted to kill himself in front of his girlfriend, but then, unable to do so, he turned his hostility against her and hoped to be killed, himself, by the police. This case could be considered a failed murder-suicide. He was sentenced to life in prison.

Klein,[99] Mahler,[98] and Bowlby[102] explained the jealous paranoid type of violence as the expression of the killer's unconscious and unresolved, symbiotic, ambivalent feelings for the mother, and of displaced ambivalence towards the partner who is seen as an extension of the self.

The above manifestations of interpersonal violence illustrate the intricacies of human relationships, often a mixture of hatred and love, at times at unconscious levels, and of people's reactions of despair when faced with emotionally unbearable situations. One could certainly ask whether this violence is an expression of a personal reaction to deeply felt feelings of rejection or is the expression of an unconscious rejection of life itself and a desire to be autonomous and omnipotent.

While it is generally agreed that destructive hostility is at the basis of violence, in the case of the altruistic murder or murder/suicide this does not seem to be so, as the action is felt by the perpetrator to be beneficient and compassionate. That hostility is present, however, in the other types of murder above mentioned, and may be repressed but obvious from the actions of the perpetrators of the crimes, as in the case of the serial killer, or may be openly expressed, as in the case of the uncontrolled mass murder-suicide or of the jealous paranoid killer.

Most of the sadistic killers, like Dahmer, do not suffer from any obvious mental illness; however, their violent behavior is so destructive that one may wonder whether at its basis there is a disease that is actually more serious than schizophrenia. It seems that their negative emotions are so strong that they cause the release of what Barbusse termed "monsters" from their unconscious.[212] This is certainly remindful of the meaning that Freud gave to the Id—a place in which negative instincts are located and to which negative emotions are later removed. This monstrosity is due not only to an exaggerated, disquieting pseudo-hypersexuality, but also to an exaggerated desire to control others.

The FBI well summarized the traits of the serial killer: They have "a sense of social isolation, preferences for autoerotic activities and fetishes, rebelliousness, aggression, chronic lying, . . . lack of trust and commitment to a world of rules and negotiations. . . . Their personal affective life becomes dependent on fantasy . . . [and] fantasy becomes the primary source of emotional arousal and . . . a confused mixture of sex and aggression."[208] Holmes and DeBurger[207] estimate that there may be 350 serial murderers at large in the United States, responsible for 3,500 unsolved homicides.

We can theorize that the dehumanized, robotized, technological society in which we live may be conducive to the development of destructive hostility in some individuals who use their fantasy to overcome their feelings of worthlessness and exercise pseudo-omnipotent control on their fellow humans.

Chapter Eight

THE RAVAGE OF RAPE

While the dictionary definition of rape states that it is a sexual violent act imposed with force, threat or trickery on subjects who are either unable or unwilling to give valid consent because of a state of physical or emotional submission, the F.B.I. gives a much more succinct definition: " . . . the carnal knowledge of a female forcibly and against her will."[222 p.2] What ever the definition, rape is one of the most devastating experiences that a woman can be subjected to. Ellis, in *Theories of Rape,* stated that rape "refers to a physically forceful attempt at sexual intimacy when one of the individuals involved chooses not to become sexually intimate,"[223] and then added that a better term for rape, already in use in many jurisdictions throughout the country, would be forced sex or sexual assault.

However, since the sexuality of such an act is probably only a vehicle of hostile aggression, I personally prefer to continue to use the term rape. The word, indeed, comes from the Latin *rapere* which in its Latin meaning, especially in the past participle and derivative noun raptus, portrays the rapidity of the action and the physical possession which is akin to the invasion of a person's private self. The actual act of rape should be distinguished from the similarly traumatizing act of lascivious behavior, both of which belong to that larger category of lustful conduct.

From a legal point of view, a distinction is made as to whether the sexual act has been consummated, with the penetration of the genital organ of the aggressor into the genital organ of the victim, or if there has only been the manipulation of the victim's body with a concomitant sexual excitation. The quality of the violence exercised does not necessarily have to be, "*a vis atrox,* i.e., a violence of such a force as to overcome any possible resistance, but simply a violence capable of overcoming the resistance of the victim . . . limiting and annulling the free determination of its victim . . . ,"[224] as in cases in which the dissent could not be expressed because of the rapidity or insidiousness of the aggression or because of the psychic trauma of which the victim is the object.

The above opens the door to the inclusion under the terms rape or sexual assault that of any sexual abuse carried out with or through violence, threat, or subtle persuasion, and regardless of the relationship between the victimizer and the victim. It includes marital rape as well as those situations wherein any dispenser of help has sexual contact with the person in need of help: teacher-student, lawyer-client, doctor-patient, etc. The rape of a minor, an unconscionable and unfortunately not infrequent happening, is frequently part of domestic violence. Bureau of Justice Statistics regarding rape victims in thirteen of the United States and the District of Columbia, report that "girls under 18 were the victims in 51 percent of rapes in 1992 even though girls at that age made up only 25 percent of the female population."[225] The same report stated that more than half the rapes reported to the police happen to girls under age eighteen. Girls under twelve years represent 16 percent of reported rape victims, and one in five of those is raped by her father. Usually, the younger the rape victim, the more probable it is that the rapist is a relative or acquaintance.

While rape may occur not only as male to female, but also as male to male—a frequent happening in correctional institutions—or woman to child or adolescent, or woman to woman, present day national and international legislation deals primarily with the classic case of male versus female rape, either adult or child.

Since the act of rape is a dyadic rapport, not only the typology of the rapist must be taken into consideration but also that of the victim, with special attention to her mental and physical condition. In a case in which the victim of rape suffers from mental illness, his or her capacity to resist the aggression must be considered. Mental illness *per se* does not necessarily cause the total incapacity to oppose resistance to the attack, but the mentally ill victim of such aggression may have a reduced capacity for understanding the significance of the physical and moral aggression he or she is subjected to, and this may lead to impaired decisional capacity.

Rapists and their victims both tend to be under twenty-five years of age,[110] after which age there is a decline in the frequency of the sexual assaults.[226] Rapists are usually married.[227]

"They are . . . poor at budgeting and managing their accommodation, [adding to their stress], frequently bored and often use alcohol to excess . . . [reducing] their inhibitions against sexual assault."[228] Together with other violent offenders, they tend to have a lower IQ.[229] A neglected aspect of their interpersonal functioning is their lack of concern for others.[228] Their victims are usually young, often inexperienced, physically normal females, and are frequently either students or persons employed outside of their homes, thus necessitating mobility in their lives.

Conklin,[230] in reviewing studies on rape, reports four categories of rapists. The first is described as being exploitative, with rape being a spur of the moment, impulsive and predatory act. The compensatory rapists often feel inadequate and are obsessed with sexual fantasies. The third type, the displaced anger rapists, as the name implies, express their displaced anger and rage. The fourth type of rapist, the sadistic rapist, because his sexual feelings are linked to his aggressive act, becomes more violent as he becomes more aroused.

The present day complexities of social living have become a breeding ground for the possibility of this type of invasive victimization. People are tense, insecure and dissatisfied, and are prone to give vent to verbal and physical, and at times sexual, aggression, especially when under the influence of drugs or alcohol. Scholars have proposed various theories in their attempt to explain this social phenomenon. The feminist theory, supported by Mehrhof and Kearon[231] and Brownmiller,[232] proposes rape as being primarily an act of male aggression resulting from an atavistic male dominance and female submission in a political and economic ecological system that perpetrates social inequality between the two sexes. There is no doubt that rape is " . . . the result of a male's decision to behave towards women in a possessive, dominating and demeaning manner. . . . a pseudo-sexual act . . . motivated largely out of desires for power and a hatred of women rather than by passion," as Groth and Burgess reported.[233] The feminist theory of rape is fundamentally a socio-political theory, however, which does not take into consideration the deeper psychological conflicts usually present in the rapist, the effect of hormonal influences to which he is subjected, or the devastating influence that drugs and alcohol may have on his moral decisions.

I doubt that it is possible to correct, or even diminish rape in society, by reducing the frustrating political and economic inequality that exists between men and women. This may even create a state of frustration in some men who might then use rape in order to reestablish their "lost male supremacy." I strongly believe, in fact, as stated in the chapter on domestic violence, that this subtle reaction may be one of the causes of rape. It is even possible to hypothesize that some men, especially in today's socio-economic environment, while misperceiving women as competitors, castrating, to use a psychological term, may attack them sexually as an unconscious attempt to regain their male dominance and to reestablish an archaic role differentiation.

Today, the presence of women in an interactive social and professional life is more common than in the past, and many men are still ambivalent about having them as working colleagues or as competitive rivals. In these circumstances women may be more exposed to tempting situations and/or frequently be a source of temptation for men while sharing with them the social and professional arena. They tend to familiarize with men in a much more open way than in the past and at times may inadvertently provoke men's desire by sending unconscious mixed messages which reawaken man's attraction to them. This may sound like male chauvinism, but I believe it to be an objective appraisal. Complete desensitization to possible unspoken parasexual behavior in the working place may never be reached, but this failure should never justify any sexual misconduct.

The social learning theory of rape implies that repeated exposure to any stimulus tends to promote a certain positive attraction towards it. Bandura[23] has extensively reported that aggression is learned basically through imitating role models and is strengthened by reinforcement—reminiscent of Pavlovian conditioning. Rape, in fact, being an act of aggression, is also subject to conditioning influences. Young people who witness in their role models, their friends and/or family members, macho, lustful attitudes are left with the impression that rape is the normal praxis to follow in an interpersonal relationship, a type of conduct that they believe is expected of them.

The evolutionary theory considers rape to be due to a natural masculine drive to copulate with different partners and the concomitant desire to impregnate large numbers of women. In so doing, the male hopes to achieve the transmission of his genes to a potentially vast number of offspring without having to gestate or nurture them, ensuring his personal projection into the future. The consequences of rape could be particularly disastrous if the rape results in a pregnancy and the rapist is a psychopath, which is often the case, and if we assume that biology in some way influences human behavior. Women, obviously, tend to resist this type of forced sexuality since their desire is generally for a monogamous relationship and eventually to have children with men capable of supporting their offspring. This evolutionary theory of rape is mindful of animal behavior and of the so-called syndrome of the player-of-women attributed to disadvantaged groups where males focus their attention on their masculine body—valuing it in a narcissistic way—and assert their maleness by forcing the female into unwanted sexual relationships.[234]

Since rape is a form of victimization, we should devote some attention to reviewing human thought regarding it through the years. Hans von Hentig[235] pioneered victimology and recognized the important role victims play in any debasing sexual assault against them, affirming the innovative and thought provoking idea that the behavior of the victims themselves may actually lead to their victimization. Schaefer[236] strongly supported the above and agreed with von Hentig's ideas, further stating that the study of crime is not complete without considering the role played by the victim. While Gasser, too, expressed the belief that the isolated study of the offender's personality was not sufficient for a thorough understanding of a criminal act, Dobrotka pointed out that the personality of the criminal and the psychological determinants of the offense could be better explained by understanding the personality of the victim, her relationship to the offender, and her role in the genesis of the crime.[237]

One may say that the victim is to the criminal as was Eve to Adam, and that victimology was born out of criminology. The word victim derives from the Latin "victima," and the Sanskrit "vinakti"—he sets apart; and is akin to OHG—vih-holy. Among its meanings, are those of someone or something killed, destroyed, or sacrificed under any of various conditions; and one that is subjected to oppression, hardship or mistreatment.[192] In ancient times, both people and animals were sacrificed as victims to appease the gods. An interpretation of this early ritual could be that humankind's personal or collective unconscious, riddled with hostile feelings, was projected outwardly and identified with an angry power entity or God whose wrath had to be appeased. The young, the beautiful, especially the virgin woman and the lamb, were usually the object of these offerings. Those ancient ceremonies, even though crude, did not have the brutality that is usually a part of rape, however, and there was actually an aura of religious reverence surrounding the sacrifice.

The social milieu, with its complexities, plays a role in victimization. In present-day society, for example, alcohol, drug addiction and socio-economic distress are some of the major co-factors contributing to the soaring wave of victimization. During times of war, rape is a frequent occurrence, and since recorded history women have been a part of the spoils demanded by—or given to—victorious soldiers. Millet, in an investigation of sexual victimization, believed that violence and social patriarchal tradition were strictly connected.[238]

Striking and peculiar reactions are observable in people's assessments of the violence suffered by women. At times, ambivalence, suspiciousness and downright prejudice are expressed when judging these victims. This is probably an atavistic attitude, since ancient Babylonian and Hebraic law already considered a married rape victim to be as guilty as the attacker and sentenced both victim and victimizer to death for adultery. In the Middle Ages, also, raped women were automatically considered to have contributed to their being attacked, either consciously or subconsciously.

The dominant role of men over women throughout the centuries, and the traditional concept of strong male victimizer and weak female victim, is believed to have influenced the behavior of both offender and victim.[232] The proposal that males are influenced by the so-called virility mystique that accents the aggressive, forceful, domineering traits which are similar to those of a predatory animal, clashes with the inner insecurity and inadequacy of many a rapist.[239]

The woman who is victimized shows a psychobiological reaction similar to a stress reaction,[240] and may show a fight, a flight, or a frozen attitude. In addition to any bodily injury, the various degrees of psychological distress which the victim suffers from, such as fear of loss of control and feeling that her most intimate self has been violated, are the most tragic and traumatizing aftermath of rape. The reaction one observes in victims of rape is similar to the reaction of combat soldiers described as post-traumatic stress disorder (PTSD). To this effect, the *DSM-IV* reads in part: "The person experienced, witnessed, or was confronted with an event or events that involved actual or threatened death or serious injury, or a threat to the physical integrity of self or others . . . "[241] The traumatic event may be persistently re-experienced as a recurrent, intrusive, distressing recollection of the event or as a recurrent distressing dream. The victim may, at times, have a sense of reliving the experience with illusions, hallucinations and dissociative-flashback episodes; these usually occur upon awakening or if she is intoxicated. There may be intense psychological distress at exposure to events that symbolize the attack, such as the anniversary of the trauma, or that resemble some aspect of it, such as viewing a similar attack on television.[241] In fact, the victim has a tendency to avoid thoughts or activities which may arouse a recollection of the trauma, and, as a defense mechanism, may unconsciously develop amnesia for the event itself. Avoidance is a basic defense mechanism and a precursor of denial.

Victims may regress to an earlier developmental level, or become constricted in their affect or unable to relate affectively to others. They may feel estranged and disinterested in their future. At times, disruption of sleep patterns, difficulty in concentration, irritability and anger ensue. Hyper-vigilant behavior may be manifested by a heightened startle response, and physiological disturbances such as vertigo, headaches, and insomnia also may be present. Depression, anxiety, impulsive behavior, failing memory, difficulty in concentrating, emotional lability and painful guilt feelings are the most common psychological and psychiatric symptoms. At times the rape victim compulsively and abruptly changes her residence or her life-style. Rape may even lead to severe depression and suicidal attempts in the victim.

Together with other forms of victimization, rape shares a psychological reaction that may be immediate, short term or long term. Bard and Sangrey call the immediate reaction the impact-disorganization stage.[242] At first the individual reacts with numbness, disorientation, disbelief and denial. Then loneliness, depression, vulnerability and helplessness set in. Symonds described a first reaction of shock, disbelief, temporary paralysis and denial, followed by frozen fright, pseudo-calm and regressive behavior.[243] One study found similarities in the immediate reaction between rape and burglary victims,[244] while another found that victims of rape, like robbery and assault victims, saw themselves as weak, frightened, helpless, out of control, anxious, insomniac, and suffering from nightmares, headaches and diarrhea.[245] Herman and Julia Schwendinger[246] stated that rape victims may suffer from self-recrimination and undue remorse if not properly handled by investigators, and if no emotional support is available their reaction may become chronic. Indeed, family support, when available, is essential for the psychological reintegration of these victims. Many of them also form support groups with others who have experienced a similar type of trauma, where they are able to discuss their feelings and help each other find methods of coping with them.

A stage of recoil, occurring from a few hours to a few days after the assault may last for several months. During this stage, fear alternates with anger, sadness with elation, self-pity with guilt. In this stage, rape victims fear additional attacks, and their mood fluctuates according to their trust in their ability to defend themselves from future attacks. Following a short-term acute phase of disorganization, rape victims often go through a "controlled style reaction" or an "expressive style reaction" during which the victim shows anger, anxiety, weeping and tension, and she is afraid, feels humiliated, embarrassed, revengeful, and self-blaming. Victims of violence, no matter what type, experience loss of identity and self-respect. A reorganization phase with attempts at behavioral changes, such as changing phone number and residence, eventually takes place, even though the victim may still be suffering from nightmares and phobias, and still seeks support from family and friends.[247]

Personal reorganization is evidenced by an adaptive phase with gradual dissipation of negative feelings and symptoms, usually within six months to a year. When, in some cases, this does not take place, a maladaptive phase with an early or delayed onset ensues, with the persistence of negative symptomatology.

Even though society attempts to help these victims in their reintegration and to minimize, as much as possible, the impact of their exposure to this type of invasive violence, a sizable number of rape victims report not having recovered from the attack four to six years later. They show decreased sexual activity, difficulty in experiencing orgasm, less pleasure in their life, low self-esteem, guilt and depression.[248] Successful coping may serve as a growth-promoting experience and during this stage of reorganization many victims establish more effective, vigilant behavior, revision of values and new attitudes towards life.

Predatory rape, i.e., an attack by a stranger, has the greatest probability of being reported to the police. The following case illustrates this type of rape.

> A twenty-two year old, black male was charged with five counts of first degree sexual assault, two counts of attempted armed robbery and sixteen more counts of armed robbery. Even though he had never been hospitalized for mental illness or alcohol and drug addiction, he admitted to a long history of illicit polydrug addiction since age thirteen. He also had a history of paraphilic behavior in adolescence. Among the worst of his crimes of sexual assault was that in which he entered a hospital at 2 A.M. and managed to reach the obstetrics department without being seen. While holding a nurse at gunpoint, and after having pulled the telephone line out of the wall, he sexually abused her twice. He pleaded not guilty by reason of insanity. He was diagnosed as an antisocial personality disorder and sexual sadism. He was found guilty and legally sane and was sentenced to life in prison.

The number of reported cases of rape in the United States is the highest in the world: twice as high as in Canada; three times higher than that in England, West Germany, Sweden and Denmark; five to ten times higher than in France, Holland, Belgium and Japan. However, rape, such a devastating experience for any woman, is believed to be vastly underreported.[223]

Estimates of cases of rape are nearly twice as high as the number actually reported to the law enforcement authorities. In 1950, the United States Department of Justice reported that 25/100,000 women were raped. By 1985, that number had risen to 70/100,000.[223] In 1988, according to the F.B.I. Uniform Crime Report, 92,486 rapes of women were reported to the police.[249] By 1990, the number of offenses was 102,555, or 41.2/100,000; in 1991, that number had increased to 106,593, or 42.3/100,000, an increase of +3.9 percent and +2.7 percent respectively. Part of this increase is thought to be due to better reporting. In 1991, the regional distribution of rape in the United States was 89/100,000 in the midwestern states; 88/100,000 in the southern states; 81/100,000 in the western states; and 55/100,000 in the northeastern states. The rate was 67/100,000 in metropolitan areas; 46/100,000 in rural areas. The greatest number of rapes are reported during the summer.[222]

In 1992, the highest rate of reported rape among selected United States cities was in Minneapolis with 179.68/100,000 population, followed by Cleveland with 166.31/100,000; Atlanta with 152.6/100,000; Detroit with 117.32/100,000; Los Angeles with 51.78/100,000; New York with 38.17/100,000; and Washington, D.C. with 35.31/100,000 population. The states with the highest number of reported rapes were Michigan, with 2,247/100,000 cases, 311 were under age eighteen; New York followed with 2,225 cases, of which 327 were under eighteen; Illinois had 1,056 cases, 250 of which were under age eighteen; Georgia reported 897 cases rape, 101 of which were under age eighteen; and the District of Columbia had 122 cases, of which twenty-seven were under age eighteen.[172]

The United States Bureau of Census in cooperation with the United States Bureau of Justice Statistics compiles a yearly victimization report from data based on selected samples of residents in housing units, and the information is gathered directly from the people.[166] Unfortunately, even this type of collecting victim data does not reflect the reality of the issue at hand because of under and overreporting.

JAMA[223] reports Koss's[250] national sample study of students in higher education that found that at least 20% of adult women, 15% of college women, and 12% of adolescent girls have experienced sexual abuse and assault during their life time. He quite aptly entitled his paper, "Hidden

Rape." Ellis also reports that Russell,[251] following a study done in San Francisco, estimated that over a lifetime approximately 24 percent of women will be raped and while another 20 percent will experience an attempted rape; estimates for rape in African American women are even higher.[252]

Victims of rape react in many different ways, but, as previously stated, rape is usually followed by stress and anxiety. The victim appraises what has happened and attempts to realize its significance—harm, loss, threat or challenge. Victims of rape share similar demographic characteristics with women subjected to other types of victimization. Victims without a previous history of exposure to severe stress have been found to be more vulnerable to an ensuing maladaptive reaction to victimization. Younger women appear to experience more immediate symptoms. Divorced or separated females, are, together with unmarried women, more likely objects of crime than those who are either married or widowed. People over the age of twenty-five with college educations are more likely to be the victims of violent crimes than people who are less educated.[166] It must be noted that rape and/or sexual assault among the higher social classes is steadily increasing but often goes unreported.

The theory of the violated self, the equity theory, the theories of safety and invulnerability, and the perception of the self as deviant have all been proposed in a search to further understand the reaction of women to this devastating type of aggression.

The theory of the violated self proposes that the stronger the ego or sense of self, the less likely it is for the victim to experience long-term self fragmentation (anxiety and/or obsession). People with poor emotional equilibrium react badly to any form victimization, but to rape in particular, not only because of their unconscious, unresolved conflicts, but because of the reality of their trauma—the forceful, usually sudden and unexpected, invasion of their privacy. Lister,[253] in discussing victimization in general, wrote of the so-called regressive reaction in which the victim tries to overcome fear and anxiety by compliance with, and dependence on, the assailant. This may be an explanation for the compliance of the victim in cases of domestic violence, as I have observed in many young girls who had been sexually assaulted by their fathers and step-fathers over long periods of time. This is remindful of the Stockholm reaction seen at times in victims of political terrorism. Rape is also a terror inducing criminal offense!

The equity theory suggests that victims tend to feel angry and distressed according to the degree of emotional and/or physical harm suffered as recipients of an action they consider to be unfair.

The vulnerability-invulnerability theory is based on the belief that some individuals may have a sense of personal invulnerability. A victimized woman who had previously felt immune to any kind of violent act, feels humiliated, depressed, angry and revengeful. As in the equity theory, she feels she has been treated unfairly and is understandably anxious about her future vulnerability. This reaction is even stronger in those women who had been adopting security rules prior to victimization. "And now what else can I do?" they often say.[254] I believe that the feeling of invulnerability has both positive and negative effects. While on the one hand the individual is protected from the stress and anxiety associated with the threat of a possible attack by the illusion of invulnerability, on the other, the person who feels invulnerable may be slow in recognizing and reacting to a potentially dangerous situation or to an attacker who preys upon her. Friends or relatives of victims may be secondarily involved when they sympathize with the victim and may question their own sense of invulnerability—"It might happen to me too!"

The hypothesis of the deviance theory supports the tenet that the raped woman begins to feel different, loses her self esteem, and believes she has been stigmatized as a rape victim. Feelings of self-pity may ensue and are compounded by the victim's attributing the victimization to some personal, characterological factors: they feel, therefore, different from others or deviant, as the name implies.[255]

Ellis applies the arousal theory in his explanation of the behavior of the rapist, and claims that it has a genetic basis and is neurologically mediated.[223] This is also used as an explanation for some psychopathic conduct. In fact, Ellis believes that the rapist, like the person suffering from an antisocial personality disorder, has a low arousal level which necessitates strong emotional stimuli in order for him to act out. Envisioning a rape or actually committing a rape arouse and disinhibit him.

A six foot tall, undernourished, young-looking, thirty-four year old white male was arrested for sexually molesting two young girls, seven and eight years old, in a city neighborhood. At the time of his examination he was coherent and relevant, and his ideas progressed logically. He grew up in a dysfunctional family and claimed to have been frequently physically abused by his father and sexually abused by strangers. He had a tenth grade education. He claimed that he had never dated a girl or had any heterosexual experiences. His criminal charges consisted of pedophilic behavior involving the two young girls. He had a history of this type of conduct since age eighteen and he had spent eight years in a correctional institution because he had been found guilty of pedophilic conduct. He stated that he had been released from prison six months before the present offense. He was depressed, concerned about his future trial and fearful that he might have to return to prison. Asked why he repeated the offense that had led to his previous incarceration, he stated, "I didn't know what I was doing. I gave them a few pennies and I asked them to sit down by me and that is when I touched them." He explained, upon my request, that he felt comfortable with little girls and was able to get an erection while touching them. A diagnosis of pedophilia and reactive depression was made. There was no presence of any major mental illness. He is serving a ten year sentence at the same prison from which he had been discharged six months prior to his offense.

Ellis also states that the stimulating effect of sex hormones (androgens) on the hypothalamic-limbic center throughout intra- and extrauterine development, creates a tendency to hypersexuality. When this hypersexual drive surpasses the average copulation threshold, forced copulation may ensue. The following case illustrates the above.

A twenty-eight year old black male was charged with five counts of first degree sexual assault with a weapon and three counts of robbery. The police complaint stated that during a period of six weeks the defendant had sexually assaulted and robbed four different people, three of them owners of small shops and one the owner-manager of a beauty salon whom he raped twice on two consecutive weeks. He was able to enter the crime scenes when no one else was present and held his victims at knife point. At the time of his examination he was coherent and relevant and his ideas progressed logically. He admitted to two of the charges but claimed not to remember the other three. He claimed that he had been using cocaine and needed money. His affect was blunted and he did not appear to be remorseful. There was no presence of psychotic thinking or behavior. The defendant had spent time in jail for similar offenses during the past few years. He was classified as antisocial personality disorder with cocaine use and abuse. He was found to be competent to stand trial and adjudicated guilty.

This may assume various manifestations according to the circumstances, as in date rape, marital rape, or stranger rape. This theory, however, does not address the problem of rape in its totality. There is much more than just the primitive structure of the brain and the effect of androgens in the determination of man's sexual behavior! There are the neocortex with its higher intellectual center and epicritical faculties, and, not to be underestimated, those ethical-moral overstructures acquired through years of exposure to society's mores and dictates.

Many victims of sexual abuse do not seek treatment for the abuse per se but for other symptoms such as depression, nightmares, sexual identity issues, substance abuse, suicide attempts, or body mutilation. Usually these victims have difficulty in revealing their traumatic experience and it is not easy to elicit from them a history of abuse because of their shame, guilt, or "magical thinking," such as, "If I don't speak of it, it never was." It is interesting to note that among psychiatric hospital in-patients sexual abuse prior to hospitalization has been found to be much higher than among the general population. One study found that 51 percent of a sample of one hundred and five female state hospital patients reported having been sexually abused as children or adolescents.[256] One can wonder if that abuse in any way contributed to the eventual development of their illness, was only a coincidental factor, or has actually been overreported.

In the case of incest, which can be considered a form of rape, a child is abused by an adult in a parental role or by other family members. This is particularly disturbing within a family where the father is suffering from psychosis. Freud stated that there was a history of childhood sexual abuse by the father in his cases of hysteria, and although he later retracted this theory, some studies seem to show that it may have been correct.[257] Statistics vary, but according to Goodwin,[258] 5 percent of women in the general population have experienced incest with a father or step-father.

A twenty-nine year old Hispanic American male was charged with first degree sexual assault of a child. At examination, he appeared pensive, somewhat slow in his reaction time when questioned and with some loss of memory; however, he was coherent and relevant. His affect was blunted. He was poorly oriented as to time and had difficulty remembering dates. He had had previous contacts with mental health professionals because of his inappropriate outbursts of anger at home. He stated that he was charged with raping his two daughters. He claimed that he did not have any memory of his actions and claimed his estranged wife was setting the children against him. He had a past history of dependence on alcohol, marijuana, and cocaine. He also claimed that on one occasion while he was driving he collided with another car and a friend who was a passenger in his car was killed. They were both drunk at the time. He was unable to abstract the usual proverbs and seemed anxiously childish and possibly paranoid. He was classified as organic personality syndrome, supported by his attitude of unconcern, apathy, affective instability, and impaired social judgement, and with polysubstance dependence from his history.

The presence of a step-father, regardless of socio-economic class, may carry a chance of sexual abuse of the step-daughter and, even, occasionally, of the step-son, as I have seen in many forensic cases. Some children undergo, unfortunately, hundreds of sexual assaults. Some of them view this as attention given by the offending parent and may, at times actually experience the act as pleasurable.

The child, at the time of his/her incestual interaction, may be prey to a fear for his or her life and/or the loss of an important emotional tie with the supposedly protective parental figure. The children are often threatened with the possibility of disrupting the family if they talk about the incestual relationship. I have examined many young people who have been sexually abused during their childhood by a drunken or psychopathic father on many occasions, and often, when they did speak up about it, their mothers did not believe them.

Unfortunately, some cases of rape eventuate in the death of the victim. Sadistic killers of women often include rape as an initial part of their destructive behavior. This can be seen in the chapter on serial killers.

Women are most often raped by a current or former partner, but the rape by an unknown assailant is probably the most traumatizing type of attack.

Often, even among marital or other emotionally involved couples, rape is part and parcel of an aggressive assault by the male partner. In 1982, Russell[223] found that 14 percent of married or previously married women reported that they had been assaulted by their husbands, and "sexual assault is reported by 33 percent to 46 percent of women who are being physically assaulted by their partners,"[252] who may be the husband or cohabiting or dating friend. The use of physical violence to subdue the woman and force her to accede to sexual requests is primarily an act of aggression and control, the only purpose of which is to demean and insult the woman by the invasion of her most private self.

Date sexual assault and rape is frequent and is increasing steadily among females from age sixteen through twenty-four. The number of rapes of women at age twenty-four is fourfold that of the rate for all women. The Council on Scientific Affairs of the American Medical Association reports that "a survey of over 6,000 college students found that 42 percent of women students reported some type of sexual contact, attempted rape, and completed rape." Ellis[223] reports the study of Koss in which he found that 38 percent of college women reported sexual victimization consisting of rape or attempted rape, and another study of Lott, Reilly, and Howard,[259] in which they found that 6 percent of college males report being sexually assaulted, most often by female offenders. He also reports that from 10 percent to 15 percent of them (college males) forced their dates to have sex against her will. In addition, he reports that Koss, Gidycz, and Wisniewski[260] reported that 28 percent of women reported having experienced rape or a rape attempt since the age of fourteen.

Different degrees of violence were applied by the abusers in order to subdue the women. The majority of these are cases of date rape or cases in which there is, or has been, some romantic involvement between the two persons. The definition of date rape is appropriate in those cases where the aggressor, usually the male, willfully programs the rape of the victim. It is my opinion that many cases of so-called date rape represent the inability of generally young men to restrain their sexually aroused impulses during the heat of passion or, especially, when under the influence of alcohol.

The sexual victimization of women, including young girls and adolescents, has been increasing during the past twenty years. It is difficult to explain the reason for this when, at the same time, a climate of easy communication exists between the sexes. Perhaps, as previously mentioned, this type of easy communication at times conveys to some men double meaning-messages, an obviously incorrect perception of the woman's easy availability. Or perhaps the act of rape, at a subconscious level, is the male's reaction to women's present day independence and expression of resentment for the apparent abandonment of what he considers to be their primary role—that of wife and mother. With present-day economic conditions often being very difficult and many people finding themselves unemployed, many men may also resent female competition in the job market and feel displaced by them. Is it possible that unconsciously men's sexual aggression against women conveys this type of rivalry?

Even though it is an interesting theory, and probably true in some cases, basically rape reflects the absence of morals in the rapist's character. At its roots are deep psychological conflicts in the aggressor, conflicts that usually arise within the family and are later acted out in the larger relational arena of the community. It is usually the expression of rejection, feelings of inadequacy, anticipated or real failure in dealing with others, and a profound defeatist attitude towards life itself. As stated at the beginning of this chapter, whatever the definition, whatever the cause, rape is one of the most devastating experiences that a person can be subjected to.

Chapter Nine

THE PLAGUE OF DOMESTIC VIOLENCE

The rate of family violence has reached epidemic proportions as will be seen later in this chapter. "People are more likely to be killed, physically assaulted, hit, beaten up, slapped, or spanked in their own homes by other family members than anywhere else, or by anyone else, in our society."[261] Family violence is not restricted to any particular social or economic group, nor are sex, age or gender limiting factors. In order to understand the agony and the despair suffered by the victims of family violence, one should be reminded of what any person, either at a conscious or an unconscious level, expects from his or her living within a family. My long professional experience with people who have struggled with emotional or existential problems allows me to state that the majority of people look upon, and expect, the family to be a nurturing and protecting micro-community. It is within the family unit, ideally an aggregate of people sharing similar biological backgrounds or strong physical and affective ties and interests, such as can be observed between spouses, and between parents and children, that each individual expects to be loved, to be nurtured and to be respected in his or her own privacy.

The family is the fundamental unit upon which society is built. Its functions are basic and vital, even though its structure has moved from a fixed and static one to a more flexible variance in order to assure the continuity of an evolving society—the *gesellschaft* of the German sociologists—whose purpose is to bring together diverse ethnic, social groups into harmonious functioning.

In searching for the etymological roots of the word domestic, defined as "relating to the household or the family,"[192 p.374] we are reminded that for the ancient Greeks, the word *domos,* and for the Romans, its equivalent *domus,* referred not only to the physical structure of a house but also to what today we call home; just as *domesticus* meant pertaining to the family. Violence, on the other hand, as frequently mentioned in this book, deriving from the Latin *vis* and *violentia* is the intentional use of force exercised by one against another. The force may be physical, psychological or moral, and its purpose is usually to inflict physical harm, psychological pain or moral constriction. Usually, the violent action is a source of gratification for the victimizer.

With this semantic background we are on better grounds for an understanding of what domestic violence actually means to the aggressor. When we talk about domestic violence we are referring to violence within the family, generally of one of its members against another, with the specific intention of exercising control. I question, however, whether a dyscontrolled individual, and in this case, a violent one, is able to achieve control in such a situation other than that of the short-lived frightening or intimidating effect on the victim. The definition of domestic violence must have at its core the intention of the victimizer to harm another member of his or her own family. Obviously, when using this particular definition we have to extend the perimeter of the household, and include the concept of familiarity among the persons involved and include persons having strong emotional and physical ties but who, for various considerations, live separately. While not underestimating its importance in interpersonal relationships, I do not consider pertinent in this context, the occasional explosive expression of emotional feelings in the heat of an argument which is known as verbal violence.

Domestic violence in its various forms of aggression towards spouse, children and the elderly may be continuous, cyclical or sudden in its manifestations. As family violence is often a recurrent situation and often unpredictable, even though usually specific in type, it is easy to understand the anxieties and the despair in the minds of the victims who wait in anxious anticipation for the next explosive act, usually by abusing partner or a father. The deleterious effect of family violence does not stop at the suffering and agony of the helpless victim, but tends to influence the present and future behavior of all the other family members. Indeed, it has been reported that over two-thirds of men who physically abuse their partners come from homes in which there was parental violence and approximately half of the abusers were, themselves, abused as children.[262]

Violence appears to beget violence, to divide the members of the family into partisan groups, to create psychosomatic problems in both adults and in children. The behavior of these children may at first be oppositional, but later in life may develop into antisocial psychopathic aggression. Extreme rage against parental figures, at times eventuating in the tragedy of murder, is often seen as the sequelae of continuous maltreatment or, rarely, may be due to mental illness.

Sexual abuse consisting in spousal rape, sexual assault of biological children—usually girls—or of adoptive children by the man of the house is a frequently reported event at the basis of adolescent or young adult drug addiction, alcoholism and prostitution. One must wonder whether the retraction by Sigmund Freud of the possible sexual molestation of his female patients by their fathers was only a politically correct and convenient action on his part during that historical period.

It is natural to wonder whether either the aggressor or the victim of family violence has particular psychodynamics which make this type of offense recurrent and unfortunately under-reported. The family is, as a rule, housed in a structure the boundaries of which are well defined and that is generally far from the scrutiny of neighbors or passers-by. The members of the family usually develop strong emotional feelings towards one another, either positive or negative, or, at times, ambivalent. No one could find a better laboratory for the study of emotions than in the family. It is within the family that the newborn infant, the developing child—future adult—develops his or her primary, basic feeling self.

The persons involved in family violence usually have a particular type of personality. Generally, men who assault their female partners claim to have been subjected in childhood to sexual abuse, to have witnessed violence, and to have witnessed their father abusing alcohol and illicit drugs. They, themselves, have often done the same at a much higher rate than in non-abusive males. It has been my personal experience that the perpetrators of violence are usually insecure and inadequate, and are poor achievers who feel incapable of living up to expected standards within a relationship with their partner, and who often attempted to hide their incompetence as a provider or co-provider in the family. At times, arguing with a partner or other family members makes them acutely aware of their fear of being "found out," and because of that, they strike out against those people whom they feel to be a threat to their marginal emotional homeostasis.

It has been estimated that, on the average, within a twelve month period in the United States, approximately 2,000,000 women are seriously assaulted by their male partners.[252] Other studies point out that the above estimate is far below the possible 4,000,000 severely assaulted women.[263] And that does not take into consideration the aggression towards minors and the elderly within a home. Lansky,[264] in "Family

Genesis of Aggression," states that shame is of central importance in the determination of impulsive and violent behavior. It is equated, he says, to humiliation and loss of self esteem. He claims that some people have a particular proneness to shame that leads to excessive reliance on others for the maintenance of their self-esteem. He believes that this is due to having grown up in a dysfunctional family in which the child was made to feel inadequate. This person, as a result of these feelings of inadequacy, is often filled with semi-repressed rage and acts out his or her hostile feelings.

As we all know, it is not the well balanced, self-assured, strong individual who strikes out at members of his family or at others, but rather the anxious, inadequate person who feels intimidated, powerless, shamed, and helpless. It is usually the weak who react in a violent fashion, not the strong.

The person prone to violence, in order to avoid impulsive actions may use various defense mechanisms. One of these is to keep his spouse or other members of the family at a certain emotional distance; this is why some explosive people often appear to be emotionally detached and are often loners. Their rage is usually controlled by camouflaged behavior, initiated as a protective mechanism to avoid feelings of shame.

The individual who is prone to violence often finds in his home ambience a ground that greatly facilitates his offensive conduct. First of all, the other member of the family, the victim or victims in this case, often are seen by the victimizer as "easy prey." Indeed, the victim, even though partially able to express feelings of anger, and frustrated by the mistreatment, is often unable or unwilling to report the violent behavior because of ambivalent emotional feelings, rationalizations, practical economical factors, discomfort about disintegrating the family even further, and last, but not least, because of a fear of retaliation. Indeed, "The risk of assault is greatest when a woman leaves or threatens to leave an abusive relationship."[265] p.14

In reviewing the literature, it becomes evident that women in the United States are more likely to be victimized through "assault, battery, rape or homicide by a current or former male partner than by all other assailants combined."[266] p.3190 One in-depth study of all one-on-one murder and non-negligent manslaughter cases across a five year period found that over half of female victims were killed by male partners.[267] The innocent victims in such cases are the children who witness these parental homicides and are "emotionally traumatized, stigmatized, and deeply scarred by the terrifying event. They often exhibit debilitating symptoms comparable to those of posttraumatic stress disorder,"[268].

> I remember the vicious destructive rage of a forty-three year old male whom I examined for competency to stand trial. He had been charged with one count of false imprisonment while armed and one count of second degree recklessly endangering safety while armed. The victim, the wife of the defendant, stated that her husband had grabbed her by the shoulders and began shouting at her. He then began to push her and threw her against the refrigerator, after which he first grabbed her collar tightly, causing her to choke, and then continued choking her with one hand while opening a silverware drawer with the other, eventually pulling out a fork. He was shouting words to the effect that he was going to kill her for destroying his mind. As he continued to choke the victim, the defendant stabbed her face with the fork. The victim was able to fend off numerous blows by raising her arm but the defendant struck her numerous times in the face with the fork, causing lacerations and abrasions. The victim managed to get away momentarily but the defendant chased her out on to the front lawn where he tackled her and ripped off some of her clothes, forcing her to remain partially disrobed. Eventually, the victim managed to break free and run for help. She had been held without her consent for approximately two hours, and a portion of the above described actions were observed by her children who were extremely upset, frightened and disturbed by the actions. The defendant was found competent to stand trial but diagnosed as suffering from chronic schizophrenia, paranoid in type.

Research on domestic violence shows that half of all women will experience some form of violence from their partners during marriage, and that more than one-third are battered repeatedly every year,[263] and that women are six times more likely than men to be victims of violent crime in intimate relationships. In 1991, more than ninety women were murdered every week. Nine out of ten were murdered by men.[269] Even though violence against women is more prevalent in the home, abusive husbands and lovers harass 74 percent of employed battered women at work, either in person or over the telephone, causing 20 percent to lose their jobs.[263]

Even though most battered women do not report the abuse they receive because of fear and/or rationalizations, they frequently visit physicians because of their injuries and/or various other symptoms that are due to the violent family situation in which they find themselves. In fact, already in 1985, it was reported that battering accounted for one-fifth of all medical visits by women and one-third of all emergency room visits by women in the United States each year.[270] The authors of that report also stated that domestic violence was the largest single cause of injury among women seen in the emergency rooms and was more common than auto accidents, muggings, and rapes combined. Their symptomatology varies, and may consist only of vague physical complaints such as muscular or abdominal pains, headaches or difficulty with sleeping. "Between 22 percent and 35 percent of women presenting with complaints in emergency departments are suffering injuries or symptoms caused by ongoing abuse . . . [and] 25 percent of female emergency psychiatric patients are battered by a male partner; and up to 64 percent of female psychiatric patients are abused as adults."[266 p.3191]

Unfortunately, even physicians are not always able to recognize the disguised or masked battered-woman syndrome. Indeed, it is reported that "in only eight percent of the cases in which explicit information about abuse (e.g., patient's statements about abuse) or very strong indications of abuse were recorded in the medical chart," were physicians able to discharge their patients with the correct diagnosis of spousal abuse.[266 p.3191]

The possibility that damage to the frontal lobe structures of the aggressor might be at the basis of violent marital behavior towards the spouse should be entertained. In 1989, Rosenbaum and Hoge,[271] reporting the possible connection between head injury and marital aggression in offenders, found that out of a group of thirty-one violent marital offenders, nineteen had a history of severe head injury. They also found that alcohol imbibition, as reported by the offenders they studied, was present in slightly more than 48 percent (48.4%) of the sample. In fact, it has been my experience that physical abuse is most common following excessive use of alcohol or illicit drugs.

That the episodic dyscontrol syndrome due to organic factors may be at the basis of the violent behavior of a person against his spouse or other family member is also a possibility; however, in my estimation it is somewhat rare. The dyscontrol is usually a reaction to eco-psychological stressors.

Whatever the factors that are at the basis of violent behavior of a spouse, organic or psychodynamic or both, statistics show that 30 percent of all women will be victimized in some way during the course of their lifetime by their partner, and, as previously stated, more than one-half of the women murdered in the United States are killed by their partners.[267,271] The problem of battered women, the bulk of domestic violence, is both puzzling and depressing. Statistics reveal the quandary in which these women find themselves. Although divorced and separated women compose only 7 percent of the population in the United States, they account for 75 percent of all battered women and report being battered fourteen times as often as women still living with their partners.[272] Women who leave their batterers are at a 75 percent greater risk of being killed by the batterer than those who stay. Up to 50 percent of all homeless women and children in this country are fleeing domestic violence and after being sheltered, 31 percent of abused women in New York City returned to their batterers primarily because they could not locate longer-term housing.[263]

It appears that women are at a risk of greater danger in their homes than in the streets.

> This thirty-eight year old black male, a good provider for his family but with a long history of alcohol addiction and cocaine use, became increasingly suspicious of his wife's fidelity. He became so intolerable that she obtained a restraining order that relegated him to living quarters in the basement of their home. In a jealous paranoid raptus, he climbed a ladder to the second floor of the house, at 2 A.M., thinking that he would surprise his wife with her lover. He was armed with a kitchen knife. Entering his wife's room, he engaged in a struggle with her and with his son, wounding both of them, his wife severely. He was finally subdued by his other children. He was found to be suffering from a paranoid delusional disorder, jealous type, and found to have been insane at the time of the offense. Six months later his delusional ideas were still present, even though he appeared more relaxed about them.

The Supreme Court of Mississippi, in 1824,[273] followed by Maryland, Massachusetts, and North Carolina, decided that a husband has the right to use moderate physical chastisement towards his wife. However, since 1920, all states have abolished the above legal sanction allowing this type of treatment. Nonetheless, even though a completely different legal point of view exists today, the abuse of wives still continues in the United States, possibly due to deeply rooted and antiquated socio-cultural ideas of possessiveness and superiority of the male sex.

There is still a certain reluctance on the part of the police, the judicial system, and even of the population at large, to interfere with any marital discord. Domestic violence is part of a multifaceted relationship, and the relationship between the batterer and the victim is very important, often appearing to be of a sado-masochistic type. Even though the above mentioned fear of the aggressor of being found inadequate is important, the quest for power and control is a major motivating factor behind this type of aggressivity, often showing in the assailant's controlling attitude over his victim. This control, frequently used to intimidate the victim, may also be psychological or economic. "Controlling behaviors of batterers typically involve issues of money, choice of friends, and contacts/resources outside the homes."[274]

Already in 1958, Wolfgang,[275] reporting the results of a study in Philadelphia, stated that the most common homicide in a family is uxoricide, followed by filicide.

> A 52 year old, six foot tall, black male, weighing over two hundred pounds, was charged with first degree intentional homicide while armed. The shocking murder took place just outside of a courtroom while his estranged girlfriend was attempting to enter the courtroom in order to request a restraining order against him. He stabbed her to death, plunging a large kitchen knife into her body eighteen times. He was apprehended in the courthouse shortly afterward. The man exhibited a sullen, negativistic, uncooperative behavior. He apparently felt that the woman was not only abandoning him but was also allowing his adult children to cheat him out of his money and possessions. He continued to assume an evasive and malingering attitude. Eventually he pled guilty and was sentenced to life in prison without possibility of parole.

The above shows that domestic violence may also take place outside of the home.

A survey[275] of the homicides that had taken place in Philadelphia between 1948 and 1952, found that 25 percent involved members of the same family; of a group of 136 victims of homicide, 100 were wives and seventeen were children of the murderer. Pittman and Handy[276] reported in 1964 that either the wife or the husband were victims of aggravated aggressions in 11 percent of the cases they studied. In 1972, Palmer[277] reported statistics similar to those of Wolfgang, stating that 29 percent of all the homicides that had taken place in 1966 involved members of the same family.

One can appreciate the complexity of the problem of domestic violence, not only because of the sado-masochistic relationship which is often a part of this type of violence, but also because the persons involved, frequently husband and wife, bring into their relationship their own life experiences prior to their marriage.

Gifford,[278] already in 1975, reported that a high rate of separation between spouses (81%) was present among a group of one hundred battered wives. He added that in 54 percent of the one hundred families considered, the violence had extended to the children. He also reported a high degree and frequency of alcoholism and antisocial behavior among the abusive husbands. Hotaling and collaborators[279] also reported that the risk of child abuse is significantly higher when the partner is also assaulted. Walker[280] wrote that nearly half of the men who abuse their female partners also abuse their children.

Strauss and collaborators,[281] in *Behind Closed Doors: Violence in the American Family,* reported that 6,100 married couples out of 100,000, had abused one another physically in a violent way during the year of their study. The study further pointed out that during the same period 1,800,000 wives had been seriously physically assaulted by their husbands at least once a year. In cases in which husbands are abused by wives, the wife's violent behavior may be more frequent and more serious than that reported for husbands.

In fact, violence is also perpetrated by women against their husbands. I remember an unusual case of a forty-five year old chronic schizophrenic female who, prey to paranoid ideas, after battering her husband, then sat on him to the point that the victim sustained multiple internal injuries and was crushed to death. The offender weighed 350 pounds!

However, Walker[282] stated that the data indicate that women who kill their abusers resort to such violence as a last attempt to protect themselves from further physical and mental harm. It has also been reported that 76 percent of a small sample of thirty-eight women out of fifty who had killed their husbands had used the same weapon with which they had been threatened by him, each believing that the batterer was going to make good on his threat to use it against her.[280]

It is natural to ask why either wife or husband submit to the violent behavior of which they are victims. In addition to the previously mentioned variables such as the physical fear of retaliation, complete economic dependency, fear of breaking up the family, and/or ambivalent feelings towards the partner, one may think that in some cases the battered partner realizes that the batterer, whom they probably still love, is a person who acts in a such an unacceptable way because he or she is suffering from some type of psychopathology which he or she is unable to control. In other words, the victim views the victimizer as being mentally disturbed and justifies the behavior on that basis.

Studies have been done in order to define the characteristics of persons who are victims of marital violence. Interestingly, in one review of fifty-two studies of comparison groups, only one variable potential risk marker for women seemed to be associated in a rather consistent manner with the possibility of becoming the victim of marital violence, and that was "witnessing parental violence as a child or adolescent."[252] p.3186 Another study, instead, pointed out that a very important risk variable for marital violence is that the woman had been sexually abused as a child.

Physical abuse within a marital or marital-like relationship leaves the victim with a profound sense of vulnerability, of loss, of betrayal, and feelings of severe hopelessness. These people often become very depressed, and at times abandon their homes and become part of the large cohort of homeless people. When the battering is severe, there are many physical symptoms that are reported and that require immediate medical attention. Typical injuries inflicted by an abusive person in cases of domestic violence are contusions and lacerations, usually of the head, face and neck, followed by those to the breasts or abdominal area.

Walker stated that, "A disproportionately large number of women are assaulted while they are pregnant."[280] p.51 Another report stated that "Nearly 50% of abusive husbands batter their pregnant wives,"[283] while another stated that battered women are three times more likely to be injured while pregnant.[270] The consequences of battering the pregnant woman are not only physical pain, fright and/or despair, but at times miscarriage, rupture of the uterus, and precipitated labor, often with placental complications, low birth weight babies, and injury to or death of the fetus.[270,283]

A review of domestic violence cases in the city of Milwaukee for the years 1992 and 1993 shows that in 1992 the total cases of battery reviewed amounted to 11,469, while in 1993 the number increased to 12,007, an increase of 538 units. In 1992, 11% of the offenders in these cases were charged with the offense, in 87% of the cases there was no process and the remaining (2%) were diverted. In 1993, 17% of the offenders were charged, in 82% of the cases there was no process, and the rest (1%) were diverted. During the same years, 1992 and 1993, 311 cases of domestic violence and endangering safety by the use of a dangerous weapon were reviewed. In 1992, 60 (22%) of these cases resulted in a criminal charge; in 1993, 352 (20%) offenders were charged.[284]

Violence is also perpetrated by women against women in the domesticity of their homes as in the following case.

Two sisters in their early twenties were visiting their mother who had custody of the four children of one of the sisters. The sisters began to argue about one of the children after one of the sisters had raised her voice at the other's three year old son. The aunt grabbed the son and attempted to pull him away from his mother. The two sisters began to wrestle in the dining room and one of them believing that the other was going to pick up an object with which to hit her, ran into the kitchen and grabbed a butcher knife from the sink. The two sisters then continued their wrestling match while their mother ran to call for help. A few minutes later one of the sisters was found on the couch with blood coming from a wound on her neck. Her sister was standing close to her, the knife still in her hand. The victim died shortly afterwards and the autopsy report found that a stab wound to her neck had incised her left subclavian artery causing death by exanguination.

Those who are caught in the middle in a domestic violence situation are the children. They are often abducted by one of their parents and more than 50 percent of child abductions result from domestic violence.[263] Most of these abductions are perpetrated by fathers and their agents. Battering men use custodial access to the children as a tool to terrorize battered women or to retaliate for separation.[263] Abusive partners often use children as pawns in custody fights to coerce their female partners to reconcile with them. Often, these coercive incidents occur during court-ordered visitation.[263]

When violence, especially sexual violence, is directed against children, there is, at times, a failure to properly recognize it because of the fact that it may be difficult to distinguish whether the parents were negligent or intentionally abusive. The traumatic experience of being battered or sexually abused is extremely disruptive of the normal development of the young victim. Its consequences involve the victim's physical, psychological, and spiritual dimensions, and also influence future interpersonal relationships. Nevertheless, in my professional experience I have seen many of these victims who have been able to overcome the obsessive memories of their abused childhood and/or adolescence, and have been able to enjoy a life without fear and with a realistic objectivity, depriving the haunting memory of the past of its negative powers.

I have also witnessed a curtain of denial drawn by family members in cases of violence against children. These persons are often unwilling to accept the disclosures of their victimized children or are attempting to protect one another from the possible consequences of these actions. Children, themselves, may have misconceptions about what sexual abuse is and may not reveal the abuse they have suffered. This may also be due to a deep need for the support and love which they fear would be lost if the abusive behavior is reported, the fear of disrupting their parents' relationship, or the fear of not being believed by other family members. So the child often suffers passively until the latter part of the adolescent period when he or she may try to finally stand up to the offensive parent or to leave home.

At times an incestuous relationship may continue for years and may stop only when the offending parent substitutes the grown-up victim with a younger sibling. This type of sexual abuse is a form of entrapment for children who, because of fear and threats, may become almost coparticipants in one of the worst forms of exploitation of the child's body and emotions.

Domestic abuse of children, either physical or sexual, does not depend on the socio-economic level of the family. Here again, it is essentially the psychopathology and the unconventional attitudes of the abuser that are determining factors in the offense. I remember the case of a father, chronically addicted to alcohol, who frequently abused his teen-aged daughter who justified his abuse of her by comparing it to a biblical story he claimed to have read. He voiced the idea that his abuse was like the sexual indoctrination that took place in primitive times.

The abuse of children and adolescents, as with spouses, is not only sexual, but may be physical and/or psychological. Sexual abuse comprises fondling of non-genital body parts, heterosexual and homosexual acts, molestation with genital contact such as cunnilingus, vaginal, oral, and rectal intercourse. Physical abuse may comprise any of a multitude of injuries that may be due to beating, punching, kicking, biting, burning and hitting. The neglect of a child or adolescent should be considered as an indirect form of abuse.

The battered-child syndrome was first described by Helfer and Kaempe.[285] They reported that children battered physically by their parents numbered in the thousands each year. Gil,[286] in 1971, stated that there were at least 6,000 battered children yearly. However, in 1972, *Parade*[287] reported that each year 60,000 cases of physical abuse come to the attention of medical personnel and police. Other studies, in 1974, reported an approximate number of 200,000 to 500,000 cases of battered-child syndrome per year.[288]

The physical and sexual abuse of children and adolescents should be viewed as one of the worst criminal offenses. It represents an act of violence perpetrated on a helpless individual, physically, emotionally and socially immature; an act of violence that unfortunately is all too common and that must not be ignored. As in many other forms of maltreatment involving wives or the elderly, even with children the numbers reported are usually an underestimation of the actual number of cases. In 1975, The National Center on Child Abuse and Neglect (NCCAN) of the United States reported 250,000 cases of physical abuse of children. However, in striking contrast to that number, a national survey of the American family conducted by Gelles[289] reported that during the same year, 1,200,000 to 1,700,000 children in the United States had been battered by their parents; the battering consisted in being beaten, kicked or severely pinched. He also reported that from 460,000 to 750,000 children had been severely physically abused and 46,000 had been either threatened with, or struck with, guns or knives.

Viano,[290] reporting in 1975 on the battered-child syndrome, stated that the abuse of minors is present throughout the world, not only in the United States, Canada and New Zealand, as had been reported by Maden[291] and McKeith,[292] also in 1975, and that the incidence of death due to physical abuse was high in both Western Europe and the United States. Smith[293] found it to be increasingly present in Western Europe and in the Scandinavian countries, in Australia and in Uganda during the same year.

In 1977, Scott[294] reported that in England an average of six children out of 100,000 were severely maltreated by their parents or custodian each year. Also in 1977, Kaiser[295] reported 200 to 300 hundred cases of physical abuse of children in Western Germany.

A national study on child neglect and abuse reported by the American Humane Association,[296] showed an escalation of abuse and negligence of minors from 1977 to 1979. Indeed, there were 33,546 reported cases of physical abuse of children in 1977, while by 1979 the number had risen to 58,772. Cases of negligence were 55,127 in 1977, and in 1979 had risen to 111,162. Other forms of maltreatment in 1979 amounted to 21,135 cases. The total number of cases reported to the police in 1979 was more than triple that of 1977, respectively 110,117 and 33,927.[297]

The American Association for Protecting Children[298] showed an increase of 225 percent in child abuse reporting between 1976 and 1987. In 1992, there were 2.9 million reported cases of child abuse and neglect in the United States.[263] Of the reported cases, 27 percent involved physical abuse, 17 percent involved sexual abuse, 45 percent involved neglect,

7 percent involved emotional abuse, and 8 percent were classified as "other" which includes abandonment and dependency.

The original observations of child abuse by Kempe and his pediatric group, in 1962, gave a great deal of impetus to its detection, not only by pediatricians but also by emergency room personnel, visiting nurses, and social workers during home visitations. Their observations concluded that 15 percent of children below the age of five had been maltreated, and in the 749 cases that came to their attention, the group of maltreated children reached a mortality rate of more than ten (10.4%) percent.[297] Unfortunately, the actual number of cases of battered children was probably tenfold, and Kempe's statistics may have been a gross underestimation of the actual number. Nonetheless, the report alerted public opinion to the problem of child abuse which, until then, had only been touched upon in some medical-legal literature such as the study by Tardieu[299] in 1860 and that of Parristo and Cossad[300] in 1929. Prior to Kempe's study, few people had suspected the frequency of maltreatment and physical abuse of children and of its consequences. In 1946, Kaffe,[301] however, had reported in his a paper, "Multiple Fracture of the Long Bones of Infants Suffering from Chronic Subdural Hematoma," that he suspected that the cause of the above radiologically demonstrable lesions may have been due to physical abuse. In 1951, Silvermann[301] described various bony fractures in children, and his belief was also that they were the result of physical abuse received from their parents. In a report by Gil[286] regarding the period 1967–1968, the child abuse ranged between 8.4 and 9.3/100,000 children under the age of eighteen, while the reported rate by Light was only 1 to 4 percent of 1,000 families.[288]

By 1992, as reported above, there had been a progressive increase in the reported cases of child abuse, reaching the number of 2.9 million cases. The above may be due to a greater awareness of the problem leading to better detection by indivdiuals and by public agencies. This detection, however, needs better planning for better results. In 1992, 1,261 children died—37% as a result of physical neglect, 58% as a result of physical abuse.[263] Children often attempt to defend their mothers from an abusive male partner, and the National Coalition Against Domestic Violence reports that 62% of sons over age fourteen were injured when they attempted to protect their mothers from attacks by abusive male partners.[302]

Bland and Orn[112] reported that "Baldwin and Oliver, in a British study, using detailed and specific definitions, found annual rates of about 1/1,000 for severe abuse in children under four years old."[p.134] In their discussion of the above study, they stated that of the 1,200 persons in their own study, 2.6 percent of the parents admitted abusing a child. The results of their study reveal that a fairly high proportion of people exhibiting violent behavior suffer from a psychiatric illness, and, more specifically, the rate of violent behavior of those with psychiatric diagnoses reached 54.4 percent. They claimed that particularly high rates for violence were found among people who were diagnosed as antisocial personality disorder and who also were addicted to alcohol, or among those who suffered from a recurrent depression with occasional suicidal attempts. In their statistics, the rate of depression combined with antisocial personality disorder and alcoholism reached 80 to 93 percent among those people exhibiting violent behavior within the family.

Psychiatric illnesses ranging from schizophrenia and bipolar illness or recurrent depression are at times at the basis of some violent behavior within the family, and the type and intensity of this behavior is at times of serious significance.

A seventeen year old Puerto-Rican male was bound to adult court by the children's division of a local circuit court and charged with first degree intentional homicide. Reportedly, on Nov. 22, 1992, he entered a woman's home under the pretext of wanting to make a telephone call. The woman, 40 years old, was a friend of his mother. He stated to the police that he was in love with her and wanted to make love to her. He had misunderstood her motherly kindness. He asked her for a kiss and the woman consented to it but she refused his further advances and while trying to ward him off she yelled at him that she would tell his mother about his behavior. The defendant grabbed a kitchen knife and furiously tried to stab her and a struggle for the knife ensued between the two. Finally, the young man got hold of the knife and while he continued telling her that he loved her he closed his eyes and started pushing the knife into her. He did not remember how many times he stabbed her. When he stopped, he ran out of the house and heard her last words of penance addressed to God: "Forgive me for all of my sins and other things I did bad." Following the killing, the defendant became withdrawn, confused, unable to recall, deeply depressed. He had a long history of mental illness and had been treated with Thorazine and attended special classes while in school. He appeared to be highly dependent on his mother, with a tremendous amount of hostility towards his rejecting father. He was angry and had superficial ideas of reference. He was reported to be suffering from epilepsy of a grand mal type. He appeared self-conscious and prone to panic. The defendant was diagnosed as suffering from schizo-affective psychosis.

Much more common, however, in my experience, is the occurrence of violent behavior with serious consequences perpetrated by people who can be classified as personality disorder of the antisocial type with drug and alcohol addiction, and people with a paranoid delusional disorder.

> A thirty-eight year old white male was apprehended by the police and charged with aggravated battery against his live-in girlfriend. Following an argument over money at their home, the victim was suddenly attacked by the defendant who slapped and punched her repeatedly in the face and head areas. The attacker grabbed her by the neck with both hands and choked her until she fell to the floor unconscious. He continued to kick her repeatedly about the body, especially in the area of the torso, held her down and caused her to gag on her own blood. He ripped her clothes and sexually assaulted her. The victim was taken to the emergency hospital where she was diagnosed as having two broken ribs, contusions to both orbital and nasal regions, lacerations and edema of the mouth, laceration of the neck area, numerous bruises and contusions in the torso region and on the arms. She also had several bite marks. She required hospitalization. The offender was classified as a paranoid personality disorder with explosive behavior.

A very sad example of this type of abuse is that of a two year old child who came to my attention during an autopsy examination. Because of his incessant crying, he was grabbed by the intoxicated boyfriend of his mother, and swung around by his ankles, hitting his head against the wall with such force that he sustained a skull fracture and brain laceration that caused instant death. Unfortunately, many cases of physical abuse of children end in the morgue.

Infants and children are not new to physical abuse. In ancient societies they were not only frequently mistreated, but the infanticide of deformed or unwanted children was not an uncommon practice. During the reign of the Emperor Justinian in Rome, in 529 A.D., special homes were established for children who had been abandoned or who had no parents. Throughout the centuries, very young children were used as cheap labor, and not until the eighteenth century was public opinion sensitized to the physical and psychological maltreatment incurred by these children. This brought about the institution of children's homes as protective shelters. However, even there the children were occasionally battered.[301] Unfortunately, even at the end of the twentieth century, the reliance on child labor is still common in some countries.

In the case of domestic abuse, the mother is more often the batterer in the physical abuse of the child, probably due to the fact that she is more likely to be in contact with the child during the day, or she may be frustrated by her inability to cope or by what she feels to be an impingement on her liberty. However, "for the most serious forms of violence (beating up; kicking, biting, punching; using guns or knives), men and women are approximately equal in their disposition to use these modes of violence on their children."[289] p.589 Gelles states that this is one of the few situations in which women and men are both likely to use a similar type of violence.

Of the 2.9 million reported cases of child abuse and neglect in the United States in 1992, 17 percent involved sexual violence.[263] The abuser is often the father, but at times it may be other male figures in the household, such as brothers, uncles or friends of the family. Kendall-Tackett and Simon[303] found that most perpetrators of the abuse of the persons taken into consideration in their study had been the fathers or father surrogates (62%), while that of other male family members was found to be relatively low (cousins or uncles [10.7%] and brothers [9.3%]). This was in contrast to the results of Finkelhor's[304] study which had found that most perpetrators were brothers and male cousins, while fathers and father surrogates were a small percentage of the perpetrators. Kendall-Tackett and Simon theorize that the difference can be accounted for by different data collecting methods.

Sexual abuse of children is often present in lower socio-economic classes where many children are crowded into a single room and on a single bed, or at times sleep in the same bed with their parents. It has been reported that adolescents experience maltreatment at rates similar to or even higher than that for younger children. However, because of their older age they are often perceived as being responsible for this maltreatment. Adolescent girls are reported as victims more often than boys, especially in cases of sexual abuse.[305] In my professional experience, I have found the sexual abuse of adolescent girls has been perpetrated equally by fathers and step-fathers, who are usually under the influence of alcohol at the time of the offense, removing the last vestiges of any moral control.

In order to understand the higher incidence of adolescent abuse and maltreatment, one must be reminded of the growing surge of rebelliousness in the child entering the teens and into late adolescence. This is a struggle for independence and control, duties and rights, that often eventuates in a chaotic situation, and even though temporary, may be destructive of family relationships. It is not surprising that at times parents of adolescents feel confused and angry because they are unable to control their children's behavior.

The attitude of adolescents towards their parents may be of an oppositional or defiant type. Occasionally they may be involved in antisocial type of behavior or in drug or alcohol experimentation or addictions. We are all well aware of the clash between parental dictates and the rebelliousness of these young people, and of the possibility that parents, mostly fathers, may try to exercise control of the child, and at times some form of physical control. This is often felt by the child to be abuse and at times he or she may run away from home because of it. The adolescent may rebel against the parent who is believed to be aggressive to the point of antisocial conduct. In fact, "incarcerated youths, homeless or runaway youths, and youths who victimize or assault parents have been shown to have high rates of prior maltreatment."[305 p.1950]

It is reported that between 1980 and 1986, the rates of physical abuse among adolescents almost doubled while the rates of sexual abuse actually tripled. In 1990, more than 208,000 youths between the ages of twelve and seventeen "were reported to child protective service agencies as victims of abuse. These represented 25 percent of all cases reported."[305 p.1851] Except for sexual abuse the overall incidence of abuse and neglect in adolescents is no higher than that in childhood and the injuries in older children are less serious than in the younger ones. This can be explained by the fact that the older child usually reacts to the aggressor, whoever it may be.

Children often deny being abused by their parents, possibly feeling that they provoked the abusive incident. In one study where abuse of adolescents was clear, 40 percent of the abused children described themselves as deserving maltreatment.[306] While boys younger than twelve years of age are reported to show higher rates of physical abuse than girls, the situation reverses itself when adolescent girls are compared to adolescent boys.[305] This may be due to the concern of parents for the consequences of the increasing autonomy of girls and/or their fear of possible sexual misconduct, as well as a lower propensity in girls to engage in a defensive physical fight with a paternal figure. The opposite is true for adolescent boys who may be thought to be able to ward off physical attacks.

We can probably term some families, "families of abuse." Indeed, the causes of physical and sexual abuse are not to be found only in the serious intrapersonal problems of the abuser, but also in a dysfunctional, chaotic family situation. Either extreme independence or excessive dependence has been found to be present in members of this type of dysfunctional family, and both authoritarian families and overindulgent families may be abusive at different times during the period of adolescence.[305]

The majority of abusers of children, as with spousal abuse, are persons having a particular personality makeup. These persons are usually dissatisfied with themselves; they have a poor sexual identification; they have a great deal of ambivalence towards the female figure stemming from a poor relationship with their mothers; they are unable to relate properly to their wives; they are shy, timid and fearful of rejection. They have often been battered by their father and frequently sexually molested. They suffer from feelings of jealousy towards their own children, especially those of the same sex, and have a fear of being supplanted by the children in their relationship with the children's mother. Their battering and their sexual abuse are an unsuccessful attempt to assert their fragile masculinity.

Domestic violence does not restrict itself to women and children. Approximately one out of every twenty-five elderly persons is victimized annually. Of those who experience domestic elder abuse, 37% are physically abused. Of those who perpetrate domestic elder abuse, 30% are the adult children of the abused person.[263]

The topic of domestic violence would not be complete if I did not mention the infrequent but present victimization of parents by their younger children. I am not referring here to the unruly, uncivil behavior of many young people towards their parents, or to young people's truancy, use of alcohol, drugs and participation in misdemenant or felonious behavior away from home, behavior which obviously creates in parents anxiety, concern, depression, and the frequent disruption of the family's daily routine. I am referring to the killing of parents by their children, usually during their adolescent period, but, as the case below describes, even at a later age.

A twenty-three year old Puerto Rican male was observed by a passer-by to be beating a woman with his fists as she stood on the porch of a house. The beating continued for some time and at the end the woman was seen to be sitting on the floor of the porch next to the porch railing while the young man, the defendant, kept striking her in such a way that she was hitting the railing with her head. The defendant was yelling, "She killed my brother." On apprehension by the police, the defendant stated that he had suddenly had an explosion in his behavior and began throwing things around—a pillow, the telephone and pictures and followed his mother who ran out of the house. He took off his clothes in the living room, ran outside, caught up with her on the porch and hit her with his fists, slamming her head into the railing of the porch. He claimed that it was just anger. He was found to be suffering from paranoid schizophrenia of long standing. He was charged with first degree reckless homicide.

Almost five hundred cases of parricide are reported annually in the United States. The killing of one's parents, either father, mother, or both, represents the breaking down of one of the sacred taboos in the history of mankind. However, it is also as old as the history of mankind and writers such as Sophocles, Shakespeare and Dostoyevsky remind us of that in their writings. Freud,[307] in *Totem and Taboo,* attempted to explain on the basis of the Oedipal complex this tendency which he claims is almost inborn in the developing child. These adolescents are usually sensitive, insecure, ambivalent, frightened and emotionally deprived. They have usually sustained a great deal of physical, and at times sexual, abuse at the hands of their parents. However, as we justly castigate their parents' behavior as unnatural and offensive, we should look upon the behavior of these children in a similar way. There is no justification for *anyone* to abuse, victimize, or murder another person.

We should not absolve the adolescent from the responsibility for similar crimes since we know that by the age of thirteen the majority of children, especially in present day society, should have acquired cognitive and moral development relatively adequate for social interaction, and only when found to be suffering from a psychotic condition, do they usually lose the capacity to make choices.

Chapter Ten

ALCOHOL AND PSYCHOACTIVE DRUGS AND VIOLENCE

The short term and long term effects of mind-altering substances such as alcohol and cocaine, the two major psychoactive substances used today, are very important in the assessment of violent behavior. Both of them may influence human conduct in a negative way, creating a state of acute mental confusion or a chronic mental impairment manifesting itself with physiological, cognitive, and behavioral dysfunctions. The question of whether the use of alcohol or cocaine is the primary cause of criminal conduct or is only associated with criminal behavior, and whether both antisocial behavior and psychoactive substance abuse stem from a certain primary psychopathology, is a debatable one. A recent survey of state prison inmates[165] reports that 31 percent of the inmates surveyed committed their offense while under the influence of drugs and 32 percent committed their offense while under the influence of alcohol. It is my opinion that psychoactive substances are basically suppressors of self-control and facilitators of those antisocial propensities which may be already present in the make-up of the violent individual.

When addressing the issue of alcoholism in our society one cannot help but be struck with the biblical words regarding some motivation for its use. In Psalm 104:15 we are told that "wine . . . makes glad the heart of man"; and in Proverbs 31:7 we are reminded, "Let him drink and forget his poverty and remember his misery no more." However, in other sections, the wisdom of the biblical writer tells us dependence on, or untimely use of alcohol is to be avoided, as when, in Isaiah 5:11, one can read, "Woe unto them that rise up early in the morning, that they may follow strong drink;" or, when we are reminded of its devastating consequences as stated in Proverbs 23:21, "The drunkard and the glutton shall come to poverty."

The use of alcohol is as old as mankind. Various investigators believe that it was already used during the Neolithic age. At that time, alcohol, in the form of wine and beer, usually derived from honey, and its use was convivial or ritualistic. In 1926, at Nineveh, an anonymous account of the Flood was found which recounts that Noah took not only food in the Ark, but also beer and wine in large jars.[308] The Old Testament was even more specific about Noah's use of alcohol when it states, "And he drank of the wine, and was drunken."[309] At the time of the Mesopotamian and Egyptian civilizations, wine was part of banquets, and people apparently frequented taverns where they would "drink wine to rapture." Fermented grain and honey were well known and frequently used in the Orient, and already in 650 B.C., in the *Canon of History,* or *Shu Ching,* was written, "Men will not do without beer."[309] p.170 It added, however, warnings regarding its use in moderate amounts.

The Jews of the Old Testament denounced drunkenness, but occasionally, under special circumstances, allowed the use of alcoholic beverages, usually diluted with water. The Greeks, referring to wine as the nectar of the Gods, and the ancient Romans, also used wine diluted with water. Euripides is reported to have said in his *Bacchae,* that wine "removes the cares pressing upon the minds of sorrowing mortals. . . . There is no other like cure for all their troubles."[308] p.170 Plato advised moderation in drinking, while Pliny the Elder recognized its excessive use throughout the world he knew.

The distillation and isolation of alcohol, around 800 A.D., is credited to an Arabian alchemist, Jabir ibn Hayyan (Geber). However, its practical properties were first recognized by Arnaldus de Villanova, at the University of Montpellier near the end of the thirteenth century. At the time it was known as aqua vitae—the water of life or immortality—and Arnaldus considered it to be "the philosopher's stone, the universal panacea, the key to life everlasting."[308] p.170

The use of whiskey seems to have been present since the fifteenth century, and during the seventeenth century, brandy and gin came into use and spread throughout Europe. This was followed by the development of scotch, rum, and, eventually, around the middle of the eighteenth century, in the United States, by rye and bourbon.

At present, the consumption of alcoholic beverages is widespread in our culture. A 1991 survey reported that 103 million Americans had used alcohol in the month prior to the survey.[310] Many problems arise in conjunction with its excessive use, be they the various acute and chronic pathological effects of its abuse, its relationship to marital discord, its influence on driving and/or the facilitation of people's misdemeanant or felonious behavior. In fact, violence is often precipitated by alcohol consumption. Drinking alcohol, and particularly beer, is a part of the interaction in many groups of young people, and adolescents, wanting to become part of a group, frequently adapt to its drinking habits. It then often occurs that because of the tension relieving appeal of alcohol, they may become abusers of it and eventually addicted to it. It is also a part of the adult socialization process and has, indeed, often become a source of an Hamletian dilemma—to drink or not to drink is a question forced on almost everyone at some time in their life.

Alcoholic beverages may have a salutary effect on both body and mind when drunk in minimal amounts but excess use and abuse of it may have deleterious, even devastating, effects. Pace aptly stated, "We have to change our views on the patron god of drinkers from Bacchus to Janus. I think we are dealing with a two faced problem."[311] p.87 Indeed, even though alcohol is often used in convivial situations as a mild disinhibitor of human conduct and in essence is a facilitator of interpersonal relationships, carrying no untoward mental or physical consequences; alcoholism, instead, viewed as the excessive and continued use of an acceptable naturally derived substance, must be considered a social disease. Helzer reports the definition of Keller and collaborators that alcoholism should be considered "the repetitive intake of alcoholic beverages to a degree that harms the drinker in health or socially or economically, with indication of inability consistently to control the occasional amount of drinking."[312] I would like to add that the intake not only harms the drinker but also harms the family, and often society at large, because of the intoxicated drinker's frequent antisocial behavior. Indeed, the following statement undoubtedly refers not only to drugs but also to alcohol which is also a substance of abuse and dependence: "As the number one health problem in the country, substance abuse places a major burden on the nation's health care system. . . . [and] on American society as a whole. It can harm health, family, life, the economy and the public safety. . . . [It] affects all segments of society . . . "[310] p.8

The consumption of alcohol in the United States has fluctuated through the years. In previous centuries Americans, by and large, drank more alcoholic beverages, and one of the factors that brought about Prohibition was that it served to call attention to the necessity of limiting its consumption. In fact, while high peaks were reached during periods of major wars, its consumption was low during the period of Prohibition and also during the depression. A recent review, in fact, reveals that in

1934, during the depression, alcohol consumption was at its lowest—0.9 gallons of ethanol/person age fourteen or older; instead it was highest—2.8 gallons/person in and around 1980, after the drinking age became eighteen in most of the states. "The consumption of distilled spirits which has a high ethanol content decreased substantially over the past fifteen years; beer consumption remained relatively stable; and wine consumption increased slightly."[310 p.10]

Alcohol is reported as a major cause of premature death due to cirrhosis, cardiomyopathy, and alcohol related motor vehicle fatalities and obviously antisocial behavior, even homicide. The above report states that "one-half to two-thirds of homicides and serious assaults involve alcohol."[310 p.42] Recent statistics state that 35 percent of Americans abstain from alcohol consumption, 55 percent drink fewer than three alcoholic drinks per week, and 11 percent drink more than one ounce of alcohol daily.[313] It is reported that males consume three times as much alcohol as females; their use of alcohol starts earlier in life and by age fifteen three-fourths of adolescents have consumed alcohol. The cost to the United States economy of alcohol abuse is 10.5 billion dollars annually. The impact on the individual and the family is also high. In my experience, three-fourths of the offenders who are charged with major crimes (felonies), including homicide, rape, assault and battery, had used alcohol prior to their offense, and alcohol was found in their blood and urine and frequently in that of their victims who had been drinking with them at the time.

In order to better appreciate the frequent association of major crimes with alcohol ingestion, the character of those persons who drink excessively should be taken into consideration. The personality of the chronic alcoholic often shows an immature attitude with strong frustrated dependency needs, a dysfunctional family background, a self-centered attitude and a tendency to become easily anxious, angry and frustrated. The alcoholic often harbors deep neurotic conflicts, inhibited sexual and aggressive drives, and an ambivalent attitude towards family members and/or significant others. I have also found that those individuals who manifest explosive behavior, or who abuse their wives and children during their intoxicated states, struggle with deep feelings of inferiority and inadequacy. Their bravado, was in fact, often just a facade.

The alcoholic personality can be divided into five types, alpha, beta, gamma, delta, and epsilon. The gamma, delta, and epsilon alcoholics are the most frequently associated with criminal actions. The gamma alcoholic usually lacks control and is unable to stop his drinking. There may be remissions and exacerbations throughout the alcoholic's life.[314] Wolfgang,[275] in 1958, established what today appears to be confirmed, that alcoholic indulgence and homicide are more frequent during weekends.

There is no doubt that alcohol must be viewed as a facilitating factor in crime, along with illicit drugs. Its importance as a cofactor in crime is supported by the previously mentioned data from a 1991 survey of state prison inmates, from the Bureau of Justice Statistics, showing that just over two-fifths of inmates convicted of homicide or assault had committed their current offense under the influence of alcohol or combination of alcohol and drugs.[165] The study also found that violent inmates had been drinking (an average of nearly nine ounces of ethanol) before their offense, and that they had been drinking for a period of six hours or more prior to the offense. Nine ounces of alcohol is equivalent to three six-packs of beer or to a quart of wine. Wolfgang,[275] in 1958, had already reported that offenders who had been drinking prior to their offense perpetrated more violent and brutal crimes than those who had not been drinking.

Alcohol use indeed, is frequently associated with felonies, and at times it is responsible for the reflexive homicide committed by a robber who has been discovered during his criminal action. Many homicides take place in or outside of taverns and may involve innocent bystanders or drinking companions. Women and children are often at the mercy of their inebriated husbands or fathers. Alcohol victimization is also often a part of gang rivalry. Even though violence, per se, is not attributed to alcohol the association between alcohol intoxication and violent crime is supported by many studies.[275,315,316]

Macdonald,[193] took a middle view in his appraisal of the relationship between alcohol and crime, and stated that while crimes, especially murder, are not caused by alcohol they are often associated with its use. His review of ten major research findings regarding the relationship between alcohol and criminal homicide in the sixties, found that the use of alcohol by offenders prior to their offense ranged from a minimum of 19 percent to a maximum of 83 percent, with an average of 55 percent.

In 1986, Lindqvist[317] reported a study of alcoholism and criminal homicide in northern Sweden for the period spanning 1970 to 1981. After reviewing seventy-one cases (sixty-four offenders) he concluded that: "Mutual intoxication was a feature in 44 percent of the cases . . . The majority of the victims were related by blood or marriage to the offender [and] 63 percent of the offenders had previously been subjected to psychiatric care. Thirty-one percent were considered mentally diseased at trial and another twenty-two percent also had a co-existing abuse or personality disorder."[317] p.36

"The mind-brain problem plagues all our endeavors to account for human actions. It is particularly pertinent to alcoholism, to drug abuse, and to recent theories of violence. . . . If mental states are somehow reducible to brain states then scientific accounts of the brain could in principle provide full accounts of human psychology."[318] Lindqvist reported that in Sweden alcohol abuse is reported to be much higher at a national level, and that his study does not reflect the overall presence of alcohol abuse in criminality. In his paper he stressed "cultural heritage, social stability, and attitude to overt violence" as significant factors in homicide, in addition to the fact that violent persons may also be intoxicated at the time of the homicidal act.

In 1987, it was reported that 10 percent of drinkers use 50 percent of the total amount of alcohol and drinking patterns vary with age and sex. Above sixty-five years of age only 7 percent of males and 2 percent of females are considered to be heavy drinkers. The age range of twenty-one to thirty-four shows the highest consumption of alcohol, and the male to female ratio is two to five times more in the male.[313] This age pattern of drinking corresponds roughly to the highest occurrence of antisocial criminal violent behavior which is, as we know, from age eighteen to thirty-four. The significance of this is probably self-evident. Homicide and violent behavior usually take place among people of a similar age bracket and often among people who have been using alcohol to excess within a home or in and outside of a tavern.

The Italian criminologist, Di Tullio,[319] considered chronic alcoholism to be part of a constitutional habitus of the delinquent individual. Schneider,[320] on the other hand, believed it to be a part of the psychopathic personality. Interestingly, Wolfgang[275] reported that in a group of 364 homicide cases the blood alcohol level was elevated in 75 percent of the victims and/or victimizer. This seems to agree with Di Tullio's assertion that there is a typical alcoholic personality with profound alteration of mood, affectivity, emotionality, impulsivity and a tendency to violent and histrionic manifestations of behavior, with frequent moral debasement and social dysfunctioning.

Alcohol can unleash repressed destructive hostility as in the following case.

A forty-two year old, somewhat obese, white male with a history of rebellious behavior, alcohol imbibition, and drug experimentation as an adolescent, was examined by me for competency to stand trial. Frequent rows with his father had led him to move out of his parents' home at age eighteen. He had only worked sporadically. He drank alcoholic beverages excessively, and used drugs, mostly marijuana and LSD. At age twenty-three he was diagnosed as suffering from a psychotic condition for which he was prescribed antipsychotic medication. For long periods of time he did not take his medication but continued to drink alcohol to excess. He lived on the street and his existence was marginal. One day during winter, while it was snowing heavily, he went to his mother's home. She let him in and even though she made him a sandwich she refused him permission to stay in the house for a few days. He was extremely resentful and thought of killing her came to his mind. He went to the basement and drank some whiskey. In the basement, he got some shells for his father's shotgun (his father had died), took the gun from the closet, loaded it, and approached his mother, saying, "Is this the way you wanted it?" He remembered that his mother said to him, "You wouldn't want to kill your mother." He fired one of the four shells and killed her. He then went to his sister's house and told his brother-in-law what he had done. One hour later he was arrested. The offender was a chronic paranoid schizophrenic who felt unwanted and looked down upon by his mother with whom he had an ambivalent relationship. He is currently awaiting trial on charges of first degree intentional homicide.

Just as alcohol may unleash aggression in those persons with a tendency to violent behavior, it may also produce a helpless type of behavior on the part of the victim, often the aggressor's drinking companion.

A recent study by Cook and Winnekour[321] states that chronic use of alcohol may bring about dysfunction of expected social roles, family violence, loss of job, abuse and/or neglect on the part of the alcoholist. They also believe that there is evidence for genetic heritability of alcoholism, and believe that genetic factors must be included as contributing factors in the dysfunctions in families burdened with alcoholism. It is also their belief that having a biological member of the family suffering from alcoholism is a socially predisposing factor to alcoholism.

There is no doubt that when taking a personal and family history of the alcoholics who come to our attention because of their violent behavior we are often confronted by the fact that very often at least one of the parents of these offenders, and often some of the offender's siblings, has been an alcoholic. It is difficult to dismiss the possibility that in addition to environmental and family factors, genetic-biological ones may play a predisposing role in the development of the addiction and the behavior of these individuals.

Schuckit,[322] in an editorial in the American Journal of Psychiatry in 1994, stated that "data supporting a genetic basis for alcoholism are as strong as the data supporting a genetic basis for any other psychiatric disorder in which inheritance is complex and multifactorial . . . and an important part of the variance is probably explained by the environment." Biological and genetic data also appear to be contributory factors in the genesis of violent behavior. Therefore, it can be presumed that alcohol, in order to contribute to violent behavior, must act upon individuals whose psychopathology already predisposes them to violence.

The accepted notion that alcohol intoxication induces aggressivity, or, better, that it allows dormant aggressive tendencies to come to light, is supported by a laboratory experiment on mice done by Callieri and Greco.[323] In their study, mice were isolated in individual cages for a period of three or four weeks. Subsequently, one group of two mice was intubated gastroesophageally with 0.5 cc. of a 10% Ringer's solution and placed in a separate cage. Another group of two mice was ingested with alcohol to intoxicated levels, and also placed in a separate cage. While both groups engaged in fighting, the intoxicated mice showed a shorter latency period for, and a longer period of, aggression. At the same time, their capacity for orientation and exploration, already reduced by isolation, was made worse by the alcohol.

Could this experiment on mice be applied to human behavior? There is no doubt that isolation in humans may create an aggressive attitude and disorientation, leading, at times, to a psychotic break. Assuming that people showing explosive violent behavior are basically shy, withdrawn and have difficulty in relating to others, and frequently are unable to contain their negative emotions, it can be theorized that alcohol ingestion could progressively disinhibit them in accordance with the alcohol blood level reached, allowing the manifestation of their hostility.

Ethnicity should be taken into consideration when assessing alcoholism and crimes of violence against persons. In 1991, Helzer and Burnham[312] in an epidemiological study of alcohol addiction in the United States, reported that the rates of alcoholism among white males in the eighteen to twenty-nine year age bracket is more than twice the rate among blacks of the same age group. However, they reported that blacks start increasing their alcohol intake from age thirty to forty-five, and when they are between forty-five to sixty-five years old they drink more than whites. After age sixty-five, they found the rate of alcohol addiction to be twice as high in blacks when compared to whites. Black and white women usually follow the same pattern as their respective male groups. Present-day younger offenders often use alcohol concomitantly with the use of cocaine. Actually, alcohol is used to "come down" from a cocaine high, as many inmates state.

Helzer and Burnham, in their above mentioned study, report that one out of every seven persons meets the criteria for alcoholism. They state that it is predominantly a male disorder with a male to female ratio of over five to one, and that the life prevalence for men is 23.8 percent while that for women is 4.6 percent. The fact that the rate of alcoholism in younger whites (eighteen to twenty-nine year age bracket) is twice as high as that for blacks, while the presence of violent crimes of African-American alcoholics is usually higher than that of whites, seems to point to different causative factors in black offenders. Indiscriminate violence is never justifiable, but it may be partially explained by the many frustrations that are encountered more by blacks than whites in their daily lives, to the degree of hopelessness that they envision for their future, and to a deep sense of futility.

A review of an epidemiological study of alcohol addiction and its damaging effect on the liver in the United States and in nineteen European countries, not including Russia, may be used to compare the alcohol intake and the rate of crime at an international level. The study reveals that crime against persons is much higher in the United States than in France, Portugal and Italy, even though the alcohol consumption in the United States is approximately one-third that of France, and slightly less than that of Portugal and Italy.[312]

The study comparing twenty-five European countries to the United States for the period between 1960 and 1973, reveals that during that period of time, the alcohol consumption in liters of absolute alcohol per capita for those age fifteen and older increased in most European nations with the exception of France and Italy which showed slight decreases. In the United States, the percentage of consumption was 7.8 percent in 1960, and had grown to 10.6 percent in 1973.[312]

A recent statistic concerning the pro-capita consumption of alcohol among the population of the European community (alcohol 100% in liters pro-capita), and comparing 1970 with 1989, reveals that alcohol consumption is decreasing in Belgium, Denmark, France, Ireland, Italy and Spain, while it is increasing in the United Kingdom, (the former) West Germany, Portugal, Greece and Belgium. Alcohol consumption in Russia, in 1989, was three and one-half times higher than the level of 1965, with a total of 4,528,000 intoxicated persons requiring institutional care. Alcohol consumption in Russia currently seems to have stabilized at a high level. However, it appears from a recent report that the constrictions placed on alcohol consumption have brought about the widespread use of illicit drugs.[324]

More recent studies show that in France, from 1970 to 1989, the pro capita alcohol use continued to diminish, falling from 17.3 liters to 13.2 liters. Italy showed a similar diminution, with 16 liters pro capita in 1970 and 9.7 liters in 1989. It is well known that southern European countries use more wine than hard liquor, and their alcohol ingestion is well integrated in their cultural way of life, to the point that, notwithstanding occasional violence associated with alcohol intoxication, drinking in southern European countries does not bring about the amount of violence seen in the United States or northern European countries.[325]

What are the metabolic and biochemical effects of alcohol on the central nervous system? Alcohol is apparently involved in the activation of noradrenergic neurons, blocks the release of acetylcholine at the presynaptic cleft, modifies the cerebral metabolism of serotonin and possibly increases GABA—gaba amino butiric acid—in the brain. It is well known to cross the hemato-encephalic barrier in the nervous system rapidly, thus creating the various manifestations of alcohol intoxication.

Even though alcohol belongs to the group of sedatives, anxiolitics and hypnotics, when its ingestion reaches high levels there is, in some people predisposed to it, a disinhibition of behavior, with violent aggression. Excessive alcohol ingestion may lead to well defined psychiatric syndromes such as acute alcoholic intoxication, alcohol hallucinosis and paranoid delusional syndromes. In addition, some individuals may have a so-called idiosyncratic alcohol intoxication even though they ingested only small quantities of alcoholic beverages.

The following case illustrates alcohol idiosyncratic intoxication:

A sixty-two year old black male, a quiet law-abiding citizen, had recently retired from his job with the county government. His life was peaceful and his relationship with his family and neighbors was good. On a hot Sunday afternoon, he drank two bottles of beer over a period of two hours. Suddenly, bothered by the noise that his young neighbors were making, this peaceful man became agitated, went to his room, loaded his shotgun, and came out of his house shooting in an aimless way. He was restrained shortly afterwards and taken to jail. The offender had no recollection of his acting out when he awoke the following morning in the county jail. He was released, tried on a disorderly conduct charge and found guilty of the offense. He was placed on probation.

Alcohol idiosyncratic intoxication is marked by sudden behavioral changes, usually aggression against persons, due to the recent ingestion of an amount of alcohol insufficient to induce intoxication in most people. The behavior of the offender is out of character with his longitudinal personality which is devoid of any previous manifestation of violence. The individual is often reported as being shy, retiring, mild mannered, and not used to drinking. During these periods of sudden intoxication, even though the amount of alcohol ingested is minimal, these individuals may commit serious crimes, even murder. There is complete amnesia for the episode once the effects of the alcohol have disappeared. At the basis of this kind of idiosyncratic and explosive type of behavior there are, at times, temporal lobe dysfunctions or brain damage due to previous brain trauma or antecedent encephalopathies.[326] Some people have called into discussion as causative factors in this unusual syndrome unusual fatigue, debilitating illnesses and advanced age.

"The theory of paradoxical rage is part of a discourse about organisms with brains, enzymes and physical chemical reactions. The theory of appropriate behavior is part of a discourse about persons with minds, intentions, and motivated actions. In the discourse about organisms, the self disappears and paradoxical rage is caused by the chemical release of the inhibitory neural system. . . . The self is the agent who chooses, who intends to kill, and who assumes a firing position and pulls the trigger."[318] p.5

The second syndrome, alcohol hallucinosis, may manifest itself as sudden unexpected violent behavior. This syndrome shows vivid and persistent hallucinations that develop shortly after the cessation or reduction of alcoholic ingestion, usually within forty-eight hours, by a person who apparently suffers from alcohol dependence. The hallucinations are usually auditory or visual; they may be unpleasant or benign. The voices are usually unformed sounds or buzzing as in any organic hallucinations. The individual affected with alcohol hallucinosis may see his symptoms abate within weeks, but at times they may last for months, or they may change to ideas of reference or to poorly systematized persecutory ideas. During the acute phase of alcohol hallucinosis, the individual, attempting to avoid the frightening visual imagery or threatening voices may harm others or himself. In the following case the hallucinations were both auditory and visual, but the visual hallucinations appeared to be much stronger and were the ones that determined the patient's sudden and unexpected violent behavior.

> The patient was waiting to be examined by me in a psychiatric hospital. He had been drinking heavily the night before. He was about thirty feet away from me at the far end of a long corridor when I invited him to come into my office. As soon as he saw me, he impulsively ran towards me in a threatening manner. The attendants present were able to restrain him. He told me that he thought I was a bat and he was trying to catch it because voices were telling him to do so. He was obviously hallucinating. A few days later, when sober, his hallucinations, due to alcohol intoxication, had disappeared.

The organic delusional syndrome, as the name implies, has prominent delusions, the character of which varies in quality and intensity depending on the etiology and on the personal psychopathology of the individual. Mild cognitive impairment is observed at times but is not long lasting. The delusional organic syndrome may be so close to the delusional (paranoid) disorder that it may be difficult to differentiate unless a previous history of alcohol or drug addiction is available. One often finds a person who, under the effect of alcohol, develops a delusional paranoid disorder with persistent non-bizarre delusions not attributable to any other mental illness, but part and parcel of a long-standing addiction to alcohol which has also acted upon an idiosyncratic pre-morbid psychopathology. They are most commonly reported as persecutory in type, as in the case cited below.

> This forty-five year old white male, a chronic alcoholic, had experienced delirium tremens on many occasions and lived a marginal existence as a homeless individual. Even though he had incipient cirrhosis of the liver, he continued his drinking of low-quality alcoholic beverages. He was frequently apprehended by the police because of drunkenness and extreme litigiosity. He believed that there was a plot to take his money, which he obviously did not have, and to kill him, because people wanted to steal his new scientific discoveries from him. The defendant came to my attention because during one of his struggles with an unknown enemy he violently attacked and manhandled another homeless man. His ideas of persecution and grandiosity were the consequence of his long alcoholic imbibition and poor physical condition. He was civilly committed to a mental institution because he was unable to care for himself.

Another facilitator of violent behavior is the use and abuse of illicit drugs, or those drugs whose social use is proscribed by law. Various psychoactive drugs have been involved in dependence and abuse. Opium and opioids, cocaine and marijuana, amphetamines, phencyclidine, peyote, LSD, and others, have been part of a drug culture supported by philosophical and social views which often stressed extreme libertarianism and, at the same time, fostered the rejection of an authoritarian society. The use and abuse of illicit drugs has brought about the theory of "victimless crime" in which the one being killed is the user of the drug.

The most commonly abused drug in the United States, and apparently in most of the Western world is, at the present time, cocaine, seemingly having supplanted heroin. The intravenous use of cocaine is reported to be responsible for spreading HIV infections among drug users, mostly because of needle sharing. The abuse of heroin and cocaine in Europe is more prevalent in the South than in the North, even though there are sacs of drug abuse and extreme dependency present in the Netherlands and in Switzerland. Recently, it has been reported that the use of illicit drugs is rapidly spreading throughout Russia and the other republics of the former Soviet Union.

Recently, the National Institute on Drug Abuse (NIDA) conducted a survey of American drug use and found that "21 million Americans had used cocaine in their lives; 8 million had used it in the past three years; 3 million were current users; but only 300,000 use cocaine daily or nearly every day. Government statistics thus show that 10 percent of current users and 1 percent of lifetime users use the drug close to daily."[327]

The use of cocaine seems to be an integral part of the vast number of violent offenses of a felonious type, and cases of sporadic violence have been reported among LSD and phencyclidine users. In fact, any discussion of the factors at the basis of violence can not be considered complete without the inclusion of those antisocial violent behaviors following the ingestion and the effect of cocaine. In a forensic practice it is a common occurrence to have to examine those defendants who have used cocaine. They come to our attention because of aggressive behavior. At times they are also suffering from schizophrenia, depression, minimal brain disorder, hyperkinesia or bipolar illness for which they are usually prescribed medication. They are, however, often attempting to medicate their emotional/mental problems by themselves with the use of cocaine. They usually qualify for a dual diagnosis: their primary mental illness and their alcohol or drug addiction.

Cocaine abuse has achieved epidemic proportions in our country and because of the concomitant aggressive conduct of the abusers it greatly contributes to the wave of violence in our streets and homes. The symptomatology of cocaine abuse may escalate from irritability to agitation and to aggressiveness. When it reaches the level of aggressiveness, even though the violence that may ensue is usually short-lived, the disruption that follows is, at times, undescribable.

An example of that violence is the case of a 30 year old individual who entered a tavern in the early hours of New Years' Day, 1992, and, high on cocaine, behaved in an abusive way toward the female manager of the premises and was rebuked for his bully-like behavior by some male patrons who were peacefully drinking at the bar. He then left in an angry mood and returned a few minutes later with a machine gun with which he sprayed the bar-room, killing three people and wounding one. He was later apprehended and found guilty of first degree intentional homicide. His abuse of cocaine had certainly contributed to the unleashing of what may be called an intermittent explosive disorder!

The *DSM-IV*,[241] under the heading psychoactive substance use disorders, includes psychoactive substance dependence and psychoactive substance abuse. In order to qualify for the diagnosis of psychoactive substance dependence, the individual must show, over a twelve month period, three or more manifestations including showing a tolerance for the substance or exhibiting the symptoms of withdrawal. The substance may be taken in larger amounts and for a longer period than the abuser intended. Even though the user may have a continuing desire to control its use, he or she is often unsuccessful. The procurement, use and recovery from its use may take up a great deal of the abuser's time, often impinging on other activities. The abusers also continue the use of the substance even though they have physical or psychological problems because of it. Psychoactive substance abuse, instead, is diagnosed when the individual exhibits, within a twelve month period, one or more manifestations consisting in "a failure to fulfill major role obligations at work, school, or home . . . ,"[241,112] recurrent use of the substance in physically dangerous situations, or even though having had legal problems related to its use, or the continued use of the substance in spite of persistent or recurring social or interpersonal problems caused by its use.

Most of the research studies and clinical observations support the idea that the use of cocaine, usually in the form of snorting, smoking or injecting, is followed by a progression of clinical syndromes: euphoria, depression, or dysphoria, paranoid reaction, and eventually psychosis. The feeling of euphoria, or being "high" is not long lasting (only minutes at times) and thus encourages the repetitive use which may become chronic. It is accepted that the dosage and the chronic use of the drug are primary factors for the development of the above manifestations.[328]

Cocaine is a potent psychomotor stimulant in humans. It generates general hyperactivity and behavior characterized by meticulous and repetitious arrangement of objects. Cocaine has demonstrated itself to be a potent inhibitor of monoamine reuptake at the synapse but without any significant antidepressant activity.[329] Post[327] stated that the user, paranoid, usually has a clear sensorium and is neither confused nor disoriented. He or she may develop stereotyped, compulsive behavior and addicts may repetitively pursue the same actions. Genetic or pre-morbid psychopathology may be important co-factors. Addicts who have recovered from a previous delusional disorder due to cocaine usually have a clear recollection of their paranoid ideation and hallucinatory experiences. It should not be forgotten that cocaine abusers may be self-medicating a psychiatric disorder, and a dual diagnosis may be indicated.[330]

A kindling, or arousal phenomenon, facilitated by cocaine, as well as by amphetamines has been extensively and magisterly researched. It is at the level of the limbic system, a system of sub-cortical structures including the amygdala, the hippocampus, and septal regions, that kindling, or the limbic ictus, originates. These anatomical structures are not only involved in the limbic ictus, also known as episodic dyscontrol, but also may be at the basis of psychotic symptomatology or atypical psychosis, a transient behavior of a confused type.[331] Episodic neurophysiological dysfunction of the limbic system, generally of short duration, may also be involved in schizophrenic reactions. Continuous or intermittent stimulation of the amygdala in laboratory animals produces either rapid neuronal exhaustion or a kindling effect.[326]

Research on cocaine has pointed to a basic dysfunction of neurotransmitters. It blocks the synaptic reuptake of norepinephrine (NE), dopamine (DA), and its action on serotonin (5-HT) neurons is largely inhibitory. Some studies have suggested that repetitious administration of even small doses of cocaine produces an increased sensitivity over time and creates a so-called reverse tolerance thus potentiating the effect of catecholamines at the synapses.[332]

Post[327] and Resnick[333] (1984) both state that cocaine may produce a variety of psychiatric syndromes. The behavioral progressive manifestations of cocaine users usually progress in the following manner: (0) No suspiciousness (1) Irritated seclusive behavior (2) Guarded fearful behavior (3) Focused suspicion—unfounded fears; moderate hostility (4) Focused paranoid ideation (5) Overt psychosis.[334] At times cocaine induced paranoia and hallucinations may lead to violent behavior—homicidal or suicidal. Typically, shortly after using cocaine, the user suddenly becomes paranoid. Hyperexcitability and bizarre behavior is usually present. In a study reported by Spitz and Rosegan[335] 57 percent of the users experienced psychiatric symptoms marked by irritability, socially disruptive behavior, omnipotent feelings, paranoid ideas, and hallucinations. "We know from animal experiments that serotonin turnover is significant for some aspects of aggressive behavior. It is possible by inhibiting the synthesis of serotonin to transfer tame domestic cats into raging wild animals or cause rats which are nursing their offspring to bite the young to death."[336]

In a group of mostly male patients studied by Jeri[337] in a Peruvian hospital who were coca paste smokers, most were found to have developed paranoid thoughts and hallucinations. A 1990 study[330] of a group comprising 120 cocaine addicts reported that ten (8.33%) of the patents exhibited fleeting, unformed, organic delusions and hallucinations. The auditory hallucinations were described as whispering voices or unintelligible words, while the delusions were usually of a persecutory type.

In another study, Climent[338] described the major symptoms as irritability, paranoia, hostility, hallucinations and suicidal ideation. Washton and Tatarsky[339] reported that more than 60 percent of their group exhibited paranoid feelings. Post and Kopanda[340] stated, "When cocaine is abused chronically, a paranoid psychosis...can result. After acute intravenous cocaine administration the development of a paranoid psychotic state (referred to by users as the bull horrors because of the intense fear of police) can occur....After chronic cocaine administration delusions of persecution may be vague....Suspiciousness normally follows long term use."

Some historical notes regarding cocaine use may be of interest to the reader. The history of this plant goes back to the ninth century B.C., during the Pre-Inca Yunga period, when it was used by priests during celebrations to the god Khunu. Legend tells us that coca was the gift of the sun god to his son, Manco Capac, first emperor of the Incas. It was with the Spanish conquest of Peru and the Inca Empire in the sixteenth century that the "divine plant," Erythroxylon Coca, was brought to the attention of the West when the Jesuit, Thomas Orter, in 1499, first divulged information regarding the use of coca leaves. Pedro Cieza de Leon, in 1550, in the "Cronaca del Peru," also described the plant and its use and the Jesuit, Jose de Acosta, described its pharmacological properties in his "Natural History of the Indies" in 1590.

In 1567, the Spanish Inquisition in Lima, Peru, prohibited the use of coca because it was believed to be a substance without usefulness, only able to promote the superstitions of the Indios and their relationship with the devil. The Inquisition was concerned about the dangerously spreading use of the drug among European immigrants and the superstitious Indios.[341]

The isolation of cocaine, the alkaloid derived from the leaves of Erythroxylon Coca, is usually attributed to the chemist Gaedecke in 1855, although some sources name the Austrian chemist Albert Niemann as a discoverer between 1858–60. In 1864, Schraff stated that pure cocaine applied to the tongue would anesthetize it and in 1868 Tomas Moreno y Maiz, a Peruvian doctor, after experimenting on frogs, proposed the use of cocaine as a local anesthetic. Bently, in the U.S.A., used cocaine in the weaning off from morphine of soldiers during the Civil War.[342] An Italian physician, Mantegazza, pioneered the scientific study of coca and, already in 1859, had extensively written on "The Hygienic and Medicinal Virtues of Coca."[343] He was so convinced of its virtues that he stated, "God is unjust because he made man unable to withstand the continuous use of this drug." Mantegazza's unquestioning acceptance of coca was well conveyed in his statement, "I would prefer to live only ten years, 'coqueando' than a billion years without it."

In 1860, Mariani wine, medicated with coca, appeared on the scene, and the Corsican Angelo Mariani was acclaimed as a benefactor of humanity. Stewart reported, in 1885, that Dr. Louis Lewis, in 1876, in Philadelphia, had used coca cigarettes for his patients who had throat affections, and Stewart, himself, used coca cigars in patients with hayfever. He noticed both stimulant and anti-depressant effects.

In 1885, John S. Pemberton first introduced "french wine coca" and later a new patent medicine containing cocaine, advertised as a brain tonic and cure for all nervous affections. In 1884, Ashenbrandt, a German army physician, secured a supply of pure cocaine from the pharmaceutical firm Merck, and gave it to Bavarian soldiers, reporting that it decreased fatigue.

Freud read Aschenbrandt's report and wrote to his fiancée that he had tried cocaine on himself and it had changed his bad mood into cheerfulness. The July 1884, issue of the *Centralblatt für die Gesammte Therapie* published an essay by Freud on cocaine, "Über Coca," which introduced and propagandized the apparently good effects of cocaine for many conditions, among which were gastric disturbances and asthma. He also suggested its use as a local anesthetic, and, most of all, as a mood stimulant.[344]

Upon Freud's suggestion, his friend, von Fleischl-Marxow, a physician, took increasing doses of cocaine to wean himself from the morphine habit he had acquired; he developed cocaine psychosis, a syndrome which resembled acute paranoid schizophrenia. In July 1885, Erlenmayer, a German authority on morphine addiction, launched the first of a series of attacks on cocaine as an addicting drug. In January 1886, Freud's friend, Obersteiner, who had at first favored cocaine, reported that it produced severe mental disturbances. Freud continued to praise cocaine as late as July 1887, when he published a final defense of the drug.[345] Indeed, in 1886, following the accidental death of a few physicians and patients who were using cocaine, he was accused, by the medical faculty of the University of Vienna, of being unable to control the "third scourge of humanity." However, " . . . the Freud-Fliess letters clearly established that Freud took cocaine . . . in the early and mid-1890s. . . . [and] there is also evidence that [he] continued to use cocaine after 1895."[346]

During the first decade of the twentieth century, cocaine was present and sold in drug stores in a great number of different products. The market offered many different drinks which contained coca: Kos-Kola, Kola-Aid, Vani-Kola, Rocokola. Authors such as Arthur Conan Doyle, the father of Sherlock Holmes, had the famous detective snort cocaine.[347] Even Charlie Chaplin in a scene of his 1936 film "Modern Times" snorts a white powdery substance in order to get strength.

It was only in 1914, with the Harrison Narcotics Act, that cocaine was defined as a very dangerous drug, and because of federal and state pressure, cocaine went underground until the 1970's. In 1954, the American Commission on Narcotics had stated that cocaine use had sharply declined but just one year later there was again a sharp rise in its use. After World War II, the world witnessed a brief intermezzo with synthetic amphetamines whose effect was similar to cocaine but whose price was very low. This reached epidemic proportions, and Japan, Sweden, and the U.S.A. were swept by it. While the late 1960's witnessed the proscription of amphetamines, during the 1970's cocaine production from Bolivia, Peru, Colombia, and Ecuador began invading European and American markets. At present, cocaine is used by all classes of society.

The cocaine-induced organic mental disorders are well known to the practicing forensic professional. Among the various manifestations, such as hypervigilance and psychomotor agitation, extreme irritability, perceptual dysfunction or conceptual distortion and impaired judgement, we often witness in the cocaine abuser a crescendo of rage-aggressiveness and violence. At times, as I described previously, one encounters among persons acutely intoxicated by cocaine paranoid behavior in a well defined clinical syndrome which does not abate even upon abstinence from the drug. Even though the type of delusional thoughts are described as grandiose, erotomanic, somatic, jealous, persecutory, or unspecified, in my experience, among the various subtypes, the individual who is classified as delusional paranoid disorder, jealous or persecutory in type, is more inclined to violent behavior. The aggression/violence of these individuals, which is due to their delusional ideas, is not limited to their homes, often going beyond them and disrupting the normal process of community life.

In a study supporting aggressivity in cocaine addicts, Honer, Gerwitz, and Turey[348] reported that the users of crack cocaine exhibited threatening behavior towards others in 36 percent of the cases, while irritability was present in 11 percent, and agitation in 19 percent. A study of 272 defendants examined for competency evaluations found that the category of antisocial personality disorder with cocaine addiction was 23.53 percent, and that their offenses were basically of an aggressive-violent type.[131]

A survey by Gold, Washton and Dacks reported that 80 percent of callers to an 800-cocaine hotline said that one of the manifestations of their cocaine abuse was irritability[349] which is a stage prior to aggressiveness. Even though any certain explanation of how cocaine may unleash aggressiveness has not yet been established, the possible underlying disregulation of brain neuro-transmitters, as mentioned previously, seems quite promising and interesting.

It appears that cocaine blocks the reuptake of dopamine and norepinephrine and diminishes the serotonin level at the synaptic cleft. Eichelman[350] demonstrated in animal research studies that an increase of the metabolic turnover of dopamine and norepinephrine coupled with lower levels of serotonin is associated with progressive agitation and aggressive activities. And as stated by Yudofski and collaborators in their recent paper, "[T]here are correlations between violent behavior and increased cathecolamine turnover or decreased serotoninergic activity in the brain."[351] p.219

As stated in the discussion of biological factors in violence, Linnoila[352] and collaborators found low CSF levels of 5-HIAA (5-hydroxyindoleacitic acid) a metabolite of serotonin (5-HT) in people with impulsive and aggressive behavior. In 1977, Taylor and Ho[353] established that repeated doses of cocaine decrease (5-HT) serotonin and its metabolite (5-HIAA). That low levels of serotonin and its metabolite in the brain may be linked to impulsive and self-directed violent behavior with firearms was reported already in 1982 by Brown and collaborators,[354] and, more recently, by Stanley, Mann, and Cohen[355] in 1986. Goeders and Smith[356] have established that cocaine acts mostly on mesolimbic and mesocortical areas of the brain which were already recognized by Elliott[357] in 1987 as anatomical sites for the control of aggressive-violent behavior.

In 1982, Post and collaborators[358] postulated that Carbamazepin, a drug primarily used for its antiepileptic activity, may be useful in controlling limbic dyscontrol or excessive firing which manifest themselves with irritability and aggression in cocaine abusers.

Persons affected by schizophrenia, epilepsy or organic diseases of the brain, or states of primary hyperprolacteminia, who concomitantly use cocaine may be more prone to violent outbursts due to low serotonin levels or an upsurge of activity of dopamine, already high in these cases, in the limbic areas, especially the amygdala.

It is well known that the frequently encountered person classified as antisocial personality, who is already, per se, more prone to aggression, probably because of a low level of serotonin and high levels of norepinephrine, is more inclined to react violently under the effect of cocaine because the above neurotransmitter parameters are further altered. We could also speculate that a depressed individual who carries a low serotonin level in his or her cerebral spinal fluid (CSF) further decreases it when smoking or injecting cocaine, and, as a result, may impulsively act out against himself or others even to the point of suicide or homicide.

The problem of drug or alcohol related violent behavior is frequent and serious in our society. Personal, constitutional and socio-economic factors may predispose an individual to the abuse of behavior altering substances. At present, researchers are also searching for possible genetic predispositions for this type of abuse. The disregulation of brain endorphin, disregulation and/or dysfunction of brain receptors of substances that modulate human behavior, are also being investigated as possible causative factors in illicit drug use.

Other illicit street drugs may also produce belligerent, assaultive, impulsive and unpredictable behavior. One of these is phencyclidine (PCP), another is lysergic acid diethylamide (LSD), which, in addition to its hallucinogenic properties, also creates an organic delusional syndrome or an organic mood disorder. It is reasonable to assume that any of the above reactions to the abuse of alcohol, cocaine, PCP, or LSD, may trigger violent behavior, especially in individuals already predisposed to violence because of their intrapersonal or interpersonal conflicts. Their wishful escape into the nirvana of alcohol or illicit drugs is then the precipitating factor of their often destructive antisocial behavior.

Wilson and Herrnstein[229] emphasized, as well, that many young people who use drugs or alcohol to excess are predisposed to aggressive and impulsive behavior, and the effect of the psychoactive substance may increase, at least in some cases, their already high probability of deviant behavior.

Alcohol and illicit drug use and abuse, especially that of cocaine, are, at present, the most important and widespread used facilitators of violence against persons and property. They are so frequently used that they are often thought to be the prime cause of violent behavior. Violent behavior is, instead, the outcome of more profound psychopathology and of willful behavior.

Chapter Eleven

GUNS AND OTHER VARIABLES

The press and other media are frequently hosts to essays and debates on the issue of the too easy availability of guns in our society and their increasing use by violent people. A recent article[359] stated that motor vehicle accidents and gunshots account for more than 50 percent of injury-related deaths in the United States. The number of deaths by guns is steadily increasing, and while 43,536 people died from crash-related injuries in 1991, 38,317 persons died from gunshot wounds during the same period. Motor vehicle related deaths declined 10 percent from 1985 to 1991, at the same time that the number of deaths by firearms increased 14 percent. The trend was even more pronounced among fifteen to twenty-four-year-olds whose reported motor vehicle related deaths rose 18 percent, while deaths from gunshots rose 40 percent.

Guns are relatively inexpensive and can be purchased by most people regardless of age or socio-economic status. Several young offenders have told me that they can even be rented on the streets. The use of guns, and even of machine-guns, is spreading fear among our citizens and creating mayhem in many minority neighborhoods. Juveniles, age twelve to eighteen, are highly represented among the users of guns and the perpetrators of murder. "Twenty-two percent of 758 boys at 10 inner city high schools reported owning a gun in 1991, and 12 percent said they carried weapons routinely . . . "[360] The murders they commit are often part of gang violence, or they may be purposeless as in the frightening drive-by shootings. Surgeon General Jocelyn Elders recently stated that fourteen children a day are killed by guns and that violent acts killed 50,000 people in 1992.[168] This has reached epidemic proportions creating fear and insecurity in people who are often afraid even at home. Federal Centers for Disease Control and Prevention concluded that gunshot wounds are the leading cause of death for black teen-age boys and the fifth leading cause of death for all children under age fourteen. The American Medical Association, becoming increasingly aware of this situation, is insistently making the case that the nation faces a new type of epidemic.[168]

Whether this happens because of boredom, a search for kicks, or rebellion against society, is often difficult to assess. The facts are that we are witnessing a teen-age generation that is growing up both dangerous and frightened, and one that does not have the supporting influence and mentorship of its families, and that is often uninvolved with the educational system, or in the strengthening competition of the work place. These are urban youngsters who feel rejected by the mainstream society and who believe that they are excluded, marginalized, and often looked down upon as deviants. These are the adolescents and young adults who, in self-defense, assume a tough guy attitude that spreads death by means of their armed hand.

It is a fact that guns are the most commonly used weapon in violent crime, either within the home or on the streets. But it is not a fact that guns per se are the direct cause of crime. I wish to argue the point that guns are just one of the many facilitators of crime, even though the most lethal one.

The prehensile capability of the human hand has greatly facilitated humankind's adaptation and survival through the centuries. Actually, the human hand has allowed the expression of the highest creative thought, producing literary and artistic masterpieces. It has designed and built homes, schools, and cities and has laid down programs for the benefit of society. A hand is useful in caring for the young and the old, at the moment of birth and at the moment of death. However, an open hand is also used to slap or clenched to express hostile gestures or aggressive intentions.

Throughout the centuries the hand has been used to hold knives, swords, daggers, and to light cannons. This has happened during the innumerable wars that humankind has gone through. Even today, in an apparently historical peaceful period, some of our communities are at risk of becoming war zones: areas of undeclared war where there are no real enemies if not the explosive behavior of a relative, a friend, a neighbor or a passer-by.

The direct relationship often proposed between guns and violence does not take into consideration the most important factor: the perpetrator of the violent act, the one who pulls the trigger. Hostility often makes the individual reach for an easily accessible weapon, and at the present time that weapon is usually a gun, which can best be viewed as an extension of the human hand. It is reasonable, then, to assume that the aggressive violent person pulls the trigger of the gun because of the hostile thoughts generated in his or her mind.

I personally am in favor of sound legislation for gun control, since I believe that guns, while not the direct cause, are, nevertheless, the most important facilitators of lethal crime, even though some skepticism has been expressed by critics who don't believe that gun control would keep guns away from criminals or from adolescents. This seems to be supported by a recent report from the National Institute of Justice and the Office of Juvenile Justice and Delinquency Prevention stating that controls imposed at the point of gun sale would probably be ineffective in preventing the acquisition of guns by juveniles because they rarely get their guns through such customary outlets.[360] Polsby[361] also argues the point, claiming that young criminals, even with gun control, will have no difficulty in obtaining guns, and stating that firearms are not the root of the problem of violence.

In support of this assumption Switzerland offers us a human statistical laboratory. In Switzerland gun ownership is mandatory and a community duty, not a matter of individual free choice.[362] Switzerland has a very low rate of juvenile delinquency[229] and a relatively low rate of crime in general.[110] This low rate is, however, connected with a more authoritarian culture, less mobility in a homogeneous society, more parental authority, and a lack of social unrest.

How different from many of our communities at risk and from the many dysfunctional families of our society! A good functioning family, where personal and social responsibility is stressed and culture promotes virtues, does not usually breed violence.

There is a certain insanity in our gun culture, and, unfortunately, even though people talk about it a great deal many of them look elsewhere instead of addressing the problem at its roots. They look at the Middle East or at the crises in Africa, at the fact that job losses might in the future ignite white crimes, or that we need more police officers. We do need more and better trained police officers, and also more and better trained parole officers, to handle the high rate of recidivism in our criminals. However, these measures still do not tackle the problem at its roots. Unfortunately, there are 4.5 million people under correctional supervision in the United States, approximately 3,375,000 of whom are not imprisoned but on parole and living free on the streets.[363]

Juvenile violence has become a public health problem. Many young people seem to have made a routine life of violence. Their crimes become more and more violent and their age group younger and younger. Their criminal activities are extending further into the community at large.

The United States Department of Justice[364] tabulated the type of weapon or method used in homicides in 1988 in thirty-three of the seventy-five most populous counties in the United States. Among the firearms, fifty percent of the weapons used were handguns, 5 percent were shotguns and 4 percent were rifles. Other methods used were knives (21%), blunt instruments (5%), and strangulation (3%).

The same report also showed the male victims to have been killed by handguns in 54 percent of the cases, by knife in 21 percent of the cases, by shotgun in 5 percent of the cases, and in 4 percent of the cases by rifles. The female victims, instead, were killed by handgun in 36 percent of the cases, by knife in 19 percent of the cases, and shotgun or rifle were each reported to have been used in 4 percent of the cases.

When race was taken into consideration, 55 percent of black victims were killed by handguns compared to 44 percent of the white victims; twenty-two percent of the blacks were murdered by knife compared to 21 percent of whites; and shotguns and rifles were both reported as being used in 4 percent of the cases for both groups. What is appalling and frightening is the number of juveniles (under age 18) arrested in 1993. When a population of 214,000,000 was scored, out of a total of 19,491 murders, 2,829 were attributed to arrested juveniles. Juveniles were also arrested for 5,369 out of 33,385 forcible rapes. Of a total of 434,918 cases of aggravated assault, 63,777 arrests of juveniles were made, and 40,439 juveniles were arrested out of a total of 153,456 robbery cases.

"Homicide is the second leading cause of death among Americans aged fifteen to twenty-five and more of our teen-aged boys die from gunshots now than any other crime."[365] If guns were not available people would not be less violent, but they would probably be less destructive. However, aggressive hostility is driving the murderous hand of people even with the use of knives, frequent in domestic violence within the home and outside of the home. Recently, a 20 year old youth was stabbed and his head smashed with a baseball bat. One of his victimizers was his ex-girlfriend and the other was a former friend.[366]

A statistical survey by the Office of Juvenile Justice and Delinquency Prevention[367] is revealing of the upsurge in violent behavior among youths. From 1965 to 1990, juveniles accounted for 17 percent of all violent crime arrests; further, juvenile arrests for murder increased by 85% between 1987 and 1991, and three of every sixteen juvenile murder arrests involved a victim under the age of eighteen in 1991.

Juvenile violence is peaking at high levels, and hand guns, or even AK-47s, are frequently used by these young people in the commission of their violent acts. The above reported statistics considering guns and homicides for the period from 1976 to 1991 revealed that between 1987 and 1991 juvenile arrests for weapon violations increased 62 percent. One out of five weapons arrests in 1991 was a juvenile arrest. Black youths were arrested for weapon-law violations at a rate triple that of white youths in 1991. They were victims of homicides at a rate six times higher than whites. Gangs are increasing and girls are beginning to join them, too.

The F.B.I. Uniform Crime Report[180] states that individuals armed with handguns committed 930,700 violent crimes in 1992, 50 percent higher than in 1991. Thirteen percent of violent crimes were committed by individuals with handguns in 1992, a 24 percent increase over a five year period. A 1991 report stated that the arrest rate for murder increased 145 percent among black juveniles over the preceding decade, growing 48 percent for white juveniles, and dropping 45 percent for other races.[222] A 79 percent increase in the number of juveniles committing murders with guns was reported during the period between 1980 and 1990. In 1990, nearly three out of every four young murderers used a firearm.[368]

Among the other variables/facilitators of crime in general and violent crime in particular we must consider unemployment. During the sixties and seventies, crime increased in the United States concomitantly with the rise in joblessness, and this was especially true in high risk neighborhoods. "Unemployment rates are typically highest among groups with the highest rates of delinquency . . . but the causal influence of unemployment on criminal behaviour remains disputed."[105 p.180] Wilson and Herrnstein[229] reviewed various studies regarding the association between unemployment and crime. They found that Gillespie,[369] in reviewing numerous studies done between 1959 and 1975 regarding the possible relationship between crime and unemployment, arrived at dubious results, as did studies of Orsagh and Witte.[370] The same skepticism about the possible relationship between the two was reported in a 1983 study by Freeman.[371] A logical conclusion is that while unemployment and crime are not cause and effect, there is a relationship between the two.

Theories have been proposed to explain this relationship, such as that which states that when factories, shops, and other commercial enterprises leave a neighborhood, usually for practical economic reasons, jobs are taken away from people residing in those areas and the rate of crime increases. When considering the effects of unemployment on homicide, the results of a study by Brenner[372] found that at its basis there is a possible association between the increase in the young male population at risk for violence and the increase in that group's unemployment. He postulated that there is a relationship between inflation and individual earnings and claimed that the important factor to consider is the ratio of the number of unemployed youths (ages sixteen to twenty-four) compared to the total number of unemployed persons: the higher the ratio of unemployed youths, the higher the rate of homicide.

Wilson and Herrnstein[229] also report a longitudinal study conducted by Witte[373] of 641 inmates released from prison in North Carolina which revealed that, in spite of the availability of jobs, many were rearrested. The results were contrary to a study from Maryland which supported the beneficial effects of employment on future violent behavior.[374] Therefore, one could deduce from the above that it is not the availability of jobs in themselves that has a positive effect on the conduct of former inmates, but rather factors idiosyncratic to the recidivists such as a lack of motivation to take advantage of jobs that are offered, or that, even though working, the former inmates may, nevertheless, continue their previous life of crime.

Allan and Stefensmeier[375] found a relationship between arrest rates for young juveniles who were unemployed in spite of job availability and for young adults who had low paying jobs or part time jobs. In both instances the arrest rates were higher.

Affluence may positively affect crime rates because it offers more opportunities, either for education, recreation (young people have less free time available) or employment, and because members of more affluent families are less likely to have to commit a crime in order to attain those material possessions that so many young people wish to obtain. It must be realized, however, that since affluence is relative, crime may continue to be present, usually motivated by envy, greed, and dissatisfaction, and at times, in cases of spousal violence, by jealousy. Crimes of violence may be committed within any type of socioeconomic group.

Another important variable thought to be a cause of crime and violence is intelligence. Wilson and Herrnstein[229] stated that in 1914, Goddard had stated that from 25 percent to 50 percent of prisoners at that time were "mentally defective and unable to manage their affairs with ordinary prudence."[p.152] These conclusions were questioned by Murchison, who, in his book, *Criminal Intelligence,* established that the test scores of "a sample of enlisted men during World War I were lower than those of prisoners in the federal penitentiary at Fort Leavenworth."[p.152] Sutherland also considered Goddard's conclusions to be flawed, and supported the idea that criminals cannot be distinguished from law abiding persons on the basis of their intelligence tests.

In 1987, Robertson and collaborators,[376] in addressing the question of whether violence has cognitive correlates, came to the conclusion, as had a previous study of Spellacy,[377] that general intelligence "may be related to a predisposition to violent behavior but to a more modest degree than that indicated by earlier studies...[and that] no pattern emerged to implicate either hemisphere in relation to a history of violent behavior."[p.67]

Heilbrun,[378] in 1990, reported a study of 243 male prisoners convicted of murder. This study confirmed the results of a previous 1985 study by the same author which was based on an analysis of conduct reports of imprisoned or paroled offenders and in which it was found that "the combination of low intelligence and high antisociality in male prisoners was associated with more dangerous conduct...and that low IQ anti-social men tend to commit the more severe forms of violence (i.e., murder)."[pp.618-619] He also reported that the cognitively limited antisocial man "may escalate into greater violence, because the man does not have the judgement, planning resources or the self-control to prevent it."[p.625]

In support of the possible intellectual deficit in delinquent youths, a statistical study conducted by Cornell and Wilson[379] on a sample of 149 juvenile offenders—seventy-two violent and seventy-seven non-violent—found that the PIQ>VIQ (performance IQ verbal IQ) discrepancy appears to be a good indicator of intellectual deficits. The discrepancy between the performance IQ and the verbal IQ was in favor of the first and varied at least by twelve IQ points. The authors found that the above discrepancy was present in both white and minority groups and among youths convicted of violent as well as non-violent crimes.

Nestor[380] assessed neuropsychological and clinical correlates of murder and other forms of extreme violence of forty inpatients at a maximum security psychiatric facility. The group was comprised of twenty-two men with a mean age of 19.3 years at the time of the violent offense, fourteen charged with murder, two with assault with intent to murder, two with rape, two with assault and battery, one with armed robbery and one no charge, and of eighteen men with a mean age of 41.4 years comprising fourteen charged with murder, one with assault and battery, one with rape and two with only a tendency to be assaultive. He found that, "the young group exhibited significantly higher rates of both a learning disability and a history of childhood conduct disorder, whereas the older group had a significantly high rate of psychosis."[p.418]

A 1993 statistical study[381] of a sample of 258 juvenile inpatients consisting of 121 caucasian males and 135 caucasian females subdivided in non-dangerous (131), moderately assaultive (39), and severely assaultive (88) groups, concluded that "violent inpatients were more likely to be younger males whose family had a history of criminal behavior and extensive family discord. Moreover, the cognitive variables showed that violent inpatients showed differences in attention and memory, especially when they were processing aggressive stimuli."[p.731]

Hirschi and Hindelang[75] proposed that the relationship between I.Q. and crime is not a direct one but finds its catalyst in the frustrating and/or failed experiences that a young person with a low-average I.Q. may encounter in a competitive school system. That could generate an emotional impetus, or impulsivity, leading to antisocial or asocial behavior. They further believed that family occupational status, from semi-skilled to professional, usually correlates with individual test scores. Even that, however, probably does not support the status as a determinant of behavior. Nonetheless, since a "person's moral reasoning is correlated with intelligence, particularly verbal intelligence,"[229 p.169] it would be logical to think that a person's capacity for moral reasoning and for differentiating right from wrong, usually the outcome of intelligence plus exposure to family and social values, is a prerequisite for any type of good behavior, and that it's lack or diminution could lead the person to antisocial or violent behavior.

Of interest is a study by Stattin and Klackenberg-Larsson[382] regarding a group of 212 subjects, 122 males and ninety females, that measured the relationship between early language and intelligence development and the subject's future criminal behavior from birth to age thirty. Only the male subjects were reported in the study since the girl's criminality appeared to be statistically insignificant. The results of the study revealed that as early as the age of 3 years the boy's intelligence scores were significantly related to their future registered criminality which was also significantly correlated with their language ability at six months of age, at 18 months and at 24 months.

The authors of the above study stressed that the boy's early language ability could reflect not only the accepted negative correlation between verbal intelligence (VIQ) and criminality, but that since differences in language ability in the years of infancy may prognosticate later intellectual ability, it could be one factor critical to the relationship between intelligence and criminality. In their very accurately conducted analytical study, Stattin and Klackenberg-Larsson asserted that the relationship between intelligence and criminality appears early in childhood and they reported that Schonfeld[383] hypothesized that early cognitive factors or poor verbal ability in children may be determinant of their later antisocial behavior. They state that "the prevalence of registered criminality of 35.2% (43 of the 122 boys) [in their sample] of males at the age of 30 years is similar to that found for comparable Swedish longitudinal samples of males born in the mid 1950s."p.[371] In my personal experience, the results of I.Q. testing of many criminals show them to be at a low average level, even though most of them are street-wise. In this regard, one must also consider that I.Q. test results, even though supposedly corrected for such an eventuality, may be directly related to the individual's exposure to the educational system rather than an expression of inborn intelligence. Many schools in disadvantaged areas have inadequate physical structures and, at times, an unprepared teaching staff. Children and adolescents also may not be motivated by their families to attend school on a regular basis and/or are inadequately supervised with their homework. Many of them probably do not have the same cultural exposure to libraries, museums, theaters that is possible in more affluent areas and which contributes to the general educational level of the individual. Nonetheless, just as the above reasoning regarding their low-average I.Q. does not explain their violent behavior, one could argue that lack of exposure to that educational environment does not prevent the acquisition of values concerned with civic behavior.

The criminals who are apprehended generally show a lower I.Q. when compared to the more intelligent offenders who carry a low clearance rate of detection. Wilson and Herrnstein[229] believe that the crimes of less intelligent offenders are usually crimes with an immediate pay-off, or crimes of violence in which the reward is the damage inflicted on one's victim of the moment or sexual crimes giving immediate gratification.

On the other hand, the more intelligent offenders are able to program and even postpone the gratification that their offense brings. This is remindful of the impulsivity of the explosive offender compared to the programmed and calculated murderous actions of the nonsocial organized serial killer.

A recent survey of youths committed to state juvenile correctional facilities[384] showed that although their age was nearly sixteen years (the equivalent of that of a typical eleventh grade student) they had only earned ninth grade level credits. "Moreover, upon their assessment at the institutions, they tested even further behind—at the 6th grade math level and 7th grade reading level." Their average grade point [was] 1.24, the equivalent of a "D."[384 p.1] Also, 38 percent were chronically truant, 7 percent had dropped out of school entirely, and 3 percent had been expelled. Nearly one out of two youths (48%) was either learning disabled, emotionally disturbed or mentally retarded. Fifteen percent showed multiple exceptional educational needs. The majority were males (94%) and African Americans (58%). The Wide Range Achievement Test scores (WRAT) by age revealed a growing gap between the actual expected educational level and the functional level.

Age may also be considered a co-factor in crime. Violent crimes are frequently committed by juveniles in the age range from fifteen to eighteen years. These include all the major felonies, rape, aggravated assault, armed assault, and murder. These young people are frequently involved in gang violence and unpredictable drive-by shootings remindful of the political terrorism that pervaded the European climate from the sixties to the eighties.

The Uniform Crime Reports for 1991,[222] in assessing crime distribution by age, and taking into consideration 10,148 agencies with an estimated population of 189,961,000, reported a total number of arrests for all ages of 10,743,755. Of these, 556,669 were violent crimes. Two thousand and fifty-two of these crimes were perpetrated by persons under age fifteen; 95,677 by persons under age nineteen; and 460,992 by persons age nineteen and above. The percentage of total crimes for age nineteen was 4.9 percent; that for age twenty was 4.7 percent; and for age twenty-one 4.5 percent. These percentages slowly decreased for the subsequent ages twenty-two, twenty-three and twenty-four, with 4.1 percent, 3.9 percent, and 3.8 percent of the crimes respectively. However, a high peak of 17.8 percent was present in the age bracket twenty-five to twenty-nine, again slowly decreasing to 14.1 percent for ages thirty to thirty-four, and continuing down to 8.9 percent for ages thirty-five to thirty-nine, and to a very low 0.6 percent for age sixty-five and older.

Murder and non-negligent manslaughter offenses for all ages totaled 18,654, of which 302 were perpetrated by persons under age fifteen, 2,626 by persons under age eighteen, and 16,028 by persons age eighteen and older, that number remaining rather stable until age twenty-two. For offenders age twenty-three to age twenty-four, the number of cases of murder and non-negligent manslaughter dropped slightly, and then continued to rise sharply among those offenders between ages twenty-five and twenty-nine, thereafter progressively decreasing to the age of sixty-five and over.

These statistics support the contention that violent crime is usually perpetrated by individuals ranging in age from fifteen to thirty-four, reaching a peak of 17.8 percent for those perpetrators aged twenty-five to twenty-nine, which is followed by a minimal decrease for those aged thirty to thirty-four. Age itself does not have any direct causality for violence, but since the majority of violent offenders in the high rate brackets are obviously in that period of their lives where one is generally considered to be stronger and more resilient physically, it may facilitate the perpetration of violent offenses.

Territoriality, meaning a physical location that may comprise a neighborhood, street or home is another important variable strictly connected with the genesis of crimes of violence. Crime, for example, is more frequent in streets that are less trafficked by either people or vehicles. Neighborhoods that are well cared for and apparently better surveilled are less likely to be intruded upon or vandalized. A rundown neighborhood, giving the impression that nobody cares about it is a more inviting target for vandals. Well kept housing with the necessary comforts for decent living also creates in its dwellers a sense of satisfaction and human dignity. Crowded, unhealthy homes, on the other hand, contribute not only to confusion, but to promiscuity, illegitimacy, incest and violence. A satisfactory home probably lessens negative emotions.

Certainly one must also consider the media as a possible variable in the cause of crime. Although research studies give mixed reports regarding its importance, there can be no doubt that many movies and television programs present diseducational and violent messages to both children and adults. These types of programs may condition the young child to an insensitivity to violence and even to violent behavior if they are a steady diet, especially when they are viewed without the supervision of parents or parent substitutes. This is also true of adolescents (and even adults, at times) who may undergo suggestive conditioning to violence, especially when under the influence of alcohol or illicit drugs.

Blacks are over-represented among persons arrested, convicted and/or imprisoned for violent domestic and street crimes. Even though one of the theories of black crime is that many blacks have "acquired a hostile view of the larger society and its values,"[229] p.467 most of their violent crimes occur within their own neighborhoods. It can be theorized to be an expression of self-hate.

In 1980, blacks, representing about 1/8th of the total population in the United States, accounted for 1/2 of all people arrested for murder, rape and robbery. The median age of black male offenders at that time was seven years lower than that of white offenders. At the present time, blacks represent 12 percent of the American population and they account for 2/3 of all felons. Black youths, on the other hand, account for 50 percent of those persons arrested for murder or rape. Also in 1980, among the 72 percent of homicides cleared by law enforcement officials, the majority of arrestees were of the same race of the victim. In 1980, the number of homicides was 24,278, and of this number 10,283 victims were black. The FBI statistics for total arrests by race for 1991 report that out of a total of 10,516,399 arrests, 69 percent were white offenders, and 29 percent were black offenders. When, instead, violent crimes were tabulated, out of a total of 548,289, 53.6 percent was attributed to whites and 44.8 percent to blacks. The remaining crimes were evenly distributed among American Indians, Alaskan Natives, Asian and Pacific Islanders.[222]

In addition to the variables previously mentioned as possible facilitators of violence, individual temperament, impulsivity, inadequacy in socialization, or a larger subcultural deviance as proposed by Wilson and Herrnstein,[229] have been advanced in order to explain the difference in behavior in the various ethnic groups. Being a member of the black race has also been considered one of the important variables for violence. However, in reflecting on this, it appears that the concept is not only ambiguous but highly controversial, since crime is ubiquitous and is not limited to one single race or certain minority groups.

It is my belief that race per se is not directly causing crime. Indeed, how else can we explain that the majority of residents in minority communities are not involved in criminal behavior, even though they share the same ethnic origin, are participants of similar variables, often live in the same neighborhoods, and attend the same schools?

All of these variables, that I prefer to call facilitators of crimes of violence, are important in the genesis of criminal behavior and they intermix with one another impinging on the psyche of the very young, the young and the adult. They contribute greatly to the destructive expression of hostility in humankind, but they do not, essentially, determine human violent behavior against other humans. That is the outcome of a personal choice.

Crime is the expression of behavior that is primarily motivated by the criminal's psychopathology and his or her impulsivity.

Chapter Twelve

AT THE ROOTS OF VIOLENCE

During the past two decades the rapidly increasing rate of violent crime has attracted the attention of sociologists and criminologists who have painstakingly searched for its possible causes. Criminals have frequently been found to be living in an ecological system of racial discrimination, residing in poor housing, lacking education, with little possibility for employment, and offered only superficial medical care with the absence of preventive care for both physical and mental disturbances. In addition, they have been exposed to the easy temptations of the drug culture and the easy availability of guns. This has prompted myriad attempts to reduce crime through a range of policy initiatives which have attacked environmental factors thought to be linked to criminal behavior. Rehabilitation efforts have taken place with limited success.

Even though much time, effort, and money have been spent to implement this approach, violent crimes have been rising at almost an exponential rate. For instance, violent crime, where force or threat of force is involved, comprising the four major offenses of murder and non-negligent manslaughter, forcible rape, robbery and aggravated assault, was reported to be 1,820,127 offenses for the year 1990, with a rate of 731.8 crimes per 100,000 inhabitants. The following year, 1991, the F.B.I. reported that the number of violent offenses increased by five percent, reaching 1,911,767, with an increase of 3.6 percent over the previous year, with a rate of 758.1 per 100,000 inhabitants.[222]

Minorities are usually considered to be at a high risk for violence. In fact, as previously stated, blacks, the largest minority group in the United States, represent twelve percent of the nation's population but are disproportionately represented among both perpetrators of violence and victims of violence. Apparently the reasons for this are many but none fully explanatory. In 1988, Sessions,[385] in a report on crime in the United States, stated that blacks represented 51 percent of the arrestees for murder, 41 percent of those arrested for aggravated assault, 36 per

213

cent for simple assault and 63 percent for robbery. In 1991, of a total number of 10,516,399 arrestees, as reported by 10,075 agencies with an estimated population of 186,621,000, 7,251,862 were white persons and 3,049,299 were black; the remaining was distributed among Native Americans or Alaskan natives for 115,345, and Asian or Pacific Islanders with 99,893.

If the categories of murder and non-negligent manslaughter are taken into consideration we can see that the number, in 1991, reached the level of 18,096, of which 7,861 offenses were committed by white persons, 9,924 by black persons, and 143 by Native Americans or Alaskan natives, and 168 by Asian or Pacific islanders. The percentage distribution of murder and non-negligent manslaughter was 43.4 percent for whites compared to 54.8 percent for blacks, 1.1 percent for Native Americans or Alaskan natives, and .9 percent for Asian or Pacific islanders.

Looking at forcible rape for the same year, 1991, as tabulated by the F.B.I., white offenders are reported at 54.8 percent and blacks at 43.5 percent. Aggravated assault perpetrated by white persons was 60 percent compared to 38.3 percent by black persons. For other minor crimes the offenses perpetrated by blacks were more or less half of the offenses perpetrated by whites on a percentage basis.

As stated in the 1991 F.B.I. report, juvenile arrest rates underwent substantial increases from 1965 to 1990 among both white and black arrestees.[222] Juveniles are considered to be youths, male or female, whose age ranges from ten to eighteen years. In 1990, the rate of crime for juveniles was recorded as 430 crimes per 100,000 juveniles. "Of particular note is the upward trend that started in 1988 for both white and black youth as well as the downward trend for those in other race categories. Overall for the period of 1980–1990, the white juvenile violent crime arrest rate increased 44 percent compared to a 19-percent increase for blacks and a 53-percent decline for others. . . . In 1990, the juvenile violent crime arrest rate reached 1,429/100,000 black juveniles, five times that for white youths. The other rates category registered its lowest violent crime arrest rate in 1990 after peaking in 1978."[386 p.270]

If we take into consideration the major crimes of murder, forcible rape, aggravated assault, and drug abuse violation by juveniles, the statistics show that in 1990 the black youth arrests for murder increased 145 percent, compared to 48 percent for white youths, and a decline of 45 percent for other races, with a black arrest rate 7.5 times that of whites. Juvenile forcible rape arrests in the United States doubled from 1965 to

1990, going from 10.9 percent to 21.9 percent. Regarding this major offense, forcible rape, the white arrest rate of juveniles has increased much faster than that for blacks during the last decade: with 86 percent for whites versus 9 percent for blacks.

Aggravated assault registers the highest juvenile arrest rate among violent offenses. The rate for this type of offense has increased substantially for both white and black juveniles, 59 percent and 89 percent respectively in the period 1980 to 1990. Regarding drug abuse violations, there has been a markedly significant increase in juvenile arrests for marijuana and heroin/cocaine during the eighties and continuing to the present time, even though the rate of marijuana abuse has now apparently decreased. Between 1980 and 1990, the overall rate for heroin/cocaine arrests for juveniles rose 713 percent; the black arrest rate jumped 2,373 percent, followed by a 251 percent upswing for whites, and a 127 percent rise for other races.[386]

It is obvious that the above statistics are pertinent to the subject of this discussion. The majority of people involved in serious violent crimes, be they aggravated assaults, rape, manslaughter, or murder, range in age from twelve to thirty-four, with an ever increasing number of juvenile offenders. The dysfunction of the family appears to be strictly correlated with violent crime among juveniles. These young people are witness to the widespread use of illicit drugs and alcohol and individual or gang violence, both in the home and on the streets. Often lacking in their lives are good housing, good schools, and the possibility of training for a decent job. All too often they grow up in dysfunctional families that have not exposed them to good parental role models. Social, educational, and moral support are often missing. All of these factors contribute in a negative way to their conduct, but it is the thesis of this discussion that the main causative factor in their violent behavior, regardless of race or socio-economic background, is the dysfunction of their families.

In order to support this thesis, it is necessary to reflect on the function of the family unit. The family needs to be understood from bio-psycho-ecological and sociological vantage points. It seems apparent that the billions of tiny cells that form the various organs of our body are all essential. These organs are formed by groups of similar cells which are differentiated from others by structure and functioning, and each cellular group contributes to the functioning of those organs, and, thus, to the sound functioning of the entire body. It is well known that if one of these cells—only one—assumes a dysfunctional state, as in a cancerous condition, whatever affects that tiny cell tends to spread to neighboring cells, creating a state of illness which may affect the entire body.

The purpose of the above, very brief, disquisition, is to prepare the reader for a very simple analogy between the human body and its cells on the one hand, and society and its families on the other. I say the family not to detract from the importance of the individual but because, from a sociological point of view, the family is a structure that relates to many other societal structures, as groups of similar cells relate to one another in their participation in the healthy functioning of the total human body.

Viewed from an historic perspective, the family, formed by biologically interconnected individuals, as a natural institution and the basic cell of society, provided for the needs of its members and offered certain protective boundaries. Even though under different forms, it existed before the origin of the community or the city. It was, for example, authoritarian, during the early Roman period, when family name and industriousness were more important than blood relationships, and there was little demonstration of feelings among its members. Only during the middle and late medieval era did the family, becoming patriarchal in type, begin to denote a complex group whose essential function was that of protection, education, and affective support.[387] Within this evolving family structure, children were given the possibility of extending their emotional contacts to members of their family other than their parents.[388]

The family, because of its natural essence, withstood even the disruptive effects of social revolutions. For instance, even during the French revolution, when many social institutions were actually destroyed, the family maintained its basic integrity.[389] Slowly, its form became less static and, at present, the concept of family is that of a group highly flexible and adapting to intrinsic and extrinsic factors in order to maintain its adequacy in a changing world. In its dynamic system, the family regulates itself through trial and error, through willful or forced experimentation, in order to find what is good for its members. Its functions are basic and vital for its members, and consequently for society. It helps its members to internalize institutions and teaches them social and moral values and responsible roles. It passes on to them basic adaptive techniques proper to their culture, as well as, hopefully, a sense of that social responsibility that is so important for proper human development and humane civic interaction.

The family, to be beneficial to society and to be comfortable within it, must interact with other similar units, usually forming the complex social system that we call "community." Goode[390] is of the opinion that the family, throughout the world, has moved away from the traditional structure of strong and traditional kinship bonds of the extended family toward a more restricted nucleus as a way to better adapt to a changing society. He claims that it is simplistic to attribute the change in family structure to the process of industrialization. Being objective, however, we cannot dismiss the fact that the impact of industrialization, and even more so the recent technological revolution, has gradually changed our way of life, our thinking, our goals, and, unfortunately, even the way we relate to one another.

These changes have reached the point that many parents seem to have given up their very private right to raise their children in a closed, intimate relationship, and they do not appear to be, or to feel, morally responsible for their social conduct. Within an almost detached relationship, the loving care of the child is often replaced by care given out of a sense of duty. Many children feel emotionally neglected and often verbalize the lack of good role models in their parents. Obviously, those role models are necessary during the process of the psychological development of the child.

As well stated by Scott and Scott,[391] a family is as healthy as its members and the factors which make a family a healthy one are, in addition to good genetic and psychogenetic indices, trust, affection, and various degrees of autonomy within an interdependent relationship. Values are essential for the good development of its members and of the family itself. Children grow up in a particular ecological environmental situation that greatly influences their existential development. In *Beyond Conformity or Rebellion*, Gary Schwartz sensibly stated, "Children tend to react to their parents in much the same way as the parents treat them ... and at times there is a parallel between tension within the family and [tension within] the community."[392]

Today, social violence is soaring. Its presence is multidimensional. It occurs within communities at large and within individual families. Within the home, the clash between spouses or live-in members often proves to be highly disruptive to their physical and emotional well-being and to that of their children. Many members of society, both young and old, exhibit the effects of living in a dysfunctional family. They show difficulty in adaptation, in communication, in establishing relationships with others. Children find it difficult to develop their inborn capacities.

As Lidz[393] well stated, many of the insecurities in our daily living and many of our dysfunctional relationships may arise from the difficulties the contemporary family encounters in finding a secure structure and satisfactory ways of raising their children.

The interaction of children with their parents is essential for their good development. It is a well known fact that the foundations for the good development of children are laid down in their young, developing personalities during their first five years of life, when they are mostly at home and hopefully in close contact and under the loving and watchful supervision of their parents. Actually, it has usually been the mother, because of her frequent presence with the child and early adolescent, who has been the one who conditions the children to discipline and good behavior, reinforced by the spontaneous, or requested, occasional intervention of the father.

However, today the "traditional" family accounts for only a small percentage of all American families, and the sociologist would argue that the forces of social change make it impossible to bring back that type of family. In fact, today, a large percentage of mothers work outside the home, and both mothers and fathers are frequently exhausted from the demands of work and of running a household. In fact, many families have no adult as a constant presence for children. But the children and the family are materially successful. There is no doubt that the rampant consumerism and materialism present in our society contribute to this state of affairs.

However, the importance of the presence of parents in a family, in the context of today's social and economic situation, remains essential. It is well known that children internalize the moral principles of their parents and that they will behave in accordance with these internalized standards. Piaget[394] and Kohlberg,[395] indicate that the morality of children may change over the course of the child's development. Bandura[396] stressed that the child's morality is acquired through a learning process that takes place throughout his or her development. De facto, this development of a child's morals and his or her conditioning to a certain type of discipline leads to good interpersonal relationships. In fact, ideally, it is within the family that the child develops his or her social and moral maturity, either through internalization of paternal or maternal dictates, or through parental ethical principles, usually a reflection of the larger society.

Unfortunately, this is not always the case. In our present society, many families, especially among those deviant groups often seen by psychiatrists, social workers, and/or psychologists, are frequently dysfunctional and unable to provide emotional and physical support, good moral standards, and consistent discipline for their children. Many people, possibly overwhelmed by social and cultural changes, and primarily interested in the satisfaction of their personal needs and desires do not communicate with one another, even within their own families. At times families are completely destructured, and children and adolescents are abandoned to themselves or completely dependent on social assistance. Social workers, psychologists, and psychiatrists are for the most part trying to help these people deal with the desperate social situations which they face. Even though this may often be done in an inadequate manner, what alternatives are there? We should not overestimate the ability of many poorly educated and not very insightful people to solve their problems by themselves. In fact, if broad scale well being in families is to occur, the political and economic institutions in society need to be more supportive of families.

In 1963, Lidz, stated, "A larger proportion of the population is married than ever before."[393] p.37 Thirty years later things are just the opposite. The one parent family has appeared on the social scene and is steadily growing in number. Statistics clearly illustrate the frailty of the contemporary family.[397] Half of all marriages end in divorce. Births to single mothers now make up one-quarter of total births. One in four Americans over age eighteen has never married. Married couples with children under age eighteen make up 25.9 percent of American households; married couples without children are 29.4 percent; people living alone—25.05 percent; unrelated people living together—4.7 percent; other families without children—6.5 percent; other families with children—8.5 percent. Married couples with a child under age eighteen have become a shrinking minority. In 1970, married couples with a child under age eighteen constituted 40.3 percent of all American households. In 1980, that number became 30.9 percent and by 1991 it was only 25.9 percent. Concentrations of families made up of a married couple with children are primarily in areas with large numbers of Hispanic, Indian or Mormon families, in parts of Appalachia and in some suburbs.

As previously stated, in 1987 42 percent of black families were headed by a single woman,[398] and many of their children are born out of wedlock. This is often the case among offenders, particularly among black offenders. This is remindful of a new form of relationship slowly established among some societal groups, the interesting polygamous groups of Scott.[399] However, I would prefer to call them pseudopolygamous because a true basic family structure does not exist in this type of alliance, but rather various promiscuous relationships in which the woman is usually used and abused by an irresponsible man. The people involved may be black or white, are usually of low educational background, unemployed and on welfare, and may use drugs and alcohol to excess. Illegitimacy is a frequent occurrence in these situations, and the children who are born today will be tomorrow's adults.

Nisbet[400] stated, already in 1966, that the so-called *gemeinschaft*, a compound of kinship, neighborhood, and friendship, usually components of a family, had lost its importance, having been supplanted by what sociologists call *gesellschaft* — a society more detached in its interpersonal relationships. However, codified laws and certificated advisors, from mental therapists to financial counselors, can not replace the functions that are discharged by the family. We all know that good nurturing involves physical, emotional and educational aspects, and that a person's sense of self-worth and dignity, acquired through the years of childhood and adolescence, derives from the love that is received from parents when he or she is young. Parents form the character of their children, educate them to values — to honesty, to compassion, to brotherhood, to understanding, to responsibility for oneself. This is the best prevention against criminal and violent behavior.

In a family, the parents have traditionally assumed different roles. Traditionally the father has represented authority and has usually been the major financial provider, and often the dispenser of rules that were enforced by the mother. The mother, whether working at home or outside the home, usually has had a protective and understanding role, showing love and forgiveness, and guiding the children and redirecting any misconduct in a positive direction. Today, because of new philosophic views and socio-economic forces, these roles are more interchangeable or are taken over by only one parent. Step-family situations and foster homes are frequently the only alternative for some children. In addition, the ideas of feminism which have greatly influenced American women make it highly unlikely that they will want to return to their previous role. As stated above, most women today work outside the home, and most educated married women are interested both in pursuing a career and sharing family responsibilities with their husband.

Unfortunately, a great deal of juvenile violent behavior comes from children raised in families where the presence of a father is lacking, or where, even though present, he is a poor role model. Children usually learn how to behave, how to be future parents through the observation of their own parents. Because of these dysfunctional parents we already have a generation of dysfunctional adolescents and young adults. This is frequently seen in minority communities. Wilson,[401] in his book, *The Truly Disadvantaged,* stated that in 1940 only 17.9 percent of black American families were headed by women, and usually because the husband was dead. In 1980, most black females between twenty and forty-five years of age were not married or living with a spouse.[402] By 1988, it was reported that 42 percent of black families were headed by a single woman.[398] Part of this increase was not due to greater widowhood but to what Scott[399] terms "polygamous" attitudes held among certain sectors of many minority groups.

Rearing children may be too much of a task for one person only. It is difficult to be mother and father at the same time, even though the one parent family is, at times, successful in raising its children. However, a two parent family seems to be the most natural way to raise children, and it is easy to agree with Lidz's statement: "It becomes increasingly evident scientifically, as it has been through common sense, that children require two parents with whom they interact and who are, optimally, of opposite sexes in temperament and outlook, but who, together, form a parental coalition complementing and completing one another."[393 p.34]

How this progressive, gradual dissolution of the traditional family has come about is certainly an intriguing question. One can wonder whether emancipation or extreme individualism has contributed to excessive egocentrism; or whether some people are incapable of dealing with day to day social living. Many people do not have the possibility of securing a good paying job in a highly competitive technological society because they lack an adequate education or adequate training. Others have resorted to the use and abuse of alcohol and drugs, and have accepted a philosophy of defeatism and extreme dependency on welfare programs.

Perhaps the sudden and drastic social changes that society has experienced during the past few decades have created chaos and insecurity, and a progressive state of social anomie fostering inappropriate thinking and behavior in many people. This inappropriate thinking and behavior is supported in these people by their recognition of a state of social confusion and a lack of direction in their lives. These perceptions are reflected not only in their conduct in society but in the way they act out within their homes. In fact, violence is often the expression of frustration and hostility, at times generated by profound dissatisfaction with the business of life.

Domestic violence is on the rise in our communities and at times it is difficult to say whether it is motivated by environmental and socio-ecological conditions, as suggested above, or is intrinsically determined by the individual's conflicts within a poor interpersonal relationship. The basic moral values which serve to direct one's personal or group libidinal energy constructively are usually learned in those families that uphold them, and civic laws serve only to reinforce our adherence to them. But when unchecked by moral values, frustration and hostility may erupt and become a highly destructive form of violence, both within and outside of the family.

At times, social systems may also be manipulative of personal and family life. In our present society, a good percentage of its members seem to direct themselves inappropriately and unsuccessfully towards those ever changing goals that culture and society incessantly manufacture for them. In a highly bureaucratic society, rationalistic and utilitarian approaches, pressure for achievement, fear of failure, and greed for the possession of futile fleeting goods, have generated persons whose behavior can be predicted, manipulated, and controlled.[403] Being in obsessive pursuit of ephemeral goals usually brings about existential frustration, and this frustration creates insecurity, hostility and confusion. All too often this hostility and violence find their outlet in the acting out against the family itself. The home, where family members are at the highest risk of victimization today,[263] is no longer that safe and secure haven that it is supposed to be.

In this confusing and frustrating atmosphere, many children grow up controlled by a series of commercial arrangements and non-spontaneous, non-affective laden contracted relationships. Apathetic and detached behavior may be assumed by their parents, and they, the children, may grow up without any real concept of what a warm human and humane relationship is. These same children are often exposed to the unhealthy atmosphere of streets flooded with crime, gradually becoming involved in self-destructive life styles of heavy drinking, drug abuse and drug trafficking, and exaggerated interest in the accumulation of those above mentioned symbols of status or power.

Is this due to a culture crisis in the larger society, or to a crisis basically restricted to those rather large groups of disadvantaged people who are struggling with the impossible realization of wanting to live according to the cultural values of mainstream society but who are unable to do so? Is the crisis of the family with its consequences of domestic and social violence prompted by the failure of the disadvantaged to integrate the cultural values of the larger society or is it actually due to the disadvantaged person's idiosyncratic philosophy of life?

The interplay between a society in transition towards stabilization, with high technological pressures and a tendency to marginalize the "substandard" individual by relegating him or her to the large cohort of welfarism, and a family unit disrupted while trying to adapt to continuous new social demands, has created a state of social dysfunctionalism. The family, often unable to withstand these new forms of living, becomes slowly disintegrated, loses its fundamental values, and its supportive capacity for the total welfare of its members.

Pressured from within and from without, the family is often unable to hold its members together. The members themselves, confused and without a clear understanding of the situation, often misperceive their goals. For people who live in a social situation of deprivation, for people who do not have a tangible sense of belonging, either to a supporting family or to an organized community, for people who feel largely rejected as active players in the socio-economic arena of a larger society, for people who see no future for themselves, life probably assumes little or no meaning. These people may focus their attention mainly on their biological selves, and physical strength and sexual power assume a cherished role in their daily activities. Their body becomes their castle and source of status. They flaunt their physical prowess at the service of deep lying hostility and violent resentment. They violate others. They transgress rules and they even kill for meaningless reasons and in an aimless way, probably in order to enhance the value of the only thing they have, which often is an able human body for which they demand respect in the incorrect assumption that manhood can be limited to just that.

Disadvantaged communities, regardless of race, are at a high risk for domestic and extra-domestic violence. Whether this is the resultant of pressures exercised by the larger society—political, economic, social and cultural—or by their dysfunctional cultural adaptation is difficult to establish. Probably a combination of the two factors is at work.

In a climate of disintegrating families and an anomic culture crime breeds easily. In an enlightening essay, Elijah Anderson,[404] wrote that street violence perpetrated by many African-American young men is just a desperate, unsuccessful, search for respect. He emphasizes the well-known fact that many poor inner-city blacks, in particular the young ones, suffer from a profound sense of alienation from mainstream society and its institutions, and that because of that a code of the streets which amounts to a set of informal rules governing interpersonal public behavior including violence is ruling the streets of their neighborhoods. That applies, as well, to members of other groups with similar demographic characteristics.

Because of the lack of a good moral influence, because of the progressively disintegrating family in our high risk communities, and because of the inadequacy of a well concerted community approach to the problem of ghetto violence, we are witnessing the upsurge of an oppositional culture flaunting disrespect for rules and regulations, immature because of family deprivation, uneducated because of poor schooling, prone to violence against persons and property. Domestic violence and street violence are most frequently encountered in those communities at risk formed by disadvantaged persons who come from highly dysfunctional families, lacking cohesiveness among its members, lacking sharing, love, work, and emotional, physical, and spiritual support for the needs of its members. In a situation of quasi total dysfunctionalism, they are frequently subjected to physical and sexual abuse, and/or to the cancer of drug and alcohol dependence and abuse. That is the pseudo-nirvana that has poorly substituted the haven of a family.

Basic cultural patterns are usually maintained through the family in its internal socialization and its moral education. Respect and duty towards self and others are usually taught within the family and not by an often useless conditioning of laws and policing. As Duby[405] stated in 1987, the home represents a " . . . zone of immunity to which we may fall back or retreat, a place where we may set aside arms and armor needed in the public place, relax, take our ease, and lie about unshielded by the ostentatious carapace worn for protection in the outside world. This is the place where the family thrives, the realm of domesticity."

What happens to the family at risk also happens to many other people "not at risk" who come from different racial or socio-economic backgrounds. They, too, feel conscious and subconscious frustration, and move around like automatons in a highly pressurized world, running through the days and the months and the years towards the world of higher achievement like goal directed projectiles; they go through life almost unaware of their affective interactions. They, too, are frequently lonely, prey to personal conflicts and ambivalence, and anxious agitation and frustrated rebelliousness.

Is it this dysfunctional social situation we live in that at times creates rebelliousness and/or violence? Or does the basic problem lie at the roots of society—in its basic cell, the family? Present day social engineering and an ultra-rational approach to life have created an image of a "truncated . . . man, a less than fully human," stated Kendall.[403] Our highly technological society is increasingly dehumanizing those who come in contact with it, often unleashing their interpersonal aggression and violence.

These violent manifestations often occur within a family, possibly as a sign of frustrated dependency, a call for help from that place that is essentially felt to be naturally supporting. Parents become both victims and victimizers, and children are conditioned by the violence that they witness. And since violence begets violence, they, too, incorporate within their selves their parents' useless and dangerous way of coping with the problems of life.

It is a common occurrence for humans to wish to return to their place of birth at the end of their life's journey, just as anyone looks forward to coming home after a hard day's work. The reason for wishing to return to the home of their childhood, a quasi instinctual drive, could lie in a subconscious feeling that home represents for them a supporting place, where their energies were refueled, and their problems were resolved in an atmosphere of love and respect. It is there that their childhood wounds were mended, and it is there where some unfinished business was obviously left, along with memories, both good and bad, and wishes that never came true. One can argue that the desire to return to their original home is due to their recognition of the power of healing that their home offered: the opportunity to smooth out differences of opinion and the upsurge of their aggressivity as young adolescents; the supporting attention of their parents during moments of emerging social crisis in the spring of their life; the discussion of contracting a particular type of behavior, either within the family or outside of it; but, uppermost, their realization that through that loving and educational arena they were helped to form their good character. Those familiar surroundings are felt by them as being full of a healing power, a power that is intrinsic to it, a power that no rehabilitative agency could ever offer because it contains a form of unselfish love.

If years later such a mature individual recognizes the usefulness of the influence of the family in his or her life, why not assume that society should direct its attention to the reintegration and stabilization of this primary agency and use its natural force to correct the violent behavior of many young persons who grow up without the beneficial effect of a good family? It is in the family, primarily, that a person's good character is formed; it is there that one acquires those natural and desirable personal and social virtues already considered so important by Aristotle over two thousand years ago: goodness, altruism, honesty, and civility. That is the place where the foundations for preventing aggression and violence are laid down. It is the family that should address the fundamental issues concerning human behavior and misbehavior, and social agencies and the mental health industry should only play a reinforcing role in addressing the problem of violence. Humans often search for complicated solutions for their problems, when the solution may be, instead, just before their eyes.

Chapter Thirteen

CONCLUSION

I hope that I have been able to convey to the reader a panoramic view of the various causative factors at the basis of the different manifestations of violent behavior. If violent behavior, and crime in general, are a tangible expression of the moral state of a community or of a nation, we can only conclude that our moral fabric is coming apart. Even accepting the fact that crime and violence have been a part of human existence since its beginnings, the present upsurge of violence in our homes, on our streets, and in our neighborhoods needs more attentive scrutiny in an attempt to formulate better preventive measures and possible improvement of the status quo. "Sharp arguments quickly arise over such issues as special income, health, employment, housing, child care, and education assistance targeted to the poor and near poor ... often viewed as replacing family responsibilities."[406 p.195]

The factors argued to be causative of felonious crimes—poverty, lack of education, lack of employment, poor housing, use of illicit drugs and alcohol, the too easily availability of guns—even though so much a part of those communities at a high risk for crime, are important but not the direct cause of violence. The commonly held assumption that considers the above factors to be primary in the genesis of crime in general, and violent crime in particular, is a disservice to the millions of those individuals of a low socio-economic level and limited educational background who live in disadvantaged conditions but who nevertheless overcome it and are successful in living a dignified, honest life. Not poverty, nor poor housing, nor lack of education are primarily causative of crimes of violence in and of themselves. These factors may certainly cause existential discomfort and pessimism, and are frequently proposed and accepted as a justification for such types of crime. However, these negative life conditions are, as well, an incentive for many people to extricate themselves from the tentacles of their demoralizing and demotivating influence that has been so pervasive among minorities throughout the past years and to engage themselves in the competitive social struggle for a better life.

Indeed, many successful, honest people come from a poor background and one wonders what motivated them to become achievers and to overcome their disadvantages. Is it due to their intelligence? their acquired knowledge? their ambition? I am inclined to believe that their success in overcoming their socio-economic handicaps is due to the strength of their good and strong character, a character which usually is forged within the supporting boundaries of a family, a family that offers its members the loving attention and moral guidance that promote personal growth and social maturity.

I think of character in a dynamic manner, i.e., as before stated, as the personality in action. Character is the sum of assimilated knowledge, personal interests, values and self-esteem, and a sense of social responsibility and virtues are usually intrinsic to a good character. In order to achieve a good character, one should be able to integrate virtues and interests in a unified pattern of good behavior throughout life. Aristotle believed that character has to do with those attitudes, sensibilities, and beliefs that affect how a person sees, acts, and lives.[204] The Aristotelian character was strictly connected with practical reason and moral virtues well expressed in the Greek word *ethikes.* For Aristotle the development of character within a caring family was not simply necessary for personal, good choice making and deliberative capacities, but it extended outward towards the *polis,* for the good of others.

In our present society, where many families are no longer that privileged place where moral and civic education takes place, and where, almost following a Platonic suggestion, for years many schools and social agencies have been entrusted with that teaching, children seem to lack a well-defined personal character, often acquiring, instead, a communality of poorly defined interests and mores. The absence of a good character undermines generosity and good will towards others, and leads to a confused, and at times dissolute, life. Many of our criminals, especially the felonious ones, were not exposed to a wholesome, emotionally stable relationship with parental figures, or their contacts with them did not facilitate their natural emulation of a good role model. McCord's[407] 1979 study revealed that the most important predictors were maternal affection (for the boy) and parental supervision; where these were low, delinquency was high.

A recent study[408] of the family profiles of the 791 juveniles incarcerated on September 7, 1993, at the Ethan Allen School in Wales, Wisconsin, and at the Lincoln Hills School in Irma, Wisconsin, focusing on their ties with their biological parents, revealed a stark fact: only thirteen percent of those incarcerated in the state juvenile correctional facilities came from intact families. The study reaffirms the idea that the lack of a father or other adequate male role model frequently results in children and adolescents joining gangs and engaging in violent actions. Inquiry into the social behavior of the parents of these incarcerated juveniles revealed that 44 percent had never married; 29 percent were divorced; 13 percent were married; 6 percent were married and then divorced; 4 percent were married but separated. Thirty percent of the juveniles had never lived with both parents at the same time while 65 percent had lived with both biological parents at the same time at some point in their life. "Life for most boys and for many grown men is a frustrating search for the lost father who has not yet offered protection, provision, nurturing, modeling, or, especially, anointment. All those tough guys who want to scare the world into seeing them as men, and who fill up the jails . . . are suffering from Father Hunger."[409]

When people grow up with a good character and are morally sound, curious, and open to those reasonable and healthy changes usually equated with progress, and are appreciative not only of their rights but of their duties, they will be better able, I believe, to withstand the occasional social erosion of their self-esteem and the ups and downs of economic changes, as well as those rejections and frustrations that are a part of life. The presence of a moral character helps people to recognize the futility of a dissipated life and to realize the importance of directing their energy towards tangible, progressive, wholesome objectives.

At times, as previously stated, the formation of a good character is not achieved because of the lack of a family which offers role-model parental figures, or of little or no exposure to other positive role-models outside of the home environment. Or, the development of the character may be impeded by the presence of biological factors, either inherited or acquired. Numerous biological studies searching for the cause of crime and violence have defined neuro-anatomical structures whose dysfunction may trigger anger and rage reactions. Serotonergic deficits may be connected with these neuro-physiological outbursts, even though psychological environmental factors may be regarded as necessary precipitating stimuli. I cannot deny that I am attracted by the utopian possibility of finding an organic cause, hopefully controllable by drugs, at the basis of disruptive behavior. Certainly hyperactive behavior, interictal epileptic behavior, the gross pathologies of the nervous system, and the effect of sudden hypoglycemic reactions are intriguing as possible causative co-factors and are suggestive of a nexus between organic factors and violence. However, until further research and clinical applications will furnish us with sound proof of the above, we can only state that there may be a possible predisposition in some persons, at some time, and under special circumstances, to react in a way that we call violent.

As we may accept this predisposition as being due to the second brain of the triune brain of MacLean,[410] which I equate to Freud's Id,[91] receptacle of negative emotions and of the removed past, we should realize, as well, that humans have been blessed with the acquisition of a thinking brain, the neo-cortical structures, whose functions should be used to curb their tendency to violence. This influence should not be looked upon as inhibitory but rather as modulating the expression of negative, often destructive, emotions into acceptable conduct. This modulating influence is at its best when people, during their development, have been exposed to moral and virtuous codes of behavior. The mind does not acquire that epicritical power capable of discerning between good and bad unless the person is exposed to a value oriented group that reinforces his or her behavior through repetitive moral actions.

"The concept of 'family responsibility' is another controversial and complicated one that usually arises in debates about families and policies. It lies at the heart of many issues. Although our traditional cultural patterns hold that it is desirable for families to be self-reliant and self-supporting, responsible towards each of their members, and independent of any public aid, virtually *no* family in today's highly urbanized technological society is totally independent of the services provided by large networks of external systems, both private and governmental."[406] p.195

The microsociological unit called family is contained in a larger macrosociological system of interdependent structures composed of neighborhoods, schools, churches, government, and other social institutions. There, as parents in a family, teachers, religious leaders, managers, and elected officials exercise some measure of control and dispense a certain degree of differential socio-moral support and discipline. In such a cooperative society, the family should be looked upon as the basic nucleus, since "all human collectivities have a tendency toward closure into self containment. They seek through their authorities to establish and maintain a certain identity, to define their boundaries and to protect their integrity."[148] p.66

But our society is on a slippery road of anonymity and dehumanization, and faces us with inconsistencies and coexisting and opposing values and pseudo-values. This is frequently reflected in families, because the larger society, the federated one, attempting to take over many duties of the microsocial family unit in an all embracing cultural approach, vitiates and devitalizes its original cells. This breeds a lack of integrative directions and values at the source. In such a social atmosphere, confusion, anomic situations, the well known relativism, and lack of civility ensue. This is followed by people's lack of desire to further reinforce the development and function of their higher epicritical faculties, leaving the individual prey to basic instincts of aggression. Under such circumstances, aggression may be expressed by a gamut of unhealthy types of behavior, ranging from desiring the possessions of others to the killing of another person as a quick solution to personal or interpersonal conflicts.

The issue of family values has been widely dealt with in the press and public opinion. However, it seems that a great deal of confusion exists concerning the meaning of this term. A family unit is not just an entity that holds people from a similar biological background together for protective and nurturing reasons and for a smoother running of communities and states, but it is a group that, regardless of its structure and membership, holds within itself values and attitudes of love, respect, and responsibility for each other, part of those larger values that have come to be known as human values. These values are handed down from generation to generation, and are intrinsic to the sacred books of the world's religions. We, as a society formed by family groups, have made those values an integral part of our *modus vivendi* to the point that a family, in its purest sense, is not a family unless those values are an integral part of it. Without them, the family is just an aggregation of people, held together for biological, nurturing and protective reasons.

"Families stand at the center of society; . . . [and] building our future must begin by preserving family values."[411] The present day upsurge of violent crimes perpetrated by adolescents is an example of the failure of the family to pass on to its children good values to live by, and of the family and society at large giving them mixed value messages. In an attempt to rectify the personal and social confusion that often breeds crime and violence, laws are in a continuous flux. However, those responsible for making our laws often forget Wilson's words to the effect that, "legislation cannot save society. Legislation cannot rectify society.... [T]he law that would work.... is the successful embodiment of unselfish citizenship."[412] Wilson's words obviously divert attention from society to the individual citizen.

Good citizenship is first learned within the microcosmal structure of the family, where the child learns not only how to relate to its peers and to authority, but also those rules that modulate its conduct and which lay the foundations for ethical behavior throughout life. If the child acquires the above qualities within the boundaries of its family, making them an integral part of its character, my assumption that the dissolution of the family is the major factor at the roots of violence in our homes and neighborhoods stands on firm ground. Therefore, the reintegration of the family into a modern and functional structure, whose members uphold high moral values and show a virtuous character, is a logical goal to aim for and is central to the stabilization of present day society.

During the recent past, human rights have become the main interest for many persons, but, in the midst of a social transition toward better civic equality, selfish attitudes have often taken the place of disinterested feelings of altruism. At times it is remindful of the theoretical society of Hobbes in which the individual member assembles with his or her similars because of a desire to survive, while maintaining the right "to do what he would, and against whom he thought fit, and to possess, use, and enjoy all that he would, or could, get."[413]

At times one wonders whether social violence finds a facilitator in the incessant revindication of civil rights to the exclusion of civil duties. Wolff stated that "...the duties of a person towards others are the same as his duties towards himself... Natural obligation is absolutely unchangeable...."[414] In preparation for writing an article on the subject of duties versus rights, I was shocked, during my attempt to peruse the literature, even at an international level, to find that while there is a plethora of writing on people's rights—of all kinds—almost nothing is available regarding duties. Indeed, I was offered, time and again, Cicero's classic, *On Duties*.

There is no doubt that each individual should see him or herself as a responsible member of society who enjoys personal rights; but I believe that in order to enjoy these rights he or she must also participate in personal and group duties. Duties and rights cannot be separated one from the other and are like the two faces of the same coin.

I am of the opinion that if the family group emphasizes the values of honesty, respect, love, and personal and civic responsibility, the tendency to criminality and violence in our homes and streets will diminish. The number of prisoners in our jails, many of them young people—social offenders and often themselves victims of early emotional and affective deprivation—will also decrease. "It is necessary to go back to seeing the family as the sanctuary of life. The family is indeed sacred: it is the place in which life, the gift of God, can be properly welcomed and protected against the many attacks to which it is exposed, and can develop in accordance with what constitutes authentic human growth. In the face of the so-called culture of death, the family is the heart of the culture of life."[415] p.76 The above should not be restricted to the two-parent family, but should include the single parent family, or any group that considers itself a family.

Kendall, commenting on the precarious personal and social conditions of many disadvantaged people who live without moral-religious values, believes that they form a large cohort of incomplete people and expresses his ideas as follows: "[T]runcated beings . . . inevitably end up being mired in social disorder, because their souls are disordered and spiritual disorder leads, in the end, to social disorder. . . ."[403] p.106

In the midst of present day social confusion it is of comfort to know that the majority of American families are still united, loving and responsible. These families silently and stoically oppose their disintegration because they believe in those traditional values passed on to them by previous generations. Myriad low income families are successfully protecting their members from the ravages of drugs, alcohol, and violence because they uphold the essential virtues of honesty, civility, and morality. It is not poverty, but the lack of values and virtues in a rapidly changing society that creates the propensity to crime in an individual.

During times of social transformation such as that which we are experiencing at the end of the twentieth century, there is an even greater necessity for a strong family nucleus. Ackerman clearly pointed out that the family is an essential supporting structure for both the young and the old when he stated that even though "the essence of life is change, growth, learning, adaptation to new conditions, and creative evolution of new levels of interchange between persons and environment . . . the matrix of human relationship, whether healthy or sick, is the family."[416] p.203

I do not share Harris's thoughts that "contrary to popular opinion, there is no scientific evidence for the application of our Euro-American concepts of family, house, home or household to the entire known spectrum of human domestic arrangements."[417] People, fortunately, are not just cold data and public opinion is usually imbued with good common sense. People are driven to the formation of a family nucleus not only by biological and emotional factors, but also by social considerations. The vast majority of them are sensitive to their human condition and believe that their families are important for the welfare of the general community. They do not deny its natural importance and its value system, and they have enough common sense to place in the right perspective both statistical and scientific data.

Freud, understanding that people are inclined to aggression, was of the opinion that the family is the germ-cell of civilization, essential to counteract man's aggressive instinct. He viewed the presence of aggressive instincts in humans as a force that opposes the course of civilization. Indeed, he stated, "[C]ivilization is a process in the service of Eros whose purpose is to combine single human individuals, and after that families, then races, peoples and nations, into one great unity, the unity of mankind. . . . [but] man's natural aggressive instinct, the hostility of each against all and of all against each, opposes this programme of civilization."[96] p.122 The natural aggressive instinct, well recognized by all, is the one at the basis of much violence in both families and communities.

The important issue is the presence of many broken families in communities at risk for violent antisocial behavior. The previously mentioned Wisconsin study may be representative of the decay of the family unit throughout the United States and of its relationship to criminal behavior, often of a violent type against persons. Criminality is neither innate nor is it immutable. As revealed by research, the criminal behavior of a sociopath emerges from the trauma of neglect or abuse (or both), and anti-social behavior is often a coping mechanism, a manifestation of immature defenses. Paradoxically, these mechanisms and antisocial outbursts cover the depression and anxiety the criminals are supposedly incapable of feeling. Their subsequent behavior then takes the form of drug abuse, masochism, insensitivity to others and their possessions, and a distrust or paranoia towards mainstream society.[418, 419]

Many offenders live in impoverished conditions, lacking in education, lacking in family stability. The breakdown of the family has certainly contributed to this lack of stability in the lives of both offenders and victims and has interfered with their ability to nurture and care for others. It has also contributed to the devaluation of life. Without a strong base from which to begin, it is difficult for people to develop self-esteem and to contribute positively to their communities.

The victimizers are often victims of their social milieu which is not conducive to transcending the sad realities of their lives and they lack opportunities and proper leadership to motivate them to move forward in a competitive, technological society. This is the background of the social misfits of Reusch[420] who share a common denominator: a lack of social conscience, a lack of social and personal responsibility, a self-centered attitude, a self-indulgent outlook on life and a tendency to manipulate people and situations through deception and violence. The solution to the cogent problems of violence and crime in our cities goes much deeper. It goes to the core of society: to the family unit.[167]

Broken families bring about illegitimacy, illiteracy, welfarism, confusion of values, frustration, anger, destructive behavior and demotivated resignation. If we accept that it is not only life that originates within the family, but also behavior—normal, abnormal, or violent—society should assess anew its priorities in the war against social violence and tackle the problem at its roots. Otherwise, society will be guilty of neglect in directing its attention elsewhere, and of only applying the usual Band-Aid approach to this problem. I wonder if society is able and willing to accept this challenging task.

Obviously there are some families that cannot be reintegrated because of the unfitness of the parents or, at times, serious disturbances in the children. Any forced reunification of the family for its own sake is not desirable. However, my suggestions are strongly directed towards the educational, religious, and governmental leaders of our country, who, when creating new policies and writing new laws, must do their utmost to help those young people who will be forming tomorrow's families to understand the responsibility that they accept with their union, for themselves, for their children and for society.

The answer to apparently complex problems is often of a simple nature. My idea may sound simplistic, and though reasonable, its implementation may seem an arduous, even impossible, task. Its aim is high and all-encompassing, and requires the efforts of all of us in the attempt to reach the goal. Otherwise it is only an impossible dream of a Don Quixotian quest.

In writing on the dualism of human nature, Durkheim[421] attempted to explain it stating that a human being not only *feels himself* to be double, but that he actually *is* double. "There are in him two classes of states of consciousness that differ from each other in origin and nature, and in the ends towards which they aim ... the one purely individual and rooted in our organisms, the other social and nothing but an extension of society."pp.161-162 Commenting on the painful character of this duality within humankind, since society "obliges us to surpass ourselves," and since "the role of the social being in our single selves will grow ever more important as history moves ahead," he envisioned that as civilization evolves this dualistic struggle within humankind will increase and that "it is wholly improbable that there will ever be an era in which man is required to resist himself to a lesser degree,"p.163 and live a life with less tension.

The solution to the present social violence lies in the moral fortitude of the people, in the strengthening of family ties, the building of the original cooperative community, the rebirth of a genuine love for one another. Exploitation of the poor or disadvantaged, whether by drugs or guns or political maneuvering, must be stopped. People should be helped to become responsible citizens and not kept in a dependency status.

Currie,[422] after discussing the necessity of addressing the increasing "destruction of solid labor markets" and stressing the importance of preventive social services and a response to the flood of hard drugs in the United States, stated that a new approach towards crime in the coming decades should consist in the "human-ecological" and added, "By that I mean a strategy which includes intervention on the level of individuals and families 'at risk,' but also moves beyond that level to exert social control over those larger forces which now are increasingly undermining communities and placing families at risk in the first place."p.10-11

In the final analysis, evil exists, as St. Augustine said, because love or good is absent. We must put some good into the lives of those people who are prone to violence, especially the young, and prevent them from becoming tomorrow's offenders. Good people should speak up in defense of the many victims who are part of an unending genocide and should force the makers of society to finally address the real issue at the roots of crime. It is long overdue!

EPILOGUE

After such a long journey in a labyrinth of data and opinions, it is natural to ask oneself what has been accomplished with such a painstaking investigation. Violence has always existed in the world and seems to be an integral part of human nature. It is my belief that sociological factors are facilitators of criminality and violent behavior and form their cradle and breeding ground.

I have tried to convey to the reader that one's personal psychological makeup is strictly connected to the biological self and that the two are intertwined and influence each other in facilitating crime, especially violent crime, and that the destructive hostility in humans is at the basis of all of the major manifestations of violence, be they crimes of murder, forcible rape, aggravated assault, or robbery.

I was confirmed in my ideas that crimes of violence are facilitated by a low I.Q., organic disease of the brain, the explosive dysrhythmias often undetectable by electroencephalograms, as well as by unemployment, lack of training, lack of job opportunities, poverty, alcohol and drug addiction in those persons who have a certain predisposition to antisocial acting out when faced with stressful environmental conditions or inter- and intra personal conflicts.

I am convinced that guns have become a lethal extension of the human hand because of our cultural decay and their easy availability. Their frequent use has desensitized many of us to their ominous consequences.

After such a meandering voyage searching for the one and only real cause of crime, if such a one exists, I have come to believe that violence is not primarily caused by the many variables mentioned above, which have been the object of decades of repetitious studies, but is an act of volition of the individual, who, master of his or her life for better or for worse, pulls the trigger of a gun and kills or maims fellow humans, or who physically assaults them in the act of committing crimes or during episodes of domestic violence.

The eternal dichotomy as to whether violent crimes are due to personal irresponsibility or to socio-demographic variables is still loudly knocking on the social door and is putting pressure on us for answers. That answer is, I believe, to be found within the individual's personal responsibility and in the social microstructure called the family, both of which are part of the larger society. The policy makers seem to have forgotten that society is not an abstract entity, but the composite of families, and that families are the togetherness of people, ideally bound by mutual feelings of love and protection, and of love for humanity at large. They have diverted their attention towards other goals that are important, yes, but not in and of themselves causative of violence. And this has been done in a most unsuccessful way, while the killing continues as does the disintegration of the families. The question one should ask is what does the future hold in store for us?

Recent FBI Uniform Crime Reports estimates of crime in the United States during 1993 give the murder rate in a crescendo, +3 percent higher than in 1992. The decline of −4 percent for forcible rape, and of −2 percent for robbery, with no change for aggravated assault may be an expression of underreporting and, as mentioned previously, even murder may be underreported.

The upsurge of violence among juvenile offenders is particularly worrisome. These young people often kill randomly and unexpectedly, almost in a ludic fashion. They will be tomorrow's parents!

Law-abiding citizens feel frustrated and demoralized by the present situation. A creeping fear has slowly taken hold of many of them. Their way of living has often become constricted and uneasy. Violence has interfered with our daily routines and has undermined our sense of security and well-being. Our society shows the fever of violence, the disease par excellence of the twentieth century. The decay of the moral fabric of society is spreading like a cancerous condition and, in spite of all the voiced efforts to correct the situation, and the many well-meaning approaches which have been attempted, social destabilization and the disappearance of values and virtues continues, while violence increases.

Fifteen centuries ago the grandiosity that was the Roman Empire rapidly crumbled under conditions similar to those existing today: disorganization, demoralization, lack of altruism, and social depravity. History goes in cycles, as Hegel and Vico often stated. Santayana observed that those who ignore history are often condemned to repeat it. Let us hope that good will triumph over evil!

REFERENCES

1. Zillmann, D.: *Hostility and Aggression.* Hilldale, Erlbaum, 1979.
2. Genesis 6:13.
3. Kirk, G.S.: *The Nature of Greek Myths.* London, Penguin, 1974.
4. Ecclesiastes, 1:8.
5. Williams, J.G.: *The Bible, Violence and the Sacred.* San Francisco, Harper and Row, 1991.
6. Schwager, R.: *Must there be Scapegoats?* Assad, M.L. (Trans.) San Francisco, Harper and Row, 1987.
7. Jeremiah 9:4.
8. Genesis 4:15.
9. Sanad, N.: Surat al-Ma'ith v:33, In *The Theory of Crime and Criminal Responsibility in Islamic Law: Sharia.* Chicago, University of Illinois, 1991.
10. Seneca: *The Tragedies.* Slavitt, D.R. (Ed., Trans.), Baltimore, Johns Hopkins University Press, 1992, vol I, p. 203.
11. Homer: *The Iliad.* Fagles, R.: (Trans.) New York, Penguin, 1991.
12. Saunders, Trevor J.: *Plato's Penal Code.* Oxford, Clarendon Paperbacks, 1994.
13. Shakespeare, W.: Macbeth, Act. II, Scene I. In William Aldis Wright, (Ed.): *The Complete Works of William Shakespeare.* The Cambridge Edition Text, Garden City, Garden City Books, 1936, pp. 1033–1034.
14. *The Divine Comedy of Dante Alighieri. Inferno.* Mandelbaum, A. (Trans.): Berkley, Bantam, 1982, Canto VII, p. 45.
15. Bettleheim, B.: *The Uses of Enchantment.* New York, Vintage Books, 1989.
16. Lorenz, K.: *On Aggression.* Wilson, M.J. (Trans.) New York, Harcourt, Brace & World, 1963.
17. Kou, ZY.: *The Dynamics of Behavior Development.* New York, Random House, 1967.
18. Craig, W.: Why do animals fight? *International Journal of Ethics. 31:*264–278, 1921.
19. Smith, C.U.M.: Evolutionary biology and psychiatry. *Br J Psychiatry, 162:*149–153, 1993.
20. Berkowitz, L.: The expression and reduction of hostility. *Psychol Bull, 55:*257–283.
21. Berkowitz, L.: Impulse, Aggression and the Gun. *Psychology Today, 2:*18–22.
22. Berkowitz, L.: Frustration-aggression hypothesis: Examination and reformulation. *Psychol Bull, 106:*59–73, 1989.
23. Bandura, A., and Walters, R.H.: *Adolescent Aggression: A Study of the Influence*

of Child-Training Practices and Family Interrelationships. New York, Ronald Press, 1959.

24. Johnson, R.N.: *Aggression in Man and Animals.* Philadelphia, Saunders, 1972.

25. Degler, C.N.: *In Search of Human Nature: The Decline and Revival of Darwinism in American Social Thought.* New York, Oxford University Press, 1991.

26. Carmichael, L.: The growth of the sensory control of behavior before birth. *Psychol Rev, 54:*322–322, 1947.

27. Hirsch, J.: Behavior-genetics, or "experimental," analysis: The challenge of science versus the lure of technology. *Amer Psychol, 2:*118–130, 1967.

28. Mazur, A., and Robertson, L.S.: *Biology and Social Behavior.* New York, Free Press, 1972.

29. Barkow, J.H.: Darwinian psychological anthropology: a biosocial approach. *Current Anthropology, 14:*375, 1973.

30. Willhoite, F.H. Jr.: Primates and political authority: A behavioral perspective. *American Political Science Review, 70:*1110, 1976.

31. Bollone, P.L.B.: *Cesare Lombroso: Ovvero Il Principio Dell'Irresponsabilità.* Turin, Società Editrice Internazionale, 1992.

32. Bromberg, W.: *Crime and the Mind: A Psychiatric Analysis of Crime and Punishment.* New York, Macmillan, 1965.

33. Wagner, H.: *Die Fleischfressenden Pflanzen.* Leipzig, 1911.

34. Semerari, A. and Citterio, C.: *Medicina Criminologica e Psichiatria Forense.* Milan, Vallardi, 1975.

35. Kretschmer, E.: *Körper Bau und Character.* Sprott, W.J.H. (Trans.) New York, Cooper Square, 1970.

36. Brown, S.E., Finn-Aage, E., and Geis, G.: *Criminology: Explaining Crime and its Context.* Cincinnati, Anderson, 1991.

37. Fenwick, P.: Brain, mind and behavior, *Br J Psychiatry, 163:*565–573, 1993.

38. Papez, J.W.: A proposed mechanism of emotion. *Archives of Neurological Psychiatry, 38:*725–743, 1937.

39. Luria, A.R.: The frontal lobe. In Vinken, P.J., and Bruym, G.W. (Eds.): *Handbook of Neurology,* New York, North Holland, 1969, vol. 2.

40. Jarvie, H.E.: Frontal lobe wound causing disinhibition: A study of six cases. *J Neurol Neurosurg Psychiatry, 17:*14–32, 1954.

41. Blumer, D., and Benson, D.F.: Personality changes with frontal and temporal lesions. In Benson, D.F., and Blumer, D. (Eds.): *Psychiatric Aspects of Neurologic Disease,* New York, Grune and Stratton, 1975, pp. 25–48.

42. Grafman, J., Vance, S.C., Weingartner, H., et al.: The effects of lateralized frontal lesions on mood regulation. *Brain, 109:*1127–1148, 1986.

43. Miller, L.: Neuropsychological perspectives on delinquency, *Behavioral Sciences and the Law, 6:*409–428, 1988.

44. Hill, D., and Watterson, D.: Electroencephalographic studies of psychopathic personalities. *J Neurol Psychiatry, 5:*47–64, 1942.

45. Silverman, D.: The electroencephalogram of criminals. *Archives of Neurology and Psychiatry, 52:*38–42, 1944.

46. Gibbs, F.A., Bagchi, B.K., and Bloomberg, W.: Electroencephalographic study of criminals. *Am J Psychiatry, 102:*294–298, 1947.

47. Mednick, S.A., and Volavka, J. Biology and crime. In Morris N., and Tonry, N. (Eds.): *Crime and Justice: Am Annual Review of Research.* Chicago, University of Chicago Press, 1980, vol. II.

48. Buikhuisen, W.: Aggressive behavior and cognitive disorders. *Int J Law Psychiatry, 5:*205–217, 1982.

49. Williams, D.: Neural factors related to habitual aggression: Consideration of differences between those habitual aggressives and others who have committed crimes of violence. *Brain, 92:*503–520, 1969.

50. Monroe, R.: *Episodic Behavioral Disorders.* Cambridge, Harvard University Press, 1970.

51. Bach-y-Rita, G., Lion, J.R., Climent, C.E., and Ervin, F.: Episodic dyscontrol: A study of 130 violent patients. *Am J Psychiatry, 27:*1473–1478, 1971.

52. Yeudall, L.T.: *The Neuropsychology of Aggression.* Clarence M. Hincks Memorial Lectures. Edmonton (Alberta, Canada), 1978.

53. Zilboorg, G.: *A History of Medical Psychology.* New York, Norton, 1941.

54. Delgado-Escueta, A.V., Mattson, R.H., King, L., Goldensohn, E.S., Spiegel, H., Madsen, J., Crandall, P., Dreifuss, F., and Porter, R.J.: The nature of aggression during epileptic seizures. *N Engl J Med, 305:*711–716, 1981.

55. *APA Task Force on Clinical Aspects of the Violent Individual.* Washington, American Psychiatric Association, 1974, p. 9.

56. Stone, A.A.: Violence and temporal lobe epilepsy. *Am J Psychiatry, 141:*1641, 1984.

57. Rickler, K.C.: Episodic dyscontrol. In Benson, D.F., and Blumer, D. (Eds.): *Psychiatric Aspects of Neurologic Disease,* New York, Grune and Stratton, 1975, pp. 49–73.

58. Elliott, F.A.: *Episodic Dyscontrol, Neurological Findings in 190 Cases.* Presented at Byberry State Hospital, Philadelphia, March 1980.

59. Monroe, R.: *Brain Dysfunction in Aggressive Criminals.* Toronto, Lexington Books, 1978.

60. Bear, D.: Dr. Bear replies. *Am J Psychiatry, 41:*1641–1642, 1984.

61. Binnie, C., Channon, S., and Marston, D.: Behavioural correlates of inter-ictal spikes. In Smith, D., Trieman, D., and Trimble, M. (Eds.): *Advances in Neurology, Neurobehavioural Problems in Epilepsy.* New York, Raven Press, 1991, vol. 55, pp. 113–127.

62. Engel, J., Bandler, R., Griffiths, N., et al.: Neurobiological evidence for epilepsy-induced ictal disturbances. In Smith, D., Trieman, D., and Trimble, M. (Eds.): *Advances in Neurology, Neurobehavioural Problems in Epilepsy.* New York, Raven Press, 1991, vol. 55, pp. 97–113.

63. Struve, F.A., Saraf, K.R., Arko, R.S., et al.: Relationship between paroxysmal electroencephalographic dysrhythmia and suicide ideation and attempts in psychiatric patients. In Shagass, C., Gershon, S., and Friedhof, J.: *Psychopathology and Brain Dysfunction.* New York, Raven Press, 1977.

64. Menninger, K.: *The Vital Balance.* New York, Viking Press, 1963.

65. Binder, R.L., and McNiel, D.E.: Effects of diagnosis and context on dangerousness. *Am J Psychiatry, 145:*728–732, 1988.

66. Elliott, F.A.: Neurological findings in adult minimal brain dysfunction and the dyscontrol syndrome. *J Nerv Ment Dis, 170:*680–687, 1982.

67. Mark, V.H., and Ervin, F.R.: *Violence and the Brain.* New York, Harper and Row, 1970.

68. American Psychiatric Association. Posttraumatic stress disorder. *Diagnostic and Statistical Manual of Mental Disorders,* 4th ed. Washington, American Psychiatric Association, 1994.

69. Eron, L.D.: Prescription for reduction of aggression. *American Psychologist, 35:*244–252, 1980.

70. Valzelli, L.: *Psychobiology of Aggression and Violence.* New York, Raven Press, 1981.

71. Wilder, J.: Sugar metabolism in its relation to criminology. In Linder, R., and Seliger, R., (Eds.): *Handbook of Correctional Psychology.* Philosophical Library, New York, 1947.

72. Virkkunen, M., Rawlings, R., Tokola, R., Poland, R.E., Guidotti, A., Nemeroff, C., Bissette, G., Kalogeras, K., Karonen, S., and Linnoila, M.: CSF biochemistries, glucose metabolisms, and diurnal activity rhythms in alcoholics, violent offenders, fire setters, and healthy volunteers. *Arch Gen Psychiatry, 51:*10–27, 1994.

73. Elliott, F.A.: I fattori neurologici del comportamento violento. In Ferracuti, F. (Ed.): *Trattato di Criminologia, Medicina e Psichiatria* Forense, Milan, Giuffrè, 1988, pp. 73–115.

74. Yakolev, R., and Lecours, R.: *Regional development of the brain in early life.* Oxford, Blackwood, 1967.

75. Hirschi, T., and Hindelang, M.: Intelligence and delinquency: a revisionist review. *American Sociological Review, 42:*471–586, 1977.

76. Moffitt, T., Gabrielli, W., Mednick, S., and Schulsinger, F.: Socioeconomic states, IQ and delinquency. *J Abnorm Psychol, 90:*152–156, 1981.

77. Kirkegaard-Sorensen, L., and Mednick, S.A.: A prospective study of predictors of criminality: A description of registered criminality in high-risk and low-risk families. In Mednick, S.A., and Christiansen, K.O. (Eds.): *Biosocial Bases of Criminal Behavior.* New York, Gardner, 229–243.

78. Jacobs, P.A., Brunton, M., Melville, M.M., Brittain, R.P., and McClermont, W.F.: Aggressive behaviour, mental sub-normality, and the XYY male. *Nature, 208:*1351–13152, 1965.

79. Witkin, H.A., Mednick, S.A., Schulsinger, F., Bakkestrom, E., Christiansen, K.O., Goodenough, D.R., Hirschhorn, K., Lundstein, C., Owen, D.R., Philip, J., Rubin, D.B., and Stocking, M.: Criminality in XYY and XXY men. *Science, 193:*547–555, 1976.

80. Craft, M.: The current status of XYY and XXY syndromes: A review of treatment implications. In March, F.H., and Katz, J. (Eds.): *Biology, Crime and Ethics.* Cincinnati, Anderson, 1985, pp. 113–121.

81. Nellist, C.C.: Research links impulsive aggression with genetic disorder in one extended family. *Clinical Psychiatry News,* January 1994, p. 3.

82. Mednick, S.A. and Finello, K.M.: Biological factors in crime: implications for forensic psychiatry. *International Journal of Law and Psychiatry, 6:*115, 1983.

83. Christiansen, K.O.: A preliminary study of criminality among twins. In Mednick, S.A., and Christiansen, K.O. (Eds.): *Biosocial Bases of Criminal Behavior.* New York, Gardner, 1977.

84. Coid, B., Lewis, S.W., and Reveley, A.M.: A twin study of psychosis and criminality. *Br J Psychiatry, 162:*87–92, 1993.

85. Ferracuti, F. and Ferracuti, S.: Criminology in the XXI century: A biological perspective. *Rivista Europea di Psichiatria, 2:*41–45, 1990.

86. James, W.: *Principles of Psychology.* New York, 1890.

87. McDougall, W.: *An Outline of Abnormal Psychology.* London, Methuen, 1926.

88. Adler, A.: *The Practice and Theory of Individual Psychology.* New York, Harcourt-Brace, 1927.

89. Ardrey, R.: *The Social Contract.* New York, Athenum, 1970.

90. Freud, S.: *Beyond the Pleasure Principle.* The Standard Edition. Strachey, J. (Trans.): New York, Norton, 1961.

91. Freud, S.: *The Ego and the Id.* Strachey, J. (Trans.): New York, Norton, 1961.

92. de Sousa, R.D.: *The Rationality of Emotion.* Cambridge, MIT Press, 1987.

93. James, W.: What is an emotion? *Mind, 9:*188–205, 1884.

94. Fromm-Reichmann, F.: Psychoanalytic remarks on the clinical significance of hostility. In Bullard, D. (Ed.): *Psychotherapy: Selected Papers of Frieda Fromm-Reichmann.* Chicago, University of Chicago Press, 1959, pp. 277–282.

95. Fava, M., and Rosenbaum, J.F.: The relationship between anger and depression. *Clinical Advances in the Treatment of Psychiatric Disorders, 7:*1–3, 1993.

96. Freud, S.: *Civilization and Its Discontents.* The Standard Edition. Strachey, J. (Trans.) New York, Norton, 1961.

97. Kohut, H.: The psychoanalytic study of the child. Monograph No. 4. In *The Analysis of the Self.* New York, International University Press, 1971. p. 28.

98. Mahler, M.: A study of the separation-individuation process. *Psychoanal Study Child, 26:*403–424, 1972.

99. Kline, M.: A contribution to the psychogenesis of manic-depressive states. *Int J Psychoanal, 16:*145–174, 1935.

100. Dollard, J., Miller, N., Doob, L., Mower, O.H., and Sears, R.R.: *Frustration and Aggression.* New Haven, Yale University Press, 1939.

101. Fenichel, O.: *The Psychoanalytic Theory of Neurosis.* New York, Norton, 1945.

102. Bowlby, J.: Developmental psychiatry comes of age. *Am J Psychiatry, 145:*1–10, 1988.

103. Hartmann, H.: *Ego Psychology and the Problem of Adaptation.* New York, International Universities Press, 1958.

104. Massermann, J.: *Principles of Dynamic Psychiatry.* Philadelphia, Saunders, 1961.

105. Blackburn, R.: *The Psychology of Criminal Conduct: Theory Research and Practice.* New York, J. Wiley, 1993.

106. Horney, K.: *The Collected Works of Karen Horney.* New York, Norton, 1945, vol. I.
107. Schilder, P.: *Goals and desires of man, a Psychological Survey of Life.* New York, Columbia University Press, 1942.
108. Satten, J., Menninger, K.M., Rosen, I., and Mayman, M.: Murder without apparent motive: A study in personality disorganization. *Am J Psychiatry, 117:*48, 1960.
109. Ramon-y-Cajal, S.: *Les nouvelles ideés sur la structure du système nerveux chex l'homme et chez les vertébrés.* Paris, Reinwold, 1895.
110. Feldman, P.: *The Psychology of Crime.* Cambridge, Cambridge University Press, 1993, p. 435.
111. Monahan, J., and Steadman, H.: Crime and mental disorder: An epidemiological approach. In Morris, J., and Tonry, M. (Eds.): *Crime and Justice: An Annual Review of the Literature.* Chicago, University of Chicago Press, 1983, vol 4, pp. 145–189.
112. Bland, R., and Orn, H.: Family violence and psychiatric disorder. *Can J Psychiatry, 31:*129–137, 1986.
113. Henn, F.A., Herjanic, M., and Vanderpearl, R.H.: Forensic psychiatry: Diagnosis and criminal responsibility. *J Nerv Ment Dis, 162:*423–429, 1976.
114. Häfner, H., and Böker, W.: *Crimes of Violence by Mentally Abnormal Offenders.* Cambridge, Cambridge University Press, 1982.
115. Steadman, H.J., Fabrisek, S., Dvorkin, J., and Holohean, E.J.: A survey of mental disability among state prison inmates. *Hosp Community Psychiatry, 38:*1086–1090, 1987.
116. Sivetz, A., Saline, M.E., Stough, T., and Brewer, T.: The prevalence of mental illness in a state correctional institution for men. *Journal of Prison and Jail Health, 8:*3–15, 1989.
117. Taylor, P. and Gunn, J.: Risk of violence among psychotic men. *British Medical Journal, 288:*1945–1949, 1984.
118. Taylor, P.: Psychiatric disorders in London's life-sentenced offenders. *Br J Psychiatry, 26:*63–78, 1986.
119. Strick, S.E.: A demographic study of 100 admissions to a female forensic center: Incidences of multiple charges and multiple diagnoses. *Journal of Psychiatry and the Law, 17:*435–448, 1989.
120. Snow, W.H., and Briar, K.H.: The convergence of the mentally disordered and the jail population. *Journal of Offender Counseling, 15:*147–162, 1990.
121. Lindqvist, P., and Allebeck, P.: Schizophrenia and crime: A longitudinal follow up of 644 schizophrenics in Stockholm. *Br J Psychiatry, 157:*3345–3350, 1990.
122. Hodgins, S.: Mental disorder, intellectual deficiency and crime. *Arch Gen Psychiatry, 49:*476–483, 1992.
123. Tammany, J.M., and Evans, R.G.: Personality and intellectual characteristics of adult male felons as a function of offense category. *J Clin Psychol, 46:*906–911, 1990.
124. Cattell, R.B., Eber, H., and Tatsuoka, M.: *Handbook for the Sixteen Personality Factor Questionnaire (16PF).* Champaign, IL, IPAT, 1970.

125. DeWolfe, A.S., and Ryan, J.J.: Wechsler Performance IQ/Verbal IQ index in a forensic sample: A reconsideration. *J Clin Psychol, 40:*291–294, 1984.

126. Holland, T.R., Beckett, G.E., and Levi, M.: Intelligence, personality and criminal violence: a multivariate analysis. *J Consult Clin Psychol, 4:*106–11, 1981.

127. Mueser, K.T., Yarnold, P.R., Levinson, D.F., Singh, H., Bellack, A.S., Kee, K., Morrison, R.L., and Yadalam, K.G.: Prevalence of substance abuse in schizophrenia: Demographic and clinical correlates. *Schizophr Bull, 16:*31–56, 1990.

128. Regier, D.A., Farmer, M.E., Rae, D.S., Locke, B.Z., Keith, S.J., Judd, L.L., and Goodwin, F.K.: Comorbidity of mental disorders with alcohol and other drug abuse. *JAMA, 264:*2511–2518, 1990.

129. Abram, K.M., and Teplin, L.A.: Co-occuring disorders among mentally ill jail detainees: Implications for public policy. *Am Psychol, 46:*1036–1045, 1991.

130. Hodgins, S.: Reply to: Violence in the severely mentally ill. Letters to the Editor. *Arch Gen Psychiatry, 51:*71–72, 1994.

131. Palermo, G.B., Gumz, E.J., Smith, M.B., and Liska, F.J.: Escape from psychiatrization: A statistical analysis of referrals to a forensic unit. *International Journal of Offender Therapy and Comparative Criminology. 36:*89–102, 1992.

132. Giovannoni, J.M., and Gurel, L.: Socially disruptive behaviour of ex-mental patients. *Arch Gen Psychiatry, 17:*146–153, 1967.

133. Durgin, J.R., Pasewark, R.A., and Albers, D.: Criminality and mental illness: a study of current arrest rates in a rural state. *Am J Psychiatry, 134:*80–83, 1977.

134. Swanson, J.W., Hozer, C.E., Ganju, V.K., and Jono, R.T.: Violence and psychiatric disorder in the community: Evidence from the epidemiological catchment area surveys. *Hosp Community Psychiatry, 41:*761–770, 1990.

135. Toch, H., and Adams, K.: *The Disturbed Violent Offender.* New Haven, Yale University Press, 1989.

136. Steadman, H.J., and Felson, R.B.: Self-reports of violence: Ex-mental patients, ex-offenders, and the general population. *Criminology, 22:*321–342, 1984.

137. Lindqvist, P.: Criminal homicide in northern Sweden, 1970–1981: Alcohol intoxication, alcohol abuse and mental disease. *Int J Law Psychiatry, 8:*19–37, 1986.

138. Bernadt, M.W., and Murray, R.M.: Psychiatric disorder, drinking and alcoholism: What are the links? *Br J Psychiatry, 148:*393–400, 1986.

139. Wolf, A.W., Schubert, D.S.P., Patterson, M.B., Brande, T.P., Brocco, K.J., and Pendleton, L.: Associations among major psychiatric diagnoses. *J Consult Clin Psycholo, 56:*292–294, 1988.

140. O'Farrell, K.T., Yarnold, P.R., Levinson, D.F., Singh, H., Bellack, A.S., Kee, K., Morrison, R.L., and Yadalam, K.G.: Addictive behaviors among hospitalized psychiatric patients. *Addict Behav, 8:*329–333, 1984.

141. Bliss, E.L., and Larson, E.M.: Sexual criminality and hypnotizability. *J Nerv Ment Dis, 173:*522–526, 1985.

142. Collins, J.J., and Bailey, S.L.: Traumatic stress disorder and violent behavior. *Journal of Traumatic Stress, 3:*203–220, 1990.

142. Collins, J.J., and Bailey, S.L.: Traumatic stress disorder and violent behavior. *Journal of Traumatic Stress, 3:*203–220, 1990.

143. Johnson, J.: *Removing the Chronically Mentally Ill from Jail.* Washington, National Coalition for Jail Reform, 1984.

144. Briar, J.H.: Jails: Neglected asylums. *Social Casework: The Journal of Contemporary Social Work,* 387–393, 1983.

145. Adler, F.: Jails as a repository for former mental patients. *International Journal of Offender Therapy and Comparative Criminology, 30:*225–236, 1986.

146. Phillips, M.R., Wolf, A.S., and Coons, D.J.: Psychiatry and the criminal justice system: Testing the myths. *Am J Psychiatry, 145:*605–610, 1988.

147. Quinsey, V.L., Warnford, A., Preusse, M., and Link, N.: A follow-up study of released Oak Ridge patients review board discharges. *Br J Psychiatry, 15:*264–279, 1975.

148. Shils, E.: *The Constitution of Society.* Chicago, University of Chicago Press, 1982.

149. Baumeister, R.: *The Meanings of Life.* New York, Guilford Press, 1991.

150. Clinard, Marshall B. Criminological research. In Merton, R.K., Broom, L. and Cottrell, L.S. Jr.: *Sociology Today: Problems and Perspectives.* New York, Basic Books, 1960, p. 510.

151. Glueck, S., and Glueck, E.: *Unravelling Juvenile Delinquency.* New York, The Commonwealth Fund, 1950.

152. Inkeles, A.: Personality and social structure. In Merton, R.K., Broom, L., and Cottrell, L.S. Jr.: *Sociology Today.* New York, Basic Books, 1960, pp. 249–276.

153. Shaw, C.R.: *Delinquency Areas.* Chicago, University of Chicago Press, 1931.

154. Durkheim, E.: *Suicide: A Study in Sociology.* New York, Free Press, 1966.

155. Wolfgang, M., and Ferracuti, F.: *The Subculture of Violence.* London, Social Science Paperbacks, 1967.

156. Palermo, G.B.: The 1978 Italian mental health law: A personal evaluation. *J Roy Soc Med, 84:*99–102, 1991.

157. Shaw, C.R., and McKay, H.D.: *Juvenile Delinquency and Urban Areas.* Chicago, University of Chicago Press, 1942.

158. Ogbrun, W.: *Social Change with Respect to Culture and Original Nature.* New York, Viking, 1922.

159. Merton, R.: Social structure and anomie. In Cressey, D.R., and Ward, D.A.: (Eds.): *Delinquency, Crime and Social Process.* New York, Harper and Row, 1969, pp. 254–284.

160. Kohlberg, L.: The development of moral character. In Hoffmann, M.C. (Ed.): *Child Development.* New York, Russell Sage foundation, 1964.

161. McCord, J.: Some child rearing antecedents of criminal behavior in adult man. *J Pers Soc Psychol, 37:*1477–86, 1979.

162. West, D.J., and Farrington, D.P.: *Who Becomes Delinquent?* London, Heinemann, 1973.

163. Reik, T.: *L'Impulso a Confessare.* Milan, Feltrinelli, 1967.

164. Smith, P.Z.: *Felony Defendants in Large Urban Counties, 1990.* Washington, U.S. Department of Justice, May 1993.

165. Beck, A., Gilliard, D., Greenfeld, L., Harlow, C., Hester, T., Jankowski, L.,

Snell, T., Stephan, J., and Morton, D.: *Survey of State Prison Inmates, 1991.* Washington, U.S. Department of Justice, March 1993.

166. Siegel, L.J.: *Criminology,* 2nd ed. St. Paul, 1986.

167. Palermo, G.B., Smith, M.B., DiMotto, J. and Christopher, T.P.: Soaring crime in a midwestern American city: a statistical study. *International Journal of Offender Therapy and Comparative Criminology, 36:*291–305, 1992, p. 293.

168. Lawrence, Jill. AP. Doctors active in campaign against guns. *Detroit News,* December 13, 1993.

169. Popkin, J.: Bombs over America. *U.S. News and World Report,* July 29, 1991, pp. 18–20.

170. Squitieri, T. and Kelley, J.: Bloody weekend boosts toll of killing. *USA Today,* Oct. 16, 1990, p. 3A.

171. Yellin, A.: Weapons. *American Medical News,* April 14, 1989, p. 30.

172. *Uniform Crime Reports, 1992. Preliminary Annual Release.* Washington, DC, U.S. Department of Justice, August, 1993.

173. *U.S. Bureau of Census.* Washington, DC, U.S. Government Printing Office, 1991.

174. *World Book Encyclopedia.* Chicago, 1994.

175. Imbert, P.: Policing a violent society. *Journal of the Royal Society of Medicine, 83:*425–426, 1990.

176. Imbert, P.: Policing a violent society. *Journal of the Royal Society of Medicine, 83:*425–426, 1990.

177. Plagen, P., Miller, M., Foote, D. and Yoffe, E.: Violence in our culture. *Newsweek,* April 1, 1991, pp. 46–52.

178. Major offenses known to police. *Federal Bureau of Investigation Uniform Crime Reports.* Washington, U.S. Government Printing Office, 1985.

179. Major offenses known to police. *Federal Bureau of Investigation Uniform Crime Reports.* Washington, U.S. Government Printing Office, 1986.

180. Major offenses known to police. *Federal Bureau of Investigation Uniform Crime Reports.* Washington, U.S. Government Printing Office, 1993.

181. Hackett, G., Underwood, A., and Rosenberg, D.: The bloodiest year yet? *Newsweek,* July 1990, p. 16.

182. Palermo, G.B., Smith, M.B., DiMotto, J.J. and Christopher, T.P.: Victimization revisited. a national statistical analysis. *International Journal of Offender Therapy and Comparative Criminology, 36:*187–210, 1992.

183. David, M. and Kahle, R.: Homicide rates in selected U.S. cities in 1992: homicides per 100,000 population. In *Crime in Metropolitan Detroit: A Fact Book. Local and National Comparisons.* Detroit, Wayne State University Center for Urban Studies, August 1993.

184. Index crimes against persons. City of Milwaukee 1992 Public Safety *Report.* Milwaukee, Milwaukee Fire and Police Commission, 1993.

185. Henry, A. and Short, J.: *Suicide and Homicide.* New York, Free Press, 1954.

186. Gottlieb, P., Kramp, P., Lindhardt, A. and Christensen, O.: Social background of homicide. *International Journal of Offender Therapy and Comparative Criminology, 34,* 115–129, 1990.

187. Langevin, R. and Handy, L.: Stranger homicide in Canada: a national sample and a psychiatric sample. *J Crim Law and Criminology, 78:*398–429, 1987.
188. Gillies, H.: Homicide in the west of Scotland. *Br J Psychiatry, 128:*105–127, 1976.
189. *U.S. Justice Department Index Crimes.* U.S. Department of Justice Crime Reports, U.S., Washington DC, Government Printing Office, 1994.
190. Maguire, K., and Pastore, A.: *Bureau of Justice Statistics Sourcebook.* Washington, U.S. Government Printing Office, 1992.
191. *Data Service Division, Wisconsin Uniform Crime Reports Program.* Madison, State of Wisconsin, 1994.
192. Webster's Ninth New Collegiate Dictionary. Merriam-Webster Inc., Springfield, MA. 1988.
193. Macdonald, J.M.: *The Murderer and His Victim.* Springfield, Charles C Thomas, 1961.
194. *Dizionario Enciclopedico Italiano.* Rome, Istituto Poligrafico di Stato, 1970, vol. VII, pp. 107–108.
195. Blackburn, R.: On moral judgements and personality disorders: The myth of psychopathic personality revisited. *Br J Psychiatry, 153:*505–512, 1988.
196. Healey, W., and Bronner, A.F.: *Delinquents and Criminals.* New York, Macmillan, 1926.
197. Noyes, A.P., and Kolb, L.C.: *Modern Clinical Psychiatry.* Philadelphia, W.B. Saunders, 1958.
198. Cleckley, H.: *The Mask of Sanity.* St. Louis, Mosby, 1955.
199. Blackburn, R., and Maybury, C.: Identifying the psychopath: The relation of Cleckley's criteria to the interpersonal domain. *Person Individ Diff, 6:*375–386, 1985.
200. Hare, R.D., and McPherson, L.M.: Violent and aggressive behavior by criminal psychopaths. *International Journal of Law and Psychiatry. 7:*35–50, 1984. p. 35.
201. Serin, R.C.: Psychopathy and violence in criminals. *Journal of Interpersonal Violence, 6:*423–431, 1991.
202. Engel, G.L.: *Psychological Development in Health and Disease.* Philadelphia, W.B. Saunders, 1962.
203. Hare, R.M.: Plato. In *Founders of Thought.* Oxford, Oxford University Press, 1982.
204. Sherman, N.: *The Fabric of Character. Aristotle's Theory of Virtue.* Oxford, Clarendon, 1989.
205. Palermo, G.B., Liska, F.J., Palermo, M.T., and Dal Forno, G.: On the predictability of violent behavior: Considerations and guidelines. *J Forensic Sci:* 1436–1444, 1991.
206. De Jong, J., Kirkkunen, M., and Linnoila, M.: Factors associated with recidivism in a criminal population. *J Nerv Ment Dis 180:*543–550, 1992.
207. Holmes, R.M., and DeBurger, J.: *Serial Murder.* Newbury Park, Sage, 1990.
208. Federal Bureau of Investigation. *Criminal Investigative Analysis: Sexual homicide.* Quantico, National Center for the Analysis of Violent crime, 1990.
209. Hazelwood, R.R., and Douglas, J.E.: The lust murderer. In *Criminal Investigative*

analysis: Sexual homicide. Quantico, National Center for the Analysis of Violent crime, 1990, pp. 129–133.

210. Pauvert, J.J.: *Vie du marquis de Sade.* Édition Jean-Jacques Pauvert et Éditions Gallinard, Paris, 1965.

211. von Krafft-Ebing, R.: *Psychopathis sexualis: With especial reference to the antipathetic sexual instinct. A medico-forensic study.* New York, Bell, [1869] 1965.

212. Wilson, C.: *A Criminal Hstory of Mankind.* New York, Carroll and Graf, 1984.

213. Abrahamsen, D.: *The Murdering Mind.* New York, Harper Colophon Books, Harper and Row, 1973.

214. *State of Wisconsin vs. Jeffrey Dahmer,* Case No. F-912542, 1992, trial testimony, G.B. Palermo, 1992.

215. Levin, J., and Fox, J.A.: *Mass Murder: The Growing Menace.* New York, Plenum Press, 1985.

216. Lunde, D.T.: *Murder and Madness.* San Francisco, San Francisco Book Company, 1976.

217. Hickey, E. W.: *Serial Murderers and Their Victims.* Pacific Grove, Brooks/Cole. 1991. p. 8.

218. Hegger, Steven A. A Working Definition of Serial Murder and the Reductions of Linkage Blindness. *Journal of Police Science and Administration.* 1984;12(3)350.

219. Bennett, K.A.: Victim selection in the Jeffrey Dahmer slayings: an example of repetition in the paraphilias? *J Forensic Sci, 38:*1227–1232, 1993.

220. Kernberg, O.F.: *Severe Personality Disorders: Psychotherapeutic Strategies.* Newhaven, Yale University Press, 1984; *Aggression in Personality Disorders and Perversions.* Newhaven, Yale University Press, 1992.

221. Abrahamsen, D.: *The Murdering Mind.* New York, Harper Colophon Books, Harper and Row, 1973.

222. Crime in the United States: 1991. *Uniform Crime Reports.* Washington, United States, U.S. Government Printing Office, Aug. 30, 1992, p. 23.

223. Ellis, L. *Theories of Rape: Inquiries into the Causes of Sexual Aggression.* New.York, Hemisphere, 1989. p. 1.

224. Rota, A. La Violenza Carnale. In: F. Ferracuti (Ed.) *Trattato di Criminologia, Medicina Criminologica e Psichiatria Forense.* Milan, Giuffrè, 1988. Vol. 8. p. 317.

225. Report cites heavy toll of rapes on young. *The New York Times,* June 23, 1994, p. A8.

226. Amir, M.: *Patterns of Forcible Rape.* Chicago, University of Chicago Press, 1971.

227. Langevin, R., Paitich, D., and Russon, A.E.: Are rapists sexually anomalous, aggressive, or both. In Langevin, R. (Ed.): Erotic *Preference, Gender Identity and Aggression.* Hillsdale, Erlbaum, 1985.

228. Marshall, W.L., and Barbaree, H.E.: A behavioral view of rape. *International Journal of Law and Psychiatry, 7:*51–77, 1984. p. 60.

229. Wilson, J.Q., and Herrnstein, R.J.: *Crime and Human Nature.* New York, Simon & Schuster, 1985.

230. Conklin, J.E.: *Criminology,* 4th ed. New York, Macmillan, 1992.

231. Mehrof, B. and Kearon, P. Rape: an act of terror. In: *Notes From the Third Year.* New York, Women's Liberation Press, 1972.

232. Brownmiller, S. *Against our Will: Men Women and Rape.* New York, Simon and Schuster, 1975.

233. Groth, A., and Burgess, A.W.: Rape: A pseudosexual act. *International Journal of Women's Studies, 1:*207–210, 1978.

234. Oliver, W.: Sexual conquest and patterns of black-on-black violence: A structural-cultural perspective. *Violence and Victims, 4:*257–273, 1989.

235. von Hentig, H.: *The Criminal and His Victim.* New Haven, Yale University Press, 1948.

236. Schaefer, S.: *The Victim and His Criminal.* New York, Random House, 1968.

237. Zigo, L. and Molcán, J. *Victimology 18:*227–236, 1983.

238. Volk, P., Hilgarth, M. and Kolter, J.: The contribution to the victimology of sexual offense. *Münich Med. Wockenschrift, 121:*468–476, 1979. Cite Millet.

239. Russell, D.: *Politics of Rape.* New York, Stein and Day, 1975.

240. Selye, H.: *Stress Without Distress.* Philadelphia, Lippincott, 1974.

241. American Psychiatric Association. Posttraumatic stress disorder. *Diagnostic and Statistical Manual of Mental Disorders,* 4th ed. Washington, American Psychiatric Association, 1994.

242. Bard, M. and Sangrey, D.: *The Crime Victim's Book,* 2nd ed. New York, Brunner-Mazel, 1986.

243. Symonds, M.: Victims of violence: psychological effects and after effects. *Am J Psychoanalysis, 35:*19–26, 1975.

244. Notman, M. and Nadelson, C.: The rape victim: psychodynamic considerations. *Am J Psychiatry, 133:*408–412, 1976.

245. Krupnick, J.L., and Horowitz, M.J.: Stress response syndromes: Recurrent themes. *Arch Gen Psychiatry, 38:*428–435, 1981.

246. Schwendinger, H. and Schwendinger, J.: Rape victims and the false sense of guilt. *Crime and Social Justice, 417:*13, 1980.

247. Burgess, A.W., and Holstrom, L.L.: Rape trauma syndrome. *Am J Psychiatry, 131:*981–986, 1974.

248. Silver, R.L. and Wortman, C.B. Coping with undesirable events. In Barber, J., and Seligman, M.E.P. (Eds.): *Human Helplessness.* New York, Academic Press, 1980, pp. 279–375.

249. *Criminal Victimization in the United States, 1988.* Washington, DC, U.S. Department of Justice, 1989.

250. Koss, M.P.: The hidden rape victim: Personality attitudes and situational characteristics. *Psychology of Women Quarterly, 9:*193–212, 1985.

251. Russell, D.E.: *Sexual Exploitation.* Beverly Hills, Sage, 1984.

252. Council on Scientific Affairs, American Medical Association: Violence against women. *JAMA, 267:*3184–3189, 1992.

253. Lister, E.: Forced silence: a neglected dimension of trauma. *Am J Psychiatry, 139:*872–876, 1982.

254. Greenberg, M.S., Ruback, R.B., and Westcott, D.R.: Seeing help from the police: The victim's perspective. In Nadler, A., Fisher, J., and DePaolo, B. (Eds.): *Applied Perspectives on Help Seeking and Receiving.* New York, Academic Press, 1983, pp. 71–103.

255. Taylor, S.E., Wood, J.V., and Lichtman, R.R.: It could be worse: Selective evaluation as a response to victimization. *Journal of Social Issues, 39:*19–40, 1983.

256. Graine, L.S., Henson, C., Colliver, J.A., and MacLean, D.G.: Prevalence of a history of sexual abuse among female psychiatric patients in a state hospital system. *Hosp Community Psychiatry, 39:*3, 1988.

257. Masson, J.M.: *The Assault on Truth.* Farrar, Straus, Giroux, 1984.

258. Goodwin, J.: Post-traumatic symptoms in incest victims. In Spiegel, D. (Ed.): *Progress in Psychiatry.* Washington, American Psychiatric Press, 1985.

259. Lott, B., Reilly, M.E., and Howard, D.R.: Sexual assault and harassment: A campus community case study. *Signs: Journal of Women in Culture and Society,* 8:296–319, 1982.

260. Koss, M.P., Gidycz, C.A., and Wisniewski, N.: The scope of rape: Incidence and prevalence of sexual aggression and victimization in a national sample of students in higher education. *J Consul Clin Psychol, 55:*162–170, 1987.

261. Gelles, R.J., and Cornell, C.P.: *Intimate Violence in Families,* 2nd ed. Newbury Park, Sage, 1990, p. 11.

262. Fitch, F.J., and Papantonio, A.: Men who batter: Some pertinent characteristics. *J Nerv Ment Dis, 171:*190–192, 1983.

263. National Coalition Against Domestic Abuse. *NCADV Fact Sheet.* Denver, 1994.

264. Lansky, M.R.: The family genesis of aggression. *Psychiatric Annals, 23:*494–499, 1993.

265. Browne, A.: *When Battered Women Kill.* New York, Free Press, 1987.

266. Council on Ethics and Judicial Affairs, American Medical Association.: Physicians and domestic violence: ethical considerations. *JAMA, 267:*3190–3193, 1992.

267. Browne, A., and Williams, K.: *Resource Availability for Women at Risk: Its Relationship to Rates of Female-Perpetrated Homicide.* Presented at the American Society of Criminology, Montreal, Quebec, November, 1987.

268. Burman, S., and Allen-Meares, P.: *Neglected Victims of Murder: Children's Witness to Parental Homicide.* National Association of Social Workers, Inc. CCC Code: oo37-8046/94, 1994.

269. Senate Judiciary Committee Report. *Violence Against Women. A Week in the Life of America.* October, 1992.

270. Stark, E., and Flitcraft, A.: Woman-battering, child abuse and social heredity: What is the relationship? In Johnson, N. (Ed.): *Marital Violence,* Sociological Review Monograph #31. London, Routledge and Kegan Paul, 1985.

271. Rosenbaum, A., Hoge, S.: Head injury and marital aggression. *Am J Psychiatry, 146:*1040–1051, 1989.

272. Klaus, P., and Rand, M.: *Special Report: Family Violence.* Washington, Bureau of Justice, 1992.

273. Asmus, M.E., Ritmeester, T. and Pence, E.L.: Prosecuting domestic abuse cases in Duluth: Developing effective prosecution strategies from understanding the dynamics of abusive relationships. *Hamline Law Review, 15:*115–166, 1991.

274. Freize, I., and Browne, A.: Violence in marriage. In Ohlin, L., and Tonry, M. (Eds.): *Family Violence.* Chicago, University of Chicago Press, p. 7.

275. Wolfgang, M.: *Patterns in Criminal Homicide.* Philadelphia, University of Pennsylvania, 1958.
276. Pittman, D.J., and Handy, W.: Patterns in criminal aggravated assault. *Journal of Criminal Law, Criminology and Police Science, 55:*462–470, 1964.
277. Palmer, S.: *The Violent Society.* New Haven College and University Press, 1972.
278. Gifford, J.J.: Wife battering: a preliminary survey of one hundred cases. *British Medical Journal. 1:*194–197, 1975.
279. Hotaling, G.T., and Straus, M.A., with Lincoln, A.: Intrafamily violence and crime and violence outside the family. In Ohlin, L., and Tonray, M. (Eds.): *Family Violence.* Chicago, University of Chicago Press, 1989, pp. 315–376.
280. Walker, L.: *Terrifying Love: Why Battered Women Kill and How Society Responds.* New York, Harper and Row, 1989.
281. Strauss, M.A., Gelles, R.J., and Steimetz, S.K.: *Behind Closed Doors: Violence in the American Family.* Beverly Hills, CA, Sage, 1980.
282. Walker, L.: *The Battered Woman Syndrome.* New York, Springer, 1984.
283. U.S. Senate, Committee on the Judiciary.: Ten facts on women and violence. *Hearings on Women and Violence.* August 29 and December 11, 1990, p. 78.
284. *Cases Reviewed by the Domestic Violence Unit.* Milwaukee, Milwaukee County District Attorney, December, 1992.
285. Helfer, R., and Kaempe, C.H.: *The Battered Child.* Chicago, University of Chicago Press, 1974.
286. Gil, D.G.: Violence against children. *Journal of Marriage and the Family, 33:*637–648, 1971.
287. Therapy for child abuse. *Parade,* April 4, 1972, p. 10.
288. Light, R.: Abused and neglected children in America: a study of alternative policies. *Harvard Educational Review, 43,* 556–598, 1974.
289. Gelles, R.: Violence toward children in the United States. *Am J Orthopsychiatry, 48:*580–592, 1979.
290. Viano, E.C.: The battered child: A review of study and research in the area of child abuse. In Drapkin, I., and Viano, E. (Eds.) *Victimology: A New Focus,* Lexington, Heath, 1975, vol. 4, pp. 145–164.
291. Maden, M.F.: *Toward a Theory of Child Abuse: A Review of the Literature.* Ann Arbor, Masters Abstracts, University Microfilms, 1975.
292. MacKeith, D.: Speculations on some possible long-term effects. In Franklin, A. (Ed.): *Concerning Child Abuse.* Edinburg, Churchill Livingstone, 1875.
293. Smith, S.M.: *The Battered Child Syndrome.* London, Butterworth, 1975.
294. Scott, P.D.: Non-accidental injury to children. *Br J Psychiatry, 131:*366–380, 1977.
295. Kaiser, G.: Child Abuse in West Germany. *Victimology: An International Journal, 2:*294–306, 1977.
296. National Study on Child Neglect and Abuse Reporting. American Humane Society. Reports of abuse or neglect of minors in 33 jurisdictions. *Source Book of Criminal Justice Statistics.* Washington, U.S. Government Printing Office, 1979, pp. 80, 81.

297. Kempe, H.C., Sherman, F.N., Steele, B.F., Droegmueller, W., and Silver, H.K.: The battered child syndrome. *JAMA, 181:*107–112, 1962.

298. American Association for Protecting Children. *Highlights of Official Child Neglect and Abuse Reporting, 1987.* Denver, American Humane Association, 1989.

299. Tardieu, A.: Etude médico-légale sur les sévice et les mauvais traitements excercès sur les enfants. *Annales de Hygiène Lègale, 13:*p. 361, 1860.

300. Parristo, P., and Caussade, L.: Les sévices envers les enfants. *Annales de Médecine Légale, 9:*398, 1929.

301. Bastianon, V., and Benedetti Gaddini, R.: Abuso e incuria verso l'infanzia. In Ferracuti, F. (Ed.): *Trattato di Criminologia, Medicina Criminologica e Psichiatria Forense.* Milan, Giuffrè, 1987, pp. 165–188.

302. Roy, M. *Children in the Crossfire.* 1988. Cited in NCADV.

303. Kendall-Tackett, K.A., and Simon, A.F.: Perpetrators and their acts: Data from 365 adults molested as children. *Child Abuse and Neglect, 11:*237–245, 1987.

304. Finkelhor, D.: *Sexually Victimized Children.* New York, Free Press, 1979.

305. Council on Scientific Affairs, American Medical Association. Adolescents as victims of family violence. *JAMA, 270:*1850–1856, 1993.

306. Garbarino, J., Shellenbach, C., and Sibis, J.: *Troubled Youth, Troubled Families: Understanding Families at Risk for Adolescent Maltreatment.* New York, Aldine Company, 1986.

307. Freud, S.: *Totem and Taboo.* The Standard Edition. Strachey, J. (Trans.): New York, Norton, 1950.

308. Roueché, B.: Alcohol in human culture. In Lucia, S.P. (Ed.): *Alcohol and Civilization.* New York, McGraw-Hill, 1963, pp. 167–182. p. 168.

309. *The Bible.* Genesis 9:21.

310. Institute of Health Policy, Brandeis University. *Substance Abuse: The Nation's Number One Health Problem.* Princeton, The Robert Wood Johnson Foundation, October 1993.

311. Pacc, N.: Present knowledge of the physiology of alcohol. In Lucia, S.P. (Ed.): *Alcohol and Civilization.* New York, McGraw-Hill, 1963, pp. 87–94.

312. Helzer, J.E.: Epidemiology of alcohol addiction: International. In Miller, N.S.: (Ed.): *Comprehensive Handbook of Drug and Alcohol Addiction.* New York, Marcel Dekker, 1991.

313. American Psychiatric Association. *Diagnostic and Statistical Manual,* 3rd ed., rev. Washington, DC. American Psychiatric Association, 1987.

314. Jellinek, E.M.: *The Disease Concept of Alcoholism.* New Haven, College and University Press, 1960.

315. Virkkunen, M.: Alcohol as a factor precipitating aggression and conflict behaviour leading to homicide. *Brit J Addict, 69:*149–154, 1974.

316. Mayfield, D.: Alcoholism, alcohol intoxication and assaultive behavior. *Diseases of the Nervous System, 37:*288–291, 1975.

317. Lindqvist, P.: Criminal homicide in northern Sweden 1970–1981: Alcohol intoxication, alcohol abuse and mental disease. *Int J Law Psychiatry, 8:*19–37, 1986.

318. Stone, A.A.: *Law, Psychiatry and Morality.* Washington, DC, American Psychiatric Press, 1984. p. 62.

319. Di Tullio, B. *Principii di Criminologia Generale e Clinica e Psicopatia Sociale.* Istituto di Medicina Sociale. 1971.

320. Schneider, K.: *Psychopathic Personalities,* 9th ed. London, Cassell, 1950.

321. Cook, B.L., and Winnekour, G.: Alcoholism as a family dysfunction. *Psychiatric Annals, 23:*508–512, 1993. p. 512.

322. Schuckit, M.A.: Editorial.: What for, alcohol research? *Am J Psychiatry, 151:*2, 1994.

323. Callieri e Greco. Alcoholismo e Criminalita'. Capitolo 15.3. in Ferracuti Trattato.

324. Kudryatsev, J.: *Alcoholism in Russia Today.* Presentation to the Milwaukee Neuro-Psychiatric Society. March 16, 1994.

325. Farrell, M., and Strang, J.: Alcohol e stupefacenti. *British Medical Journal, Edizione Italiana, 17:*266–269, 1992.

326. Monroe, R.: Limbic ictus and atypical psychosis. *J Nerv Ment Dis, 170:*711–716, 1982.

327. Peele, S.: Does addiction excuse thieves and killers from criminal responsibility? *International Journal of Law and Psychiatry. 13:*95–101, 1990.

328. Post, R.M.: Cocaine psychosis: a continuum model. *Am J Psychiatry, 132:*225–231, 1975.

329. Barchas, T.E., Berger, R.D. and Ciaranello, R.D. et al. *Psychopharmacology.* New York, Oxford University Press, 1977.

330. Palermo, G.B., and Palermo, M.T.: Clinical diagnostic considerations on cocaine abuse. *J Psychoactive Drugs, 22:*313–318, 1990.

331. Post, R.M., Rubinow, D.R. and Ballenger, J.C.: Conditioning, sensitization, and kindling: implications for the course of affective illness. In Post, R.M. and Ballenger, J.C. (Eds.): *Neurobiology of Mood Disorders.* Baltimore, Williams & Wilkins, pp. 432–466, 1984.

332. Dackis, C.A. and Gold, M.S.: Psychopharmacology of cocaine. *Psychiatric Annals, 18:*528–530, 1988.

333. Resnick, R.B. and Resnick, E.B.: Cocaine abuse and its treatment. *Psychiatric Clinics of North America, 7:*713–728, 1984.

334. Sherer, M.A.: Intravenous cocaine: Psychiatric effects, biological mechanisms. *Biological Psychiatry, 24:*865–885, 1988.

335. Spitz, H.I., and Rosegan, J.S.: *Cocaine Abuse: New Directions in Treatment and Research.* New York, Brunner-Mazel, 1987.

336. Retterstol, N.: *Suicide.* Cambridge, Cambridge University Press, 1993, p. 132.

337. Jeri, F.R.: Coca paste smoking in Latin-America: A review of a severe and unabated form of addiction. *Bulletin of Narcotics, 36:*15–32, 1984.

338. Climent, C.E. and Aragon, L.V.: Clinical aspects of coca paste smoking (basuco) in Columbia. Presented at WHO Advisory Group Meeting on the Adverse Health consequences of Cocaine and Coca Paste Smoking. Bogota, Columbia, 1984.

339. Washton, A.M., and Tatarsky, A.: *Cocaine. A Clinician's Handbook.* New York, Guilford Press, 1987.

340. Post, R.M., and Kopanda, R.T.: Cocaine, kindling and psychosis. *Am J Psychiatry,* *132:*627–634, 1976.

341. Oakley, R.: *Drugs, Society and Human Behavior.* St. Louis, C.V. Mosby, 1983.

342. Malizia, G.: *Droga '80.* Turin, Edizioni Medico Scientifiche, 1981.

343. Andrews, G., and Solomon, D. (Eds.): *The Coca Leaf and Cocaine Paper.* New York, Harcourt, Brace, Jovanovich, 1975.

344. Brecher, M.: *Licit and Illicit Drugs: Cocaine.* New York, Consumers Union Mount Vernon, 1972.

345. Clark, R.W.: *Freud – The Man and the Cause.* New York, Random House, 1980.

346. Torrey, E.F.: *Freudian Fraud.* New York, Harper Collins, 1992, pp. 11, 12.

347. Musto, D.F.: A study in cocaine: Sherlock Holmes and Sigmund Freud. In *JAMA, 204:*125–130, 1968.

348. Honer, W.G., Gewirtz, G., and Turey, M.: Psychosis and violence in cocaine smokers (Letter to the editor). *Lancet, 2:*451, 1987.

349. Gold, M.S., Washton, A.M., and Dackis, C.A.: Cocaine abuse: Neurochemistry, phenomenology, and treatment. *NIDA Research Monograph, 61:*130–150, 1985.

350. Eichelman, B.: Neurochemical and psychopharmacologic aspects of aggressive behavior. In Meltzer, H.Y. (Ed.): *Psychopharmacology: The Third Generation of Progress.* New York, Raven Press, 1987.

351. Yudofsky, S.C., Silver, J.M. and Hales, R.E.: Cocaine and aggressive behavior: Neurobiological and clinical perspectives. *Bulletin of the Menninger Clinic,* *57:*218–226, 1993.

352. Linnoila, M., Virkkunen, M., Scheinin, M., Nuutila, A., Rimon, R., and Goodwin, F.K.: Low cerebrospinal fluid 5-hydroxyindoleacetic acid concentration differentiates impulsive from nonimpulsive violent behavior. *Life Science,* *33:*2609–2614, 1983.

353. Taylor, D., and Ho, B.T.: Neurochemical effects of cocaine following acute and repeated injections. *Journal of Neuroscience Research, 3:*95–101, 1977.

354. Brown, G.L., Ebert, M.H., Goyer, P.F., Jimerson, D.C., Klein, W.J., Bunney, W.E., and Goodwin, F.K.: Aggression, suicide, and serotonin: Relationships to CSF amine metabolites. *Am J Psychiatry, 139:*741–746, 1982.

355. Stanley, M., Mann, J.J., and Cohen, L.S.: Serotonin and serotonergic receptors in suicide. *Annals of the New York Academy of Science, 487:*122–127, 1986.

356. Goeders, N.E., and Smith, J.E.: Cortical dopaminergic involvement in cocaine reinforcement. *Science, 221:*773–775, 1983.

357. Elliott, F.A.: Neuroanatomy and neurology of aggression. *Psychiatric Annals,* *17:*385–388, 1987.

358. Post, R.M., Uhde, T.W., Putnam, F.W., Ballenger, J.C., and Berrettini, W.H.: Kindling and carbamazepine in affective illness. *Journal of Nervous and Mental Disease, 170:*717–731, 1982.

359. Guns gaining on cars as bigger killer in U.S.: *The New York Times,* January 28, 1994, p. A8.

360. Rowley, J.: New laws unlikely to curb gun supply. *Detroit News,* AP. December 15, 1993.

361. Polsby, D.D.: The false promise of gun control. *The Atlantic Monthly,* March 1994, pp. 57–70.

362. Kopel, D.B. and D'Andrilli, S.: Congressional Record, April 20, 1990.

363. DiUilio, J.: *ABC News this Week with David Brinkley.* American Broadcasting Companies, Transcript #650, 1994, p. 5.

364. *Murder in Large Urban Counties, 1988.* Special Report NCJ, 140614. Washington DC, U.S. Department of Justice, May 1993.

365. *The New York Times.* Clinton links gun control to health care savings. September 25, 1993, p. 6.

366. Guns on the Streets. *Newsweek,* August 2, 1993, p. 46.

367. Office of Juvenile Justice and Delinquency Prevention. U. S. Justice Department. Federal Bureau of Investigation, Washington, U.S. Government Printing Office, 1992.

368. *Milwaukee Journal.* Juveniles committing more violent crimes. August 30, 1992, p. A14.

369. Gillespie, R.W.: *Economic Factors in Crime and Delinquency: A Critical Review of the Empirical Evidence.* Washington, National Institute of Law Enforcement and Criminal Justice. 1975.

370. Orsagh, T., and Witte, A.D.: Economic status and crime: Implications for offender rehabilitation. *Journal of Criminal Law and Criminology, 72:*1055–1071, 1981.

371. Freeman, R.B.: Crime and unemployment. In Wilson, J.Q.: (Ed.): *Crime and Public Policy.* San Francisco, Institute for Contemporary Studies, pp. 89–106.

372. Brenner, M.H.: *Estimating the Effects of Economic Change on National Health and Social Well-Being.* A study prepared for the Joint Economic Committee, United States Congress, 98th Cong., 2nd Sess., June 15, 1984.

373. Witte, A.D.: Estimating the economic model of crime with individual data. *Quarterly Journal of Economics, 94:*57–84, 1980.

374. Cook, P.J., and Zarkin, G.A.: Crime and the business cycle. *Journal of Legal Studies, 14:*115–128, 1985.

375. Allan, E.A., and Steffensmeier, D.J.: Youth, underemployment, and property crime: Differential effects of job availability and job quality on juvenile and young adult arrest rates. *American Sociological Review, 54:*107–123, 1989.

376. Robertson, P.J., Taylor, P.J., and Gunn, J.C.: Does violence have cognitive correlates? *Br J Psychiatry, 151:*63–68, 1987.

377. Spellacy, F.: Neuropsychological discrimination between violent and non-violent men. *J Clin Psychol, 30:*49–52, 1978.

378. Heilbrun, A.F. Jr.: Differentiation of death-row murderers and life sentence murderers by antisociality and intelligence measures. *Journal of Personality Assessment, 54:*617–627, 1990.

379. Cornell, D.G., and Wilson, L.A.: The PIQ>VIQ discrepancy in violent and non-violent delinquents. *J Clin Psychol, 48:*256–261, 1992.

380. Nestor, P.: Neuropsychological and clinical correlates of murder and other forms of extreme violence in a forensic psychiatric population. *J Nerv Ment Dis, 180:*418–423, 1992.

381. Calicchia, J.A., Moncata, S.J., and Santostefano, S.: Cognitive control differences in violent juvenile inpatients. *J Clin Psychol, 49:*731–740, 1993.

382. Stattin, H., and Klackenberg-Larsson, I.: Early language and intelligence development and their relationship to future criminal behavior. *J Abnorm Psychol, 3:*369–378, 1993.

383. Schonfeld, I.S.: A developmental perspective and antisocial behavior: Cognitive functioning. *Am Psychol, 45:*983–984, 1990.

384. *Academic Achievement of Juvenile Delinquents in Wisconsin.* Madison, Wisconsin Department of Health and Social Services, Office of Policy and Budget, January 1994.

385. Sessions, W.B.: *Crime in the United States.* U.S. Department of Justice, Washington, U.S. Government Printing Office, 1988.

386. *Uniform Crime Reports.* Federal Bureau of Investigation, Washington, DC, U.S. Government Printing Office, 1991.

387. Rouche, M.: The early middle ages in the West. In Ariès, P., and Duby, G. (Gen. Eds.), Veyne (Ed.): *A History of Private Life.* Cambridge, MA, Belknap Press of Harvard University Press, 1987, vol. I, pp. 411–549.

388. Duby, G., Barthélemy, D., and de La Roncière, C.: Portraits. In Ariès, P., and Duby, G. Gen. Eds.), Veyne (Ed.): *A History of Private Life.* Cambridge, MA, Belknap Press of Harvard University Press, 1987, vol. II, pp. 33–309.

389. Perrot, M., and Fugieri-Martin, A.: The actors. In Ariès, P., and Duby, G. Gen. Eds.), Veyne (Ed.): *A History of Private Life.* Cambridge, MA, Belknap Press of Harvard University Press, 1987, vol. IV, pp. 95–337.

390. Goode, W.: *World Revolution and Family Patterns.* New York, Free Press, 1970.

391. Scott, E. and Scott, K.: Healthy families. *International Journal of Offender Therapy and Comparative Criminology, 27:*71–78, 1983.

392. Schwartz, G.: *Beyond Conformity or Rebellion.* Chicago, University of Chicago Press, 1987, p. 157.

393. Lidz, T.: *The Family and Human Adaptation.* New York, International Universities Press, 1963, p. 28.

394. Piaget, J.: *The Essential Piaget.* Guber, H.G., and Vonech, J.J. (Eds.). New York, Basic Books, 1977.

395. Kohlberg, L.: Moral Stages: A Current Formulation and a Response to Critics. New York, Karger, 1983.

396. Bandura, A.: *Aggression: A Social Learning Analysis.* Englewood Cliffs, Prentice-Hall, 1973.

397. Married with children: The waning icon. *The New York Times,* August 23, 1992, sec. 4, p. 2.

398. U.S. Bureau of Census. Marital status and living arrangements: March 1987. *Current Population Reports,* P-20, No. 423, Washington DC, U.S. Government Printing Office, April, 1988.

399. Scott, J.W.: Black polygamous family formation: Case studies of legal wives and consensual wives. *Alternative Lifestyles, 3:*41–64, 1980.

400. Nisbet, R.: *The Sociological Tradition.* New York, Basic Books, 1966.

401. Wilson, W.G.: *The Truly Disadvantaged.* Chicago, University of Chicago Press, 1987.
402. U.S. Bureau of Census. *America's Black Population,* 1978–1982. Washington, DC, U.S. Government Printing Office, 1983.
403. Kendall, G.: Bureaucracy and welfare: The enslavement of the spirit. *Social Justice Review. May/June:* 104–107, 1990.
404. Anderson, E.: The code of the streets. *The Atlantic Monthly,* pp. 80–94, May 1994.
405. Duby, G.: Foreword, In Aries, P., and Duby, G.: (Gen. Eds.), Veyne, P. (Ed.): *A History of Private Life,* Vol. I. Cambridge, Belknap Press of Harvard University Press, 1987, p. viii.
406. Chilman, C.S.: Federal mental health policy: Its unhappy past and uncertain future. In Nunnally, E.W., and Chilman, C.S. (Eds.): *Mental Illness, Delinquency, Addictions and Neglect.* Families in Trouble Series, Newbury Park, Sage, 1988, vol. 4, p. 195.
407. McCord, J.: Some child rearing antecedents of criminal behavior in adult man. *Journal of Personality and Social Psychology, 37:* 1477–1486, 1979.
408. *Family Status of Delinquents in Juvenile Correctional Facilities Wisconsin.* Madison, Wisconsin Department of Health and Social Services, Division of Youth Services, April 1994.
409. Pittman, F.S.: *Man Enough: Fathers, Sons, and the Search for Masculinity.* New York, G.B. Putnam's Sons, 1993. p. 133.
410. MacLean, P.D.: On the origin and progressive evolution of the triune brain. In Armstrong, E., and Falk, D. (Eds.): *Primate Brain Evolution: Methods and Concepts.* New York, Plenum, 1982.
411. Reagan, R.: In *Attorney General's Task Force on Family Violence. Final Report.* Washington, U.S. Government Printing Office, Sept. 1984, p. 11.
412. Wilson, W.: Memorial Day Address. Arlington, Virginia, May 31, 1915.
413. Hobbes, T.: (1650) Political philosophy. In Edwards, P. (Ed.): *The Encyclopedia of Philosophy.* New York, Macmillan, 1972, vol. 3–4, p. 42.
414. Wolff, C.: Duties toward others. In Runes, D. (Ed.): *Treasury of Philosophy.* New York, Philosophical Library, 1955, 1234, 1235.
415. John Paul II.: *On the hundredth anniversario of Rerum Novarum—centesimus annus.* Encyclical Letter, Publication No. 436-8. Washington, United States Catholic Conference, May 1, 1990.
416. Ackerman, N.W.: Family therapy. In Arieti, S. (Ed.): *American Handbook of Psychiatry.* New York, Basic Books, 1966, Vol. III, pp. 201–212.
417. Harris, M.: *Culture, Man and Nature.* New York, Crowell, 1971, p. 266.
418. Schmideberg, M.: Psychotherapy of the criminal psychopath. *Archives of Criminal Psychodynamics, 4:* 724–734, 1961.
419. Magid, D. and McKelvey, C.: *High Risk: Children Without a Conscience.* New York, Bantam, 1987.
420. Reusch, R.: Social disability. The problem of misfits in society. Paper presented at *Towards a Health Community,* World Federation for Mental Health, Edinburgh, 1969.

421. Durkheim, E.: *On Morality and Society.* Bellah, R.N. (Ed.). Chicago, University of Chicago Press, 1973.
422. Currie, E.: Confronting crime: Looking toward the twenty-first century. *Justice Quarterly, 6:*7–25, 1989.

AUTHOR INDEX

SUBJECT INDEX